JAGR

An Autobiography

JAGR

An Autobiography

Jaromir Jagr
with Jan Smid

Published by 68 Productions Ltd.
c/o Civic Arena, Gate Nine
Pittsburgh, PA
15219

ISBN: 1-895629-86-1

Translation: Louis Charbonneau
Front Cover Photograph: Bruce Bennett Studios
Design: Kimberley Davison
Editorial Services: Harry Endrulat

This book was produced for 68 Productions by Mercer Digital Design Inc., a division of the Warwick Publishing Group, Toronto, Canada.

Printed and bound in Canada by Transcontinental Printing Inc.

Contents

Acknowledgments

A number of people helped us a lot in preparing this book. Let us acknowledge at least a few of them. We would like to especially thank Karel Beran, Alexandra Gross, Kell Ciabattari, Kisha Ciabattari, Raymond Haluska, Dominik Hasek, Josef Lustig, Elizabeth Modahl, Todd Morath, Craig Patrick, Nick Ruta, Zdenek Sindler, Richard Smehlik, Martin Straka, Leah Strauss and Bryan Trottier.

The Authors

Introduction

I sat in the locker room and stared straight ahead. It still hadn't hit me that it was over. Such a huge chance. I couldn't understand how it had escaped us. When Petr Nedved evened up the score and the arena crowd rose to its feet as one, I told myself, "We've made it. Now we'll beat them."

After Petr's goal, I went to the bench anticipating the flight to Denver to play for the Stanley Cup. No, I wasn't taking the victory for granted, but I allowed myself to daydream for a few seconds. But I couldn't stop thinking about the possibility of losing, either. What if they score again?

The red light went on behind Tom Barrasso to put Florida up 2-1, and in the silent arena you could have heard a pin drop. The only sound was the cheers of the celebrating Florida players. From that moment on, the game was like a dream. I desperately wanted to score a goal. To set up a goal. To turn the game around. What ifs. I still had hope.

We shook the hands of the Florida players and left the ice. Those moments before the handshake are the worst. As you sit at your locker, the last seconds of the game race through your head. What took place moments ago. Or what happened in the previous game. Moments that are etched in your memory. Moments you are helpless to change. What ifs.

Sitting in the locker room, some of the players are able to absorb the reality that it's really over. But for me it still hasn't sunk in yet.

All of a sudden, I'm aware of the terrible silence in the locker room. Why isn't anyone speaking? At least say something. I look around. Nobody is in the room.

I am utterly alone.

It's Saturday, June 1, 1996. Just a few moments ago we lost the seventh game of the Stanley Cup semifinals to the Florida Panthers, and I feel like crying. I cover my head in a towel. All at once, journalists and photographers begin flowing into the room. "I'd rather you got lost," I advise them in an unfriendly voice. "Go talk to the winners."

The city was already beginning to look forward to the finals. I occurs to me that the media will crucify me. Mario, too. After all, everybody was counting on Mario and me, and we didn't score a single goal in five games. We'll be blamed. But we deserve it. After the series against the Rangers, the media made us into deities and totally discredited our teammates. As if the two of us had single-handedly led the team. Now we're out of the tournament, and Mario and I have to take the blame.

Little by little, I'm starting to get used to these losses. When I got to the NHL, everything happened by itself. I won the Stanley Cup twice in two seasons and thought the winning would never end.

First, we got knocked out by the Islanders. It was a shock. We never imagined they could beat us. Actually, it was my first experience with losing. I sat at my locker next to Martin Straka and cried like a little boy. My knee was bruised, my eyelid was torn and my hands were black and blue everywhere from taking hits. The Islanders hammered us and then eliminated us.

We didn't even have a chance against Washington in the 1993-94 playoffs. We were tired, and Mario played in a great deal of pain. We were worn down. At that point, we couldn't possibly imagine we'd play them again exactly one year later.

The Capitals were waiting for us in the first round. And again they led 3-1. But this time we came back. It was probably my best series of the playoffs. I had an excellent regular season, winning the Art Ross Trophy for most points and plac-ing second in goal scoring behind Peter Bondra.

Trailing 2-0 in the first game, I scored shorthanded on a breakaway to beat Jim Carey. From that moment on, we were alive. This was despite the fact some peo-ple told us we might as well stay home instead of going to Washington and wast-ing money on the plane ticket and hotel room. At the end of the series, we were shaking hands with the Capitals when I came to their coach, Jim Schoenfeld. It must have been the worst of all for him since I think he too had pictured his team going to the next round. And now he had to wish his opponents well. I'll never forget what Schoenfeld said to me. I came up to him, we shook hands and despite disappointment, he smiled and said, "You're special." And then he added, "Go and take them all the way to the Stanley Cup."

But the Devils awaited us in the next round, and they handcuffed us. We were worn out from the previous series, and we lacked the stamina to survive such a tight-checking series. I recall how after the final game, Ronnie Francis sat at his locker exhausted, unable to raise his arms. And the rest of us were also pretty banged up.

The following year we felt we could win. We managed to beat Washington again, even though we lost the first two games at home. And then we totally blew out the Rangers. Florida's style didn't suit ours, and yet we came pretty close to beating them. In the fifth game we outplayed them and moved into a 3-2 lead in the series. But Florida still managed to rebound and win.

A few moments ago, the Panthers were presented the Eastern Conference Trophy on the Civic Arena ice, and in a little while, they'll be on that plane to Denver.

Instead of us.

Now I'm off to the showers. No one's talking aloud. Everybody is talking to themselves. I look around at my teammates. I probably won't be seeing some of them here a year from now. The locker room is full of journalists. The team owner Howard Baldwin arrives. He thanks me for the season and says, "You have nothing to be ashamed of." Only one small hurdle separated us from the finals. A small hurdle, but still too big for us.

Hockey is my life, but sometimes I wonder what I've been missing. Entire days on the road. Evenings before games always spent at home. Nights after defeats when I'm tossing and turning in bed with ice bags covering painful bruises. Thousands of hours on stationary bikes. But then that gratifying moment comes — the net stretching out in a beautiful arc from my shot and the arena going wild. Those are the most magical moments of all.

There is nobody left in the locker room, but I don't feel like going home. I don't want to be alone in my sadness. Dad came from the Czech Republic to watch me in the finals, but now he won't have the chance. He only saw two games against Florida in addition to Game Seven today. I remember how my folks were there waiting for me after we were eliminated last year: Dad sort of sad. Mom on the verge of tears. This year it won't be any different.

I head for the exit of the Civic Arena. I've walked this path many times before. There are always fans waiting in the parking lot. I usually autograph a few photos and posters and then take off. This time it will be faster. I tell myself, maybe they'll have all gone home. The fans were looking forward to the finals, and we disappointed them so much. Slowly I come to the heavy iron gate. Maybe a few of them will be there after all. I hope so. But then I take a look at my watch. Two hours have passed since the end of the game. Nobody will be there anymore. I make a bet with myself, pull on the handle of the big gate and there's only one thought in my head: "Will they be there?"

A huge roar erupts. I stop and can't believe my eyes. "Jaromir!" yell the fans. I look around me. Just a few hours ago we were eliminated from the Stanley Cup. It's long after midnight, and in spite of everything, hundreds of fans are there waiting for me.

I can't look at them. The tears well up in my eyes. I'm still standing in the same place, but I can't let them see me this soft. I fix my coat, though it doesn't need any fixing. I tie my shoes, though they don't need any tying. Slowly I make my way toward them. The roar doesn't get any softer. I'm unable to say a single word. I sign photos, caps, posters, programs. Somebody even waves a huge white banner at me with the words "Good luck, Jaromir!" written on it in Czech.

Now I know what I'm playing for. I wish it would start again.

Pittsburgh
June 1, 1996

One of my first photographs, maybe training on dry land?

whom I don't know continues to be difficult. But journalists weren't pursuing me in those days.

The less I expressed myself off the ice, the more I expressed myself on the ice. At practice, I won every speed race. Once I was crowned king of one-lap races. We did four laps total, and after each lap, the last four skaters were eliminated. There were fourth graders skating with us, so I had to beat boys three years older than me. However, I wasn't always that fast during games. At that time, I still didn't understand that you have to go just as fast after the puck in a game as you do in skating practice.

I've never kept it a secret that the biggest credit in my development belongs to my dad. I've listened to few others in addition to, of course, Mario Lemieux. From the time I was small, my dad taught me how to skate, how to hold a hockey stick properly, how to fake and how to pass: in short, everything in the hockey alphabet. It never occurred to me that I could play any sport other than hockey, something for which he also deserves credit. It probably also helped that Kladno hockey was in the first league, which meant the best teams in Czechoslovakia played there. Kladno soccer, on the other hand, was somewhere at the bottom of the list in the national league. But the most important thing was that my dad played hockey.

Even though he played well, my dad had to quit hockey when he was seventeen because of his family situation and problems with his knees, not to mention the overall political situation in our country. Not long ago, he founded a team at work — VKD Rozdelov — and until recently, he still played hockey for fun.

There is a quote by the Czech writer Milan Kundera that reminds me of my dad and his devotion to my hockey playing: "The characters in my novels are my own unrealized possibilities." Since my dad was never able to realize his hockey dreams, he did everything he could to make a hockey player out of me. He analyzed everything I did, pointing out my mistakes and forcing me to think about every error I made. The worst was if I was on the ice when a goal was scored by the opposing team. My dad would tell me after the game, "I'd rather eat the puck than let in a goal." He told me I didn't put up enough of a fight. That always got me really mad.

He drove me to practices and games, which he watched closely. Afterward, he always made a lot of comments. I could have scored five goals during a game, and in the car on the way home, I would have felt like I was the worst one on the ice. According to my dad, every little mistake, every imperfection was something I could learn from for future games. The other boys laughed at me because my dad was always around. He even came into the locker room to help me with my gear and skates.

My mom helped me a lot, too. We young players were given torn hand-me-down gear and uniforms. As a result, we had to repair them ourselves — which meant, of course, the parents had to do the repairs. At home, my mom sewed, patched and glued. And in the locker room, my dad checked to see that everything fit properly and that everyone's skates were on tight. Of course, my dad helped the other boys too, because our coach at that time, Karel Beran, couldn't do it alone.

Karel Beran is someone who also did a great deal for me. He was a peculiar type of coach. The majority of the men who work with the boys' leagues, especially the younger ones, are there because their own son is on the team. Karel Beran was no exception. His son tended goal for us. But in the locker room it seemed as if Beran had not one son, but twenty. He looked after us as if we were his own. He not only taught us what to do and how to do it, but he also showed us where to position ourselves and how to play with the body. He also helped us with our uniforms and gear. The kids from adjacent villages often slept at his house when we had evening practices. And in the morning, they went to school as usual.

Beran helped me by letting me play. I skated better than the others and was also the only one who could handle the puck with some precision. At that time, that was quite a skill. We were still hyper young kids who mostly fumbled across the ice. I was the only one capable of shooting the puck past the goalie, and I scored many goals.

At that time, we played in a number of tournaments, and not just in the neighboring cities, but throughout the entire republic — in Prague, Hradec Králove, Plzen (Pilsen), Pribram, Pardubice and Olomouc. During these games, Karel Beran used an interesting tactic with me. He would say to me, "Jaromir, get two or three goals and then play how you want." He always put David Cermak with me, who I really got along well with. Then he put someone else with us, someone we could play hard with. We three were on the ice constantly, and the matches were decided right at the beginning. After a short time, when the score got to be 4-0, he'd let the other boys play. It was an easy formula. We won, and everyone played well.

In little league, our team — Pracovni Zalohy /PZ/ Kladno — was hard to beat. We won all the tournaments and really got a thrill out of hockey. A number of coaches criticized Beran, saying, "You can't rely on just one player. He'll become a prima donna. The most important thing is the collective." Beran's response to that was, "If he's capable of deciding every match himself, why shouldn't we use him? How else do you expect to nurture a true hockey talent? Everybody learns how to pass, defend and follow tactical instructions. Unless we support him from the time he's young and teach him to take responsibility for winning games, he'll become as average as the others — a simple follower of somebody else's instructions."

The team and I liked Beran's philosophy. Everywhere we went, the other teams were terrified of us. As soon as we arrived, I'd hear around me: "Look. It's Jagr.

He's eating up the trophies again." I actually have a cupboard full of those medals and trophies. At every tournament, I usually got at least two prizes: one for scoring the most goals and one for being the youngest player.

At a number of places, however, people didn't like me. At one tournament, they even decided not to award me anything. All the coaches chose the best players. When Karel Beran was asked who in his opinion was the best player in the tournament, he said, "Jagr." Their response was: "No, we can't give him the prize. He gets them all the time. Let's give it to someone else." "Then I vote for nobody," said Beran. He actually didn't vote for anyone. That time the best player ended up being a goalie for some other team.

Once my mom witnessed one of those coaches' discussions about me. They all knew my dad because he usually traveled with us, but they didn't recognize my mom. And once when she brought some tea or something similar into a room where all the team coaches were, they decided in front of her on an "enough of Jagr" strategy. Of course, my mom didn't tell me this right away. She thought that I might develop a feeling of injustice. Despite all the problems I had, I have nearly eighty of those certificates and trophies at home.

I like thinking back on all those tournaments not only because we won, but also because they were a lot of fun. There was a core group of parents who were always at the tournaments. They'd all contribute to a common fund — usually ten crowns (U.S.$1 equals 28 crowns) — and buy cookies and sweets for us so we'd have something good to eat. The parents also took care of food and refreshments at the games. They made tea and sometimes sold hot dogs. It was a good group. Sometimes during the summer we went to someone's cottage for the weekend where we made a big campfire. Of course, we children just loved it.

Dad was at every one of my games, and when we went for a tournament, he was never absent. Eventually, he and Karel Beran decided that he would become the team manager. He was the obvious choice because he always helped in the locker room. He always stayed on the bench or in the stands and watched the game closely. Just how closely I always learned after the game when he analyzed everything with me. He was able to remember precisely the course of the match and all scoring opportunities. "Hey Shorty, you did this badly," or "Shorty, you should've gone there." He always called me "Shorty." He still calls me that today. Even though my dad was strict with me, he never swore at me and never once hit me. My mom occasionally gave me a smack, usually when I was being a complete brat and she couldn't take it anymore.

From the time I started playing, I learned to preserve my strength. During tournaments, when I wasn't on the ice, I slept. In the beginning, I played around with the other boys, jumped on the benches and horsed around. My dad said to me, "How are you going to play in two hours when you'll be totally exhausted? I'd like to see you on the ice. You won't be able to crawl." "But the other boys are playing too," I objected. "That's true," my dad agreed, "but they don't spend half the game on the ice like you." I have to admit that he was right. Once on the ice, I was quickly able to tell when I was rested or not. So between games, I laid down and tried to nap a little. Some of the other kids followed me as well. David Cermak almost always slept next to me.

I always really looked forward to the matches. I loved playing so much I could have slept on the ice. We practiced several times a week, and on the weekends, we had games. But that still wasn't enough hockey for me. I wanted to be on the ice all the time. In Kladno at that time there was only one ice rink. In addition to the SONP leagues, all the little league teams, the juniors and several other teams used it as well. A few schools had skating classes there, so we could only practice early in the morning or late at night. The morning practices began at 5:00 A.M., so I had to be up no later than 4:30.

Today, my mom has to wake me up at least three times before I can roll out of bed, but in those days I didn't have any problem getting up. But my dad did. Who wants to get out of bed at 4:30 in the morning? I had a simple method of getting my dad out of bed. I'd start to cry and moan that we wouldn't make practice. This always worked. My dad immediately got up and started to get dressed. In order to use the ice rink as much as possible, we practiced on Saturdays and Sundays, as well. That made it even worse for dad.

My parents always hoped that they'd get to sleep in. When the alarm clock went off and they went to wake me up, they prayed that I wouldn't want to get out of bed, so they could continue sleeping in peace. But my mom would barely touch me and I'd be out of bed and jumping into my clothes. It had to be pretty tough on my parents, waking up every day like that. In addition to that, my dad had to drive me to the stadium. Still, I don't think it really bothered him that much.

I get a lot of questions of this kind: "I want to play like you. What should I do?" I always answer with a single sentence: "You've got to have the right parents." Of course, talent and hard work are important, but at the beginning, they're not the most important thing.

I was born with certain abilities, and I loved hockey from the very beginning, but there were and are hundreds and thousands like me. But they're not playing in the NHL. When you're a kid, it's your parents who play the main role in helping you achieve your goals. In the beginning, you don't have any sense of how to use your talents. You want to play hockey, but you don't know why you have to practice all the time, particularly if you're not scrimmaging constantly. Your parents force you to do something, the point of which you grasp only later. It never occurred to me to start practicing, but my dad told me that unless I do it, the others will soon be better than me. I started training mainly because I enjoyed it.

*Uncommon picture,
I didn't fall much
on skis.*

*They used me for
shenanigans.*

One time I also tried to learn guitar, but never became a folk artist.

Jagr's here again to snarf up all the medals...

Years later I return to the place of my childhood —
this is where I practiced shooting the most...

...that's how I got strong.

When you're young, it never occurs to you that hockey could be your profession one day. And by the time you do realize it, often you can't make up for what you didn't develop when you were young.

Today I can see that everything my dad demanded of me made sense, and now I make the same demands on myself. But at that time, it was terribly important that someone forced me to do things I'd never have done on my own. It was enough for him to say, "I'll bet you can't do that." And he had a bet.

I was happiest when he was happy. It certainly helped me that from the beginning I was good, and that always motivated me to be the best. But there were times when I stopped enjoying hockey. And then my dad would come up to me and say, "Like it or not, you're going to that practice." That was it. I started getting dressed. I couldn't disappoint someone who, because of me, woke up early every day, drove me to practices and games and built his weekends around my schedule.

There's definitely more than one method of raising children to be world-class athletes — provided they have the interest, the motivation and sufficient talent. From the time I was young, I was playing against Robert Holik, who now plays for the New Jersey Devils. I remember a game when we just stared at the way his dad (Jaroslav Holik), once a famous Czechoslovakian hockey player, was shouting and spitting all over the place. He screamed at Robert the entire game, as if he was the worst one on the ice. Someone also said that he once took both Robert and his daughter Andrea to a factory at six in the morning to see the people rushing through the gates to make the morning shift. "Take a good look at them. That is, if you don't want to spend your life doing what they're doing," he told them. "You go work in the morning and come home from work in the afternoon. Day after day, eternal toil. Is that what you want? What would your prospects be?"

Andrea, who played tennis and was at one time ranked seventy-seventh in the world for women's tennis, couldn't take the pressure and gave up world-class sports. She moved overseas to be with her love, Frank Musil, who plays for the Ottawa Senators. In contrast to Andrea, however, Robert withstood the pressure and made it into the NHL. I heard that he could shoot two thousand pucks in a single practice. I run into him when we play New Jersey, but we don't talk much. Robert's not the type of player you can talk to or tease during face-offs, and after the game there's no time to talk.

Robert is the product of a different, tougher approach to hockey. My dad never tried any of the Holik methods on me. His method was to make everything a contest. He never drove me in front of any factory. It wasn't necessary. I knew hard work from our life at home. Even though Jaroslav Holik's parent's didn't have it easy, Robert grew up in a well-known athletic family. But my mom and dad had to work hard in order to support the family. Both of my parents went to work every day. In addition, we had a little farm with twelve cattle and some hens. From the time I was small, I had to go to the field and help with the feeding. Moreover, the farm was located about five miles from where we lived. To get there, my dad rode his bicycle, and I ran the entire way next to him. In the summer, we did this routinely.

Life on the farm taught me the value of hard work and of hard-earned money. I learned to take work seriously. I saw how much my parents had to do in order to provide for me and my sister Jitka. Thanks to all that hard work, we always had enough to eat and were never in need of money. My parents would simply leave money on the table, and I could take whatever I wanted. Sometimes my mom took the change out of my wallet and put a hundred crown note into it, which was a lot of money at that time. She trusted me and I learned to handle money and didn't spend it unnecessarily. I knew that I could buy a lot of things with so much money, but that very knowledge kept me from doing it. I started appreciating the value of money, and this has stayed with me up to the present day. Even now, though I have more than a hundred crowns in my wallet, I never buy stupid things just to show off my wealth. I credit my parents for teaching me so wisely.

I often liked to talk about parenting with the former assistant to Scotty Bowman in Pittsburgh, Barry Smith. Both of them are now in Detroit. In one conversation, Barry was saying that his son plays quite well, but that it is foolish to train him because it wouldn't look good. So I said to him, "If you want your son to be able to do something, then give him as much attention as you can. Give him as much as my dad gave me." At eight or nine years of age, no child has enough sense to tell himself, "All right, now I'll start practicing more than the others." Parents have to encourage a child to do this.

I don't know if Barry fully grasped what I wanted to say to him. Relationships between parents and children in America are quite different from those in Czechoslovakia. Ours are a little tighter. In America, children grow up fast and soon go their own way, while the parents support them from a distance.

My dad wanted to make a top hockey player out of me for one reason. He wanted me to have a profession that I enjoyed which would enable me to see the world a little. He forced me to invest in myself.

Once in Pittsburgh, the team had a meeting with the head of the Players' Association, Bob Goodenow, who asked us if we remembered when we started to invest in ourselves seriously. Some of my fellow players answered that they were twelve, some thirteen and others twenty-five, but then Goodenow interrupted them: "Wrong, gentlemen," he said. "You invested in yourself the moment you decided to play hockey, the moment you started to work on yourselves." And that's true. I have always loved the game, and I was always striving to be the best. With my parents' support, I invested in myself from the time I was very small, without even knowing it.

I would spend summer vacations with my sister at Grandma and Grandpa's in Sumava.

I Start Training

The method of working with children in the former Czechoslovakia — now the Czech Republic — is, in my opinion, the best in the entire world. I played organized hockey before I started going to school. I feel blessed to have been able to play in these games. I often ended up on the ice two or three times in one day. But I'm getting ahead of myself.

My dad was always inventing ways of improving my game and discussed various forms of training with everyone he met. And one such meeting later proved to be crucial to my entire hockey career. After one game, my dad met the Pilsen youth coach, Jaroslav Liska. Liska recommended that I begin to regularly work out with the weight of my own body. "Don't give him any weights to lift. That'll destroy him. If he works out with only the weight of his own body, nothing bad can happen and all his muscles will develop in harmony," Liska told my dad. So I started with knee bends.

When I look back, I have to admit that I owe my strength and balance to those deep knee bends. For skating, you mainly need strength, particularly when you take off from the edges like I do. After my dad's "historical encounter" with Mr. Liska, I threw myself into the knee bends. Of course, I had no idea that I was in the process of shaping my hockey future.

I started doing knee bends and push-ups in 1977. A year later, when I was six, I was able to do six hundred knee bends. I added the push-ups later, so I usually did around sixty. My biggest increase came when I was eight, before I started the third grade. I adhered to a daily routine of one to two thousand knee bends and one hundred push-ups. The worst was when I'd reached five or six hundred knee bends, and I felt like I couldn't go further, but I had to go on. I was often so worn out that I couldn't even lie down because everything hurt so much.

At the beginning, I was doing one hundred. Later, I increased that to two hundred and fifty. At the same time, I tried to do each knee bend in one second. I measured it with a watch, and often my dad also timed me. In the evening, he sat in the armchair and watched TV while I worked out next to him. I did one set, rested a bit, then started up again.

I did it mainly because it made him happy. But my dad also motivated me. Sometimes he did it with provocations like, "I bet you can't even do a thousand knee bends," but often he promised me something, like new skates. At that time, welded skates were a novelty, and my dad promised to buy them for me if I worked out regularly. Eventually I got used to them, and the knee bends became a regular part of my day. I no longer needed anybody telling me to do them. As a result, during games I began to sense that I was stronger and faster than my teammates.

I started working out alone. I made up a little journal that I still have stored somewhere. In this journal, I kept track of my daily routines. If I didn't fulfill my daily quota, I had to do it the next day. When I let it go several days in a row, it was agony to catch up, but I had to stick to the program. The little journal became a stricter watchdog than my dad. I couldn't pull the wool over its eyes. It was all there in black and white.

I never became very good friends with push-ups. It seemed to me more important to have strong legs, and I never really enjoyed the push-ups very much. I got the strength in my hands by natural means. I often helped my dad in the field and lifted heavy pitchforks of grass. I have to admit that in the beginning, I had difficulty just lifting the pitchfork. My dad laughed at me about that, which always made me mad. When he saw me struggling with it, he'd always burst out laughing. But I liked helping him and working the field.

Actually, I didn't just go to the field with my dad, I ran there. And sometimes when I'd run the five miles to the farm, I'd borrow my dad's bicycle and ride twenty times up and down the biggest hill in the area on the lowest gear. My dad also built a bar for pull-ups, so that I'd have something to give me resistance, but it didn't work too well for me at the beginning. It was useful later though, when I was heavier.

I did the knee bends all those years. It didn't matter at all if we had practice or not that day. Under normal circumstances, I had to reach my daily quota. Even when I was playing in the first league for Kladno, I did five hundred a day. In the morning, I woke up early and did two hundred. After practice, I added another hundred, and in the evening another two hundred.

In order to relax my tired muscles, I also went to play soccer, which I still like to do in Pittsburgh. In the summer, I look forward to going home because I get together with people like in the old days and play for two goals.

When I was around thirteen or fourteen, I devoted a lot of time to shooting at a net. What we did at practice wasn't enough, so I took my work home. My dad welded together a hockey goal with the exact hockey dimensions and covered it with some old tennis nets. He set it up in the garden and hung up an old tarpaulin on the wall so the puck wouldn't fly away or smash the plaster. He also found a platform from which I shot the puck. It was about two yards wide and three yards long and made of plastic, so the puck slid across it pretty nicely. Often my team-

A dramatic moment in front of our goal. I almost turned around into the net (training school - 8 years old).

February 1980. I score one of our six goals against Konstruktiva of Prague (training school - 8 years old).

Typical scene from elementary school, I dragged away the puck and whisked off towards the net (10 years old).

With the Captain's C in the center, my dad standing above me, to the left Karel Beran and to the right Ota Cerny.

mates came to my place, including our goalie Karel Beran (my coach's son). We all would shoot there together, mostly during the summer.

My weekend days, particularly in the summer, looked like this: In the morning I woke up and did the prescribed number of knee bends, some push-ups and chin-ups, and then I went to the garden to shoot. I took about five hundred shots and then went back to work out. After that, I returned to the garden. I enjoyed it immensely, particularly when I focused on a specific part of the net. I kept shooting until I couldn't do it anymore.

My regular workouts began to show positive effects early on. I could outskate whoever I wanted, and I scored heaps of goals. In the middle of March 1979, there was a second-grade tournament in Kladno. I was voted best shooter, and they announced that I was the youngest player. I got sixteen goals and in the game with our arch rival Sparta, which we won 4-0, I scored all four goals. Sparta Praha, the club for which Jiri Hrdina played before he left for the NHL, was a tough team and all our games with them, whether men's, junior or little league, had the character of a battle. As it's only half an hour by car from Kladno to Prague, they were our closest rivals.

In the summer of the same year, I started practicing in my backyard with boys two years older than me, and I played with both third and fourth graders. A year later in 1980, I tried playing with boys up to seven years older than me. In Kladno they were repairing the stadium, so my dad took me to the nearby town of Lovosice, where the junior leagues were starting to train. I was able to practice with the younger junior teams because the father of a friend of mine was in charge. I had new Italian Rogers boots with Swedish blades. I got used to them quickly and was able to skate superbly with them. In two-lap races, I outskated several older juniors. It was completely sensational. I was only eight years old.

In the same season, I played for the younger junior team — the "B" team, which was for fifth graders. However, you could only play in this category if you were ten or older. I was far from it at the time. In Mladá Boleslav, the referee didn't want to let me play because I was two years younger than the rule book permitted. Fortunately, my dad had an acquaintance at the central ice hockey union in the registration section — Mr. Velechovsky from Kolín. He got a stamp from the hockey regulation authority and added the postscript "Exceptional Permission To Start For The Younger Junior Team." We had to do it illegally. It wasn't possible to do it any other way since no one else in the entire country had ever been granted a similar exception. Even the Communist Party functionaries in PZ were amazed at the way my dad was able to arrange it all.

At the time, the coach of the younger juniors' "A" team was Frantisek Sebek, a known figure in Kladno youth hockey. He was a very unusual guy, particularly because he was direct and fair. However, he had significant political problems.

Sebek didn't tolerate any privileged children on his team, and because of that, he was probably a thorn in the side of many party functionaries and officials. My dad knew Sebek, and because he always wanted me play or at least practice with older boys, he went to him and asked if I could occasionally practice with them. I'm certain that if I hadn't been up to it at that time, Sebek would have gotten rid of me. But he decided to try me out.

At one of the first practices, he chose the fastest skater, Michal Cukr, and put him against me in a one-lap race around the rink. Cukr was in the sixth grade and I was in the third, and I beat him by about a yard, which was completely unbelievable. One year at that age means a great deal, and he was three years older than me.

I liked Sebek's practices. We often played scrimmages for two goals. Sometimes he played with us, too. After practice he often went up to my dad and said to him, "I played with Jaromir on the line. I haven't had such a good game in a long time."

In December 1980, Sebek actually asked my dad if I would come play for him permanently. That's when the big problems began. Theoretically, I could have played for four teams — the younger A and B junior teams and the two little league teams. Unfortunately, none of the coaches wanted to let me play for anyone else. They all wanted me for themselves.

The ice rink at that time was occupied by Zdenek Sindler, and I practiced with his junior team for a while. He made up a schedule so that the games of my various teams wouldn't overlap, thus enabling me to play as much as possible, sometimes several times on the same day. Apparently, the little league coach scheduled dates for crucial games on my days off.

There were weekends I played five games. For instance, in Kolín, I played three games in the morning and scored all the goals for our team. In the afternoon, I played two more games for both the A and B junior teams against Pilsen.

I encountered boys of my own age on the ice for the first time on Christmas day. We were playing Slavie Praha, and from the very beginning, I drew extraordinary attention. Even though they had two people covering me, we won 4-1 and I scored all the goals. After the game, the entire Slavie team was in tears. The referee wrote on the scorecard that Slavie requested the hockey union award them victory by default because "Jagr, who won the game, already plays for the juniors." Of course it was nonsense because the deciding factor is age — and I was the right age.

I looked forward to the weekend tournaments the entire week and often couldn't get to sleep because of the excitement. We won wherever we went, and I collected more and more trophies. There were ten teams at the Kladno Miner's Lamp Tournament for fourth graders, but nobody scored a single goal against us. We came away with a total combined score of 29-0 for the tournament. I was named the best offensive player.

I like recalling the tournaments at Prague Stvanice, where the best fifth-grade teams from the entire country played each other. I was two years younger than the other players, and I still managed to be named the best offensive player.

In the year-round "Sparta Tourney" which took place on weekends, I was named the best shooter. I also scored the most goals at the regional fourth-grade championship. That one was the most fun. Under Karel Beran's leadership, we beat every team. I scored tons of goals because he always let me play. During the 1980-81 season — playing for a number of teams — I potted 310 goals during the championship games.

It was the same the following year. I was in the fourth grade, I played regularly for the sixth grade and participated in the year-round "Sparta Tourney" for the fifth grade. I only played for my own grade when things were "hot." During the Christmas holidays, there was a three-day tournament in Olomouc, designated as the unofficial fifth-grade Czechoslovakian championship. During that tournament, I scored fourteen goals in three games against the strongest teams in our country.

Unfortunately, in February I experienced my first hockey injury. I broke my hand at the wrist and couldn't play for an entire month. I still managed to score 248 goals that season.

In 1982, I started preseason training with the older juniors. Once again Mr. Velechovsky had to take care of a registration permit for this age category. In the summer, I practiced with a group of even older boys led by Zdenek Sindler. I played in a group with Vladimír Kames. In September, he started playing for the adults in the first league and scored the highest number of goals on the team.

Good skating ability was all I needed at that time. I have long legs and good balance, so I always stayed up on them even when an opponent did everything he could to stop me. Through regular training I acquired a great deal of strength in my legs and increased my speed.

Our games almost always looked the same. I broke toward the goal for the puck, took off and nobody could catch me. No combinations, no passes. At that time, the decisive factors were how well you skated and whether you could do something with the puck. I only needed my teammates to cover some of the opponents to give me some free space.

I made it to the net at least ten times in every game. Sometimes I tried to end with a fake, but I usually preferred to drive the puck into the net straight away. I didn't shoot at all, particularly not from a distance, which is why I had to focus on shooting later on. It was definitely not my strong point. But at that time I didn't need to constantly shoot.

Even though we consistently won, hockey started becoming painful for me. My opponents literally hunted me down, and when they couldn't stop me by normal means, they tried other ways. So many times after games, my forearms were completely black and blue from hockey stick blows. I was covered with bruises.

Nevertheless, nobody managed to completely discourage me. Only once did I decide not to play the whole game. That was at a tournament in Pribram. I was slashed by so many hockey sticks that I couldn't even hold mine. I was crying from the pain.

Sometimes it happened that those who dealt with me so roughly actually injured themselves. Once in Olomouc, an entire team took turns checking me to try to stop me. One unlucky boy ran into me so clumsily that he ended up breaking his leg.

Of the most popular tournaments I played in during the 1982-83 season, my favorite was definitely the Martin Fric Memorial. Our biggest rival, Sparta Praha, set it up. We actually played them in the finals. For this reason it was absolutely cutthroat. But the tense atmosphere at our games disappeared right away. There was only one team on the ice: ours. We beat the Spartans 6-0 and I scored three goals. At that time, I was playing in top form. For the first time somebody wrote about me in a newspaper. The weekly magazine *Kvety,* a slightly more serious version of *People,* ran a nice article about the tournament covering two full pages, along with a lot of photos. I still have it somewhere at home.

I have fond memories of other tournaments as well. One of the tournaments with the best lineup had sixteen teams playing in four cities simultaneously. In the finals, we beat Mladá Boleslav 8-1 (I scored six goals). To reach the championship match, we crushed Litvínov with the young Slegr 8-0 (I potted six goals) and then played against our toughest opponent — Dukla Jihlava.

Robert Holik was already playing excellently for Jihlava, so the game was like a duel between Holik and Jagr. I remember how Robert's dad Jaroslav boasted that the Jihlava boys would teach us a lesson. Another hockey legend of ours, Jirí Holík, came to the tournament to watch. At the end, he praised me for my performance in the game.

Under the leadership of Karel Beran, we probably had the best team that I can remember. Even though Jaroslav Holik's voice was booming the entire game, Jihlava was no match for us. We won 5-1, and I scored four goals.

Even our coaches recall with a smile these early jousts. We always hurled insults at each other. Once it nearly turned into a fight. It's interesting that my dad was very good friends with Václav Straka who did so much for youth hockey in Pilsen. None of them at that time had any idea that their sons would meet later in the same uniform in the best hockey league in the world.

In the young junior league, I often had problems with gear. I always forgot part of it at home. When we played in Pilsen, my dad always went to the Strakas to borrow something. After Michal Straka started playing in the NHL for Cleveland, Mr. Straka (Martin and Michal's father) came to visit me a few times in Pittsburgh and often reminisced about our childhood days. "Your dad always came to me to see if he could borrow an elbow pad because his little rascal left his at home again," Straka said. "So I lent it to him, and that rascal — you! — got five goals off us."

grammar school (Czech-style junior high). I had it a total of nine years, but I can't speak it at all now. When I wanted to speak some Russian with Alex Mogilny or Sergei Fedorov just for fun, I realized I couldn't say a single sentence in Russian. I wasn't much better at Russian in school. When I was at the blackboard, the entire class got a big laugh. I was a little better at mathematics and natural history. Those two subjects I always enjoyed.

My biggest love outside of hockey was drawing. I was crazy about it, and when my parents wanted to give me a present, I always asked them for drawing paper. Apparently, when I was three years old I did a little painting in my room. Later I had a kind of painter's palette with oil paints at home, and I painted everything I saw. Once I found a sign for a sports club somewhere. I later painted a copy of it, enlarged it and embroidered it with nylon exactly as it was in the original. I also painted soldiers and tanks a lot. My mom once said to me, "All you draw is war. Paint something happier." So I drew flowers on the tanks.

I later made some attempts at hockey "art." I drew various players in their uniforms or in situations during a game, the way players stand for a face-off and so on. My parents say that some of my pictures appeared in a few school exhibitions, but I don't remember that.

What I do remember is when I was at my grandparents place in the Sumava mountains during vacation. For a change, I tried to carve pieces of wood until they started to resemble something. My favorite thing was making cutting boards, and eventually all of my mom's coworkers had a nice cutting board compliments of yours truly. I usually painted something on the cutting boards for them.

I went to the Sumava every vacation until preseason training started which took up most of the summer. I always liked it there. I had a prescribed set of exercises to do from my dad: sprints and starts. My grandfather always timed me with a watch. But I enjoyed woodcutting more than sprinting, so I always hurried to finish the exercises as fast as possible so I get back to my cutting boards.

My grandparents are over sixty and full of life. They didn't have an easy time of it earlier in life. My grandfather was put in jail because he didn't want to join the Standard Farming Cooperative and was released two years later during an amnesty. The entire family was forced to move to Kladno. Since my grandfather was a political prisoner, my mom couldn't go to the university. At first she went to a vocational school and then went into farming. Eventually the farm she worked on sent her to agricultural school.

My other grandfather, on my dad's side, had it even worse. He owned a farm and a pasture, but when the period of collectivization began in Czechoslovakia, he was forced to enter the Standard Farming Cooperative. Later he resigned from it, and the communists took everything away from him and put him in jail. He died on March 15, 1969, on the thirtieth anniversary of the Nazi occupation of Czechoslovakia. He

As an adolescent in the Poldi uniform (12 years old). With team-mates David Cermak and Radek Vins.

Man doesn't only live for hockey, I was also able to create this stuff...

was an outstanding athlete and could do everything, but he was best at gymnastics. His specialties were the rings and parallel bars. Unfortunately, he died before I was born, so I learned about him mostly from my grandmother.

A few years ago, she was still lively, but now her health is worse. It's no surprise since she's nearly ninety years old. When I was small, instead of fairy tales, she told me about my grandfather and his hard life. It was actually through her that I learned the truth about communism. The life stories of my parents and grandparents told it all. It was my grandmother who inspired me so much with her stories that immediately after the revolution, I stuck the number "68" on my helmet, the year the Soviet army occupied our country. Then I added the initials "DA." Almost nobody knew what it meant. It never occurred to anyone that these were Alexandr Dubcek's initials, in reverse order. He was the creator of the reform movement known as Prague Spring — the program of "Socialism with a Human Face" — and was still hated by the ruling party.

My grandmother was also my teacher. She sat by the radio all day long, and when I came home, she told me what had happened in the world. She was completely interested in everything — changes in the government, world conflicts, the rules of different sports or the crime pages. These days she's a little forgetful, so she makes notes and reads everything straight from the paper.

The fact that my mom's parents were forced to move to Kladno had one positive result. I was born. It happened like this. My mom went with her friends for afternoon tea and dancing on Sundays. My dad stopped by once, purely by accident, and started talking with my mom. My gentlemanly dad offered to take her and her friend home. Afterward they started meeting regularly. They got married a year after they met. My mom was nineteen and my dad was twenty-five.

The first to be born was Jitka, who's six years older than me and is my exact opposite. Jitka was not a talented athlete, but she was always an excellent student. After graduation, she went to the university and today is an economist. Two years ago, she came to Pittsburgh with her little daughter Pavlínka, who was three years old at the time. Pavlínka immediately fell in love with hockey. When she saw me on the television screen, she cried out, "Jaromir's playing!" She could already recognize the other players. When we put in a videocassette and let her watch it, Pavlínka mumbled to herself, "Look, Barrasso."

My dad couldn't study for reasons similar to my mom's. He trained to be an electrician and later went to the technical college. However, he followed in his father's footsteps and went into farming. We farmed thirty-five acres of arable land. My dad did everything after work — from drying hay and transporting it, to feeding the bulls. I helped him with just about everything, and when I got bigger, I took on heavier work as well. I could see for myself that the cattle needed to eat.

In recent years, my dad has gone into business and is the co-owner of a construction firm. He even bought the best hotel in Kladno. And as if that wasn't enough, he took up hockey again as chairman of the hockey club Poldi Kladno. I'm curious how long he'll last.

As for where I am today, my mom was just as important as my dad. She did everything she could for me. When I came to Pittsburgh, she was with me the first four months. If she hadn't been there, I probably wouldn't have survived in the unknown environment. Now she's in Pittsburgh with me constantly, and I can't imagine being there without her.

My mom not only understood my interest in hockey, but she supported me in it. Due to various training camps, I was often absent from school and missed a lot. My mom and Jitka borrowed notebooks from classmates and copied everything from that day into my notebook, so I could study it when I got home. Jitka copied the notes for the subjects requiring attention, like geometry and mathematics. In math, change a plus or minus sign around, and the whole thing comes out differently. My mom copied Czech, history and geography notes. In elementary school, we had to read a fair number of books and write reports on them. My mom always did this for me. Once she had to read the entire history of the French Revolution. She didn't enjoy it very much. Both of them helped me tremendously, but it still wasn't easy. I came home after practice completely exhausted, and I still had to study. No wonder I almost always fell asleep over my books.

I also owe my good physical condition to my mom and her cooking. It definitely helped that we had our own farm. My parents said that the polluted air we breathed was bad enough without supplementing it with more chemicals from food. We never fertilized our farm with chemicals. We always used natural manure, and we grew just about everything possible.

I didn't go to restaurants or school cafeterias very much. I always ate at home. A good and regular diet is terribly important for every athlete, and my parents knew that. I never ate any precooked or ready-made foods. I liked soups and stews and ate a lot of ham. My mom was often afraid to buy ham because of what people would say. In Czechoslovakia at the time, ham was very rare. She was worried it would set us apart — people would wonder how we afforded it. What others couldn't eat in a month, I wolfed down in a matter of days. Sometimes my mom brought home a pound of ham and I'd have swallowed almost the whole thing before she'd had a chance to open the bread. My parents never economized with food, so we always had fresh fruit and vegetables when they were available. I remember when mandarin oranges appeared in the stores, my mom always bought an entire crate.

I also really liked cakes and chocolates. In fact, I still do. I gobbled up cookies by the dozen. I often ate on the bench during games. My mom brought me cookies and I munched them while I waited to get back on the ice. I had to eat all the time. I couldn't play when I was hungry. I was almost always on the ice, and it was necessary to replace all that energy. After all, you have to replace whatever the body uses up.

One of the key moments in my career was my transfer to the junior league. Here it was finally obvious who had the right stuff. It often happens that they don't find a boy right at the beginning, so he gets discouraged by his lack of success and gives up hockey. When I was in sixth grade, I was playing with eighth graders, but then they all moved up to a higher category.

When I was in the seventh grade, the question of what to do with me came up. It was understandably more comfortable for me to play with the beginners, but my dad kept pushing me into the more difficult categories.

Frantisek Sebek had gone into the juniors as well, where he coached with Zdenek Sindler. At the time he was an extremely well-known coaching personality. After all, he had managed several Czechoslovakian national youth teams. I made it through a summer training camp with him that I'll never forget.

It was absolute hell. I couldn't stand running on a long track, and at this camp we were running constantly. As long as it was sprints, I had no problem. I could even beat the older boys at short distances, but I couldn't keep up for long distances. I was always the last. It was even worse later, when I was big and had big bones.

At this point, I also started training with boys who had already gone into puberty. They were a head taller than me and much more developed physically. It was total agony. But I survived the summer, and the season began. The coaches of the young junior teams were angry with me because I didn't go to their practices and trained with the older juniors instead, even though I could only play with the younger ones because of my age.

Then they dealt with the issue of what to do with me. "So Franta. What do we do with him?" Sindler asked Sebek once. "We have to make him older. That's the only solution." So my dad went to Prague to the central committee of the Czechoslovak Union of Physical Education. Sindler went along with him because he knew his way around the committee. I was grateful to him for that because by that time he had accepted an offer to coach a professional team; he wasn't coaching the juniors anymore. He didn't have any reason to help out at all. In spite of that, my dad didn't even have to persuade him. "He's not going to play for the young juniors," Sindler said, and that was that.

Actually, Sindler, Sebek and, of course, Beran were the only coaches who absolutely wanted me. Some people already didn't like the fact that I was moving up so fast and tried to make everything as unpleasant for me as possible. At that time, my dad warned me that a number of people were jealous of me and that they were all just waiting for me to fail. I remembered his words. Many times I have learned that he was right.

When my dad went with Sindler to Prague, they went to see a Karel Kopriva, who was responsible for registration. He simply looked at my birthdate and said, "You must be crazy. This boy is in the seventh grade, and I'm supposed to sign this? Last year old Holik was here and wanted to raise Robert's age. He was a year older than your boy, and we still refused. If he found out that I did this for you, he'd kill me." Kopriva was unyielding, so my dad and Sindler pulled out their last trump card. "But he's even got confirmation from a doctor!"

The story with the doctor is a chapter in itself. I always had serious problems getting doctors to give me a medical stamp on my registration certificate. "Don't be angry, but we can't do this for you," they told my dad. "The boy is much younger than the others, and we simply can't certify him for this age category. If something happened, they'd put us in jail." So my dad packed his things and drove to Prague to the professional sport center. At that time, the head of the center was Dr. Vladmír Urbánek. Professional hockey players went to him. He was our last hope. My dad explained to him the kind of problems I was having, and Urbánek simply said, "Bring him in, and we'll do some tests."

They put me on a bike, covered me with various suction cups and wires and started measuring everything that can possibly be measured. According to my weight, they did a fitness coefficient and because I was small and light, I had a better one than some of the professional players. "It'll be no problem," said Urbánek, and so every year I went only to him. I had already been certified by Urbánek, and that was how Sindler and my dad got Kopriva to let me play for the juniors.

"Look, even Urbánek gave him a stamp. He wouldn't do that for him if everything wasn't in order," they droned. And Kopriva finally gave up. "You guys are crazy," he said in the end. But he stamped and signed it. As they were heading out the door, he said to them, "But I don't know anything." And so I was able to play for the juniors.

That was the 1984-85 season. I was the youngest player in the entire junior league. Here they already played a completely different game than the young juniors. As a twelve-year-old, I looked like a midget and with my figure-skating hockey method I didn't have much of a chance. I certainly didn't have the reputation of being a killer. Along the boards, I mostly made sure that nobody broke any of my bones.

I had to change the style of my game. It was at this time that I started learning how to shoot. I had blisters on my hands from practicing in the garden at home. I couldn't get to the goal very easily, so I also had to practice from a distance. In those days, I rarely made it to the net.

Despite my physical handicap, I often got lucky and a few times even brought attention to myself at tournaments. My first season in the junior league was pretty successful. I played in thirty-four games, scored twenty-four goals and had seventeen assists. The following year, I improved even more. I played in two more games, scored forty-one goals and had twenty-nine assists.

1988 — sister Jitka at high school graduation...

At this point, I was also forced to start dealing with the question of what to do with my life. I completed elementary school and had to make a decision. I didn't want to go to a trade school like the majority of the boys my age. Everyone got a trade certificate without knowing much about that particular field. My dad was convinced I would eventually play professional hockey, but he also said that I wouldn't play it forever and that I'd better learn to do something else, too.

Although I spent almost all my time on the ice, I didn't have many problems at school and got all As and Bs. At that time, my dad was working at a construction firm as a joiner. He told me, "You're good at drawing and mathematics, so you should go to the technical school and learn technical drawing for the construction business. Whatever you do in life, this field will always be marketable. There's always building and every city has a construction office. Besides, you'll also have a diploma. So you can study at the university and get a deferment from the military," he said, deciding everything for me. "Go to the construction center." It was an order, so I took the entrance exam. I passed and they accepted me.

Immediately afterward, one problem appeared. There were all boys in the classroom, and my parents didn't like that. I didn't care at all. I didn't know much about girls at the time, and I was always shy around them anyway. I often crossed the street when I saw a girl from class. My parents didn't think it normal for me to be around boys all the time. So they asked the administration to place me into a mixed classroom. Not that I hung out with the girls in class. I had other problems — the material in class.

I had another problem. At that time, every male in our country who reached the age of eighteen had to do basic military service for two years. I was terrified at the thought of going into the military. That's the reason a lot of boys went to university. University students only had to go into the military for a year. I don't know what was more important for my dad: my learning something or the prospect of a military deferment. It was probably the military deferment. My dad wanted me to go to school for as long as possible. He thought that I could do one semester every two years or so. That way I'd go into the military at age twenty-seven, and nobody would be able to corrupt me very much. My dad was terrified that I would go there at seventeen and start drinking and smoking. Michal Pivonka's dad told my dad that I should study for as long as possible.

However, it wasn't very pleasant for me at school. My dad was definitely right when he said, "You have to know something. If you get injured, you'll be through with hockey, and then what will you do?" But construction was too difficult for me, even though we didn't realize it at the time. I was able to stick with my individual program until the second year, but even that didn't matter. I didn't have time for school. I practiced hockey and missed school to go to training camps, including camps for national youth teams. I'd come back from a training trip, and

I couldn't understand the material covered in class. When you aren't there for a week, you don't understand what's being taught because each lesson is connected to the previous one. And so friends began doing drawings and drafting assignments for me — secretly of course.

I also managed to turn some teachers against me. My goal was to pass the exams. I didn't care what kind of grades I got. The teachers couldn't understand why I didn't try to get better grades. One time, one of them tested me and said, "I can't give you a D. You're better than that. Come again next week." Of course, I couldn't. So I told her, "But that's good enough for me. I still have to do other exams, and if I get Ds I'll be perfectly satisfied." That infuriated her because she thought I was making fun of her.

The worst class was Russian. The entire class looked forward to the moment when I was called on. Once the teacher asked me how to say "Good day." As always, I couldn't think at the blackboard and I racked my brains for the answer. Finally, I remembered and gleefully said: "Guten Tag."

The entire class burst out laughing. "Guten Tag" is German, not Russian. In this way I stumbled through the school for four years. I stuck it out until almost the very end. To this day, I haven't graduated. I did all the exams and even have all the drawings prepared to hand in. But in the end I went to the United States and gave up on the idea of graduation. Now I regret it a bit, but I just couldn't handle both school and hockey.

I played with the young juniors for two more seasons and one more with the older juniors. We played in the first league and practiced every day. I kept winning games, but I was no longer such a standout on the ice, as I had been when I played with the beginners. It was mainly because we were playing second string and the older junior team didn't even get into the playoffs, for which twelve teams could qualify. A new star appeared on the scene at that time — Robert Reichel. At that time, Robert was outrageous. He was a superb skater so he easily got chances to score. He also had a big advantage because his team, Litvinov, was playing extremely well. Later, I began coming across his teammates in the NHL.

In those days, I devoured every piece of news from the hockey world, and almost every one of us tried to emulate Wayne Gretzky. It was interesting that none of us had actually seen him play, but everything that was said about him had an extremely strong effect on us, particularly the fact that he scored so many goals.

There was a considerable amount written about the NHL, and the WHA as well, in our country. I admired the overseas hockey players enormously, but at that time I was mostly into the Finns. My hero was Jarri Kurri. I even made my mom buy the material to sew me a Finnish flag.

In the youth divisions, I already played in several games against teams from Canada. It was a valuable hockey experience, as well as an excellent opportunity

In the uniform of league team Kladno. I play with Christian hockey sticks brought to me by Jiri Crha

to exchange souvenirs. I was probably the most daring one on the team in this way, and they often called me the "big black marketeer." I remember that as a young junior I ran to the parents of the other boys with the insignias and flags of our hockey teams and exchanged them for theirs, particularly at the training camps in Slany. Most of the swaps were for Gretzky posters, for which we were willing to give just about everything. Then in 1985, something happened which made us forget about Wayne, at least in my case.

The World Championship took place in Prague and a twenty-year-old was playing for Canada who wasn't a superstar yet, but who showed tremendous promise — Mario Lemieux. Lemieux enchanted the people of Prague. From the moment I laid eyes on him, he became my hockey hero. It never occurred to me that one day I'd be playing with him on the same team. I saw every one of his games and couldn't take my eyes off the television screen. My mom complained that it almost made her deaf. I sat in front of the television and screamed: "Mario! Mario!"

My mom was completely beside herself and asked me if I'd lost my mind.

"Why are you so hung up on that Mario? You don't even know a single person named Mario!" she exclaimed. I had to explain to her who he was. Today I don't have to explain it to her.

I can never forget how Canada, with the help of Lemieux, beat the Soviet Union 3-1. In that game, Mario scored all three goals. The World Championship ended well for Czechoslovakia. We beat the Soviet Union 2-1 and became the world champions. I was thirteen. A few months after that, I joined the older juniors, which is normally for sixteen-year-olds. The victory of our country at the World Championship that year naturally helped the cause of hockey. The stadiums were full because we were the league of world champions. I had no idea that in two years I'd be wearing a uniform with the same colors.

JAGR

A Lion Cub on my Breast

For the first time in Olomouc, there was a tournament of four national teams made up of sixteen-year-olds. I was fifteen at the time and was nominated as an alternate. In the first game against Finland, I got an opportunity to play in the last ten minutes of the game. I was able to show off quite a bit. I got one goal and had two other definite chances.

My dad was at the game to watch, even though I told him he couldn't come. I didn't want him there at all. I didn't like it when people came to watch me. It sometimes happened that someone I knew came, and I completely lost my appetite to play. I was probably a little strange in that respect.

I told my dad just to forget about going. I would have had terrible stage fright if I knew he was there. Of course, my dad didn't listen to me and secretly came to the game. However, my mom came by train to another game in the tournament with the Soviet Union. As soon as she saw me, she handed me a letter. I opened it and read: "Not bad, but you have to shoot more. Dad."

At the game with the Soviet Sborna, my mom was overjoyed because it was the first time she saw me in a Czechoslovakian uniform, with a lion cub on my breast, while our national anthem was playing. But this game didn't turn out well for me and could easily have been the last in my career.

During the game, I got a serious charley horse in my leg and couldn't move. I wasn't able to take a single step. I don't know who slammed into me that time. I couldn't even pack up my gear alone. My mom knew something had happened to me, but she was convinced it was nothing serious and took the train home after the game. My parents waited for me the next day at the train station, but Pavel Sindler, our team's masseur, had driven me home instead.

I rested for two months, but my leg didn't improve. And what was worse, it started to calcify. The doctors had no idea what was wrong with it. Some said it needed to rest, while others said I had to move it. The biggest mistake was apparently not taking the blood out of the muscle immediately after it happened. Because of that, a bump appeared and I could barely move my leg. Eventually, I went to one doctor, who examined me for a long time and said,

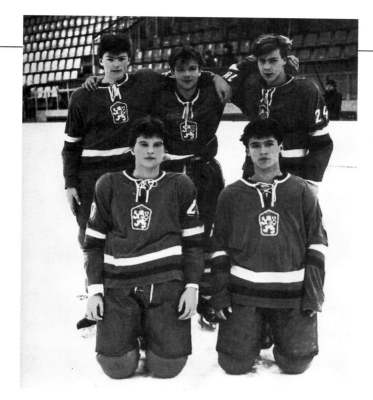

First photograph from the preparation of the CSSR "16" representational selection.

"It'll be fine. You'll be able to walk normally." But all I kept thinking was, "I want to play hockey!"

At one point they considered radiation treatments, but that would have meant that the muscle would have stopped growing, which would probably have meant the end of hockey, and definitely professional hockey. I went to orthopedic specialists in Prague, but no one could tell me what to do about it.

It eventually turned out all right. The former manager of the young junior team and current editor at Czech Television, Ota Cerny, arranged for the doctor of the adult national team, Ota Trefny, to drain most of the fluid with a hypodermic. At that time, my dad took me to the airport where the team was taking off for the World Championship in Sweden. The hypodermic procedure helped. I was able to walk again and quickly returned to the ice. Because of the injury, however, I missed the entire remainder of the season. I still have the bump on my leg, and it'll probably stay there until I die. But the main thing was that I was able to start playing hockey again.

In the 1987-88 season, I played for the older junior team PZ Kladno but started to practice with the adults. It was difficult. My longtime teammate and friend David Cermak moved onto the professional team, but I was kept in the junior league, which irritated me. It came as a blow. Even though I was two years younger than he, I was definitely ready for the adult team. It also made me angry that our junior team was weakened by David's departure. We lost every game and I completely lost all interest in playing. I just wanted to forget it all.

Representational "16" in Sweden in February 1988 at the final four championships.
Order: Sweden, USSR, Czechoslovakia, Finland.

At that time, Sparta actually made me a serious offer. They were already interested in me when I was playing for the younger teams. That was the first time I contemplated playing for someone other than Kladno. I actually didn't contemplate it much. I merely toyed with the idea. Josef Horesovsky was coaching Sparta, and he even offered to drive me to practices. And so the tug of war began.

In Kladno, there were two divisions — Poldi and PZ. The best players from Poldi automatically went from the juniors to the adults because they were players from the same club. However, PZ didn't have a men's team, which is why juniors from PZ went to Poldi if they were offered a contract. Of course, this meant that I wasn't required to move automatically to Poldi like the others. If another team offered a contract, I could go play there without anyone's consent since there wasn't actually anyone to give it.

Team officials put a great deal of pressure on my dad at work for me to sign on with Poldi, and they even hinted that he might have problems if I didn't sign. They even said it was his party duty for me to remain in Kladno. Ing. Václav Ríha, who later became the head of Czechoslovakian hockey, kept calling my dad and convinced him to not let me go anywhere else.

The fact is, I didn't have anything of the kind in mind. Daily commuting to Prague didn't seem to me like much fun, and besides, I wanted to play where I was born, in Kladno.

I played in forty-nine out of sixty-two games and got sixty-four goals and thirty-seven assists. I didn't play in thirteen games, partly because I was also starting to play in scrimmage games with the adults.

I remember my first encounter with the Kladno Matadors perfectly. I entered the locker room, but the coach at that time, Eda Novák, certainly didn't make it any easier for me. "So tell us who you are and where you're from," he said. "Jaromir Jagr, and I'm from the village of Hnidousy," I stammered. I was so scared I was shaking. But the worst was yet to come.

In the beginning, I still got dressed in the juniors' locker room. It was a little later that I moved. I was shy and didn't know where to put my things in the new locker room. My teammates sensed this, and picked on me a bit. "Do you know where there's an empty locker?" I asked. Back then, I used the polite form of address with just about everyone. "Over there. There's an empty locker," they said, pointing to one. The only problem was that was Milan Novy's locker. I placed all my things in the locker quite nicely and set up house, until Novy, the best shooter in the history of Czechoslovakian hockey with 600 goals to his credit (he even played one season in the NHL for the Washington Capitals), arrived. Novy, nicknamed "Bumpkin," was quite a bit older than me.

When he saw me, a fifteen-year-old boy, in his spot, he couldn't believe his eyes. "What are doing here, youngster?" he asked cheerfully. The entire locker room burst into laughter, and I turned beet red.

I played in my first game for the league team on January 19, 1988, in Litvinov as part of an international tournament. I was actually playing illegally — I was only fifteen at the time — so there was no Jagr on the roster. I was hiding behind the name Zdenek Hrabe. I scored my first goal right away in that game. A week later we beat Japan 5-2. I scored twice. For the first time in my life, I got some money for playing hockey after this game. I felt like a professional. I was paid 150 Czechoslovakian crowns, which was about $3.50 on the black market.

Understandably, I had some fears about entering the league. I still wasn't as physically developed as the other players, and mentally I was still a child. Some of them already had families, and I wasn't even going out with girls yet. In the locker room, I went into a corner and kept my mouth shut. Despite that, my teammates accepted me. I later learned from David Cermak that when I showed up for the very first time, someone in the locker room said, "Pretty soon they'll be bringing us kids from kindergarten."

Summer training began in the middle of May and was something I usually preferred to blow off. Especially when we had to run long distances. The runs to Kozovka were infamous. I was lucky, however, to find a "good partner" — Jarda Kames. He and I thought up a kind of scheme. Once we had a race, and Jarda and I alternated between walking and running until we were the very last ones. By then they didn't even bother timing us. There wasn't even anyone at the finish line. They'd all gone home.

Luckily we didn't run that often, so the summer practices weren't as hard as the Sindlerovská — the name we gave to coach Sindler's summer training program. The coaches' — Eduard Novák's and Bedrich Brunclík's — specialties were regular bike rides, which gave the practices some variety. It was pretty fun. We always fought over who would get to ride the fast bikes. We had a good time. At least, some of us did.

I had an old bike and didn't have the equipment my teammates had. Almost everyone had racing bikes, while I had a piece of junk with a pump and a rack. But because I was in good enough shape and had strong legs, I was able to keep up with them. It especially worked for me going uphill. Once, we were getting timed and I got lost. I didn't know the area around Kladno at all. I didn't have a clue what village I was in. That's why I usually stuck with someone — so I wouldn't get lost.

During one bike ride, I showed them that a racing bike wasn't necessarily better than an old bike. About ten kilometers before Kladno, I started to get tired and fell about twenty meters behind the group. Then I caught up with them, but I didn't switch gears. And right before the finish line, I switched into the lowest gear and passed them all. They were all irritated of course, especially Novy. They couldn't understand how a pipsqueak like me could have the nerve to pass them. When the ride was over, "Bumpkin" jumped off his bike and hit me with a pump.

At the end of August and the beginning of September, I played three games for the Czechoslovakia Under 17 team. First we tied the Under 18s from the U.S. in Frydek-Místek, and then we beat the Under 18s from Switzerland. Then the league season started.

Straight from the Field to the Season Opener

I remember the first game quite well. We played Skoda Pilsen at home, and I got ready for the game in my own way. I wasn't in bed at 10 p.m., but I wasn't at a discotheque or at the movies. I was in the field. My dad simply said we had to finish it.

The opener didn't show off my talents too much. We lost to Skoda 6-3, and then lost two more games in front of the home crowd. I scored my first goals in the seventh round when we tied Tesla Pardubice on their ice.

The break after the thirteenth round came just in time. We weren't playing well, and since we'd taken fourth place the year before, ninth place was a disappointment. David Cermak and I were the wingmen, and I scored two goals and had two assists. That's not really much, but nobody expected us to win games for them. I couldn't do anything in the next twelve games, but I was already preparing for the big trip across the Atlantic. And that was my comeback representing Czechoslovakia.

I first played for the Czechoslovakia Under 16 team, but as soon as I started league hockey, I didn't make the cut. I was going through a definite crisis at the time. I was tired and didn't like to practice. In addition, I followed my habit of not listening to anyone. But I was beating my head against a wall.

The team was coached by Pavel Siroták, and he simply hated my guts. The feeling was mutual. Siroták was a pretty big cheese, and he did nothing to hide it. He always said that there wasn't room for two hotshots on the team. Apparently he'd made up his mind to get rid of the second hotshot. That was me.

Of course, I did my best to help him make that decision. I was chosen to represent Czechoslovakia at a tournament between four countries, and I played terribly. I just couldn't do anything right. I only scored one goal during the three games, so I'm not surprised that he wanted to get rid of me. The other boys went to a training camp in Germany, and I stayed home. A little later there was a tournament in Slovakia, and my favorite coach picked me to play in it. But I just moped and sulked and tore up the invitation. What I did with the invitation was totally stupid. Eventually another invitation arrived with a note explaining that if

I didn't appear this time, I'd have to appear before a disciplinary committee. This time I went.

The most absurd thing about the whole situation was that two months after Sироták cut me from Czechoslovakia's Under 17 team, I received an invitation to play for the Under 20s. This selection was preparing me for the Under 20 World Championship. I put in a good showing in a scrimmage game against the Soviet Union's Under 20s. However, I finally agreed with the coach, Josef Vimmer, that the Under 20 World Championship in Anchorage would be a bit much for me. Besides, it wasn't clear if I would even make the team since there would be a five-person cut. So I decided it would be better to go to Canada for the Under 18 training series.

I had one of the best coaches I've ever experienced on the Under 18s. He was a great specialist and a nice person. We spent three grueling weeks in Canada. In order to pay for the trip, we had to play numerous games since the sponsor only covered part of the costs.

We played around seventeen games and were sick of hockey. We would ride in a bus for seven hours, play a game in the evening and do the whole thing over again the next day. I don't really remember the results, but I think we won quite a bit. It was my first trip overseas, and I was really taken aback by it — both by the shops full of goods and the narrower rinks. But I played well. My playing clearly benefited from the exhausting trip. I felt it when I jumped back into the league at home. In the first six games after my absence, I racked up six points — three goals and three assists. I even scored two goals against the tough Litvinov team and turned the game around. I also got a goal at home against Kosice. We won 5-2, and Peter Bondra scored both of the goals for the guests. We were also to meet again in the future.

The coaches, Eduard Novák and Bedrich Brunclík, only stayed with the team until the middle of February. We were losing, and as these things go, it was only a matter of time before we exchanged coaches. The former Kladno league players Václav Sykora and Bohumil Prosek took their places. The fight for survival was ahead of us.

Things were getting hot in the league. I received an invitation to a tournament of four Under 18 teams being held in Jindrichuv Hradec. It was in preparation for the European Championship in the Ukrainian city of Kiev. In the end, I never even went to Jindrichuv Hradec. Kladno wouldn't let me go, but other players were not allowed to go either. Their home teams needed them. Among them were Robert Holik and Robert Reichel.

We ultimately saved ourselves in the tournament, but the qualification rounds were no fun. Our performance that year had been a big disappointment, but that didn't have much to do with me. I played in a total of sixty-four games and scored twenty-one goals. I ended up fifth in points, and I couldn't have hoped for more before the start of the league season.

We played the final qualifying game at home against Olomouc. That night Jirka Vykoukal slept at our house, and the very next day we went to the airport together to fly to Kiev, where the Under 18 European Championship had already begun.

We were defending our European Championship title from the previous year. We knew that with the team we had, we could retain the gold.

We started out well. First, we beat West Germany 10-3 and then Norway 18-4. The results were like the World Championships before the sixties, when Canada beat all the other teams with similar margins. The Soviet Union pounded Romania 15-0, and Finland beat Switzerland 17-0. A tough opponent awaited us in the third game, but we defeated the Swedes, with the outstanding Mats Sundin leading the fight, by a score of 10-5. I got four goals. On the other hand, I didn't pot a single goal against Switzerland, even though we won by a record score of 19-1. I made up for it against Finland, when I scored the decisive goal to break a 3-3 tie. With that win, we had at least a silver medal.

Our toughest competitor awaited us — the Soviet Union. We went to watch when they played the Finns, and we got pretty scared. I remember that we weren't sitting in the stands alone. There were NHL scouts next to us, looking for potential players for the overseas clubs. J. C. Tremblay from the Montreal Canadiens was there along with Dan Labraaten of the New Jersey Devils, Heiki Riihiranta of the Edmonton Oilers and Inge Hammarstrom from NHL Central Scouting.

We probably had a little too much faith in ourselves prior to the game with the Soviet Sborna. We were relying on the fact our team had more stars than our opponent — Robert Reichel, Robert Holik, Jirka Slegr and the outstanding Roman Cechmanek in goal, while the home team was mainly relying on Pavel Bure and Vyacheslav Kozlov. Unfortunately, it turned out that those two were able to handle us alone.

We started the game like a hurricane and had more chances to score than our opponent. But Sergei Tkachenko, the Soviet Union's goalie, didn't let one of our sixteen shots past him in the first period. In the second period, we increased the pressure. I threw away one chance, Reichel another. Both teams were shooting, but nobody was scoring. During our biggest attack in a four-on-four confrontation, Bure and Kozlov and Eugeny Davidov slipped a goal past Cechmanek, whose vision was obstructed. We tried again, shooting from all sides, had some big chances, but scored no goals. We always breathed easier when Bure and Kozlov rotated. When they were on the ice together, everything they did left us helpless.

In the last period, we almost didn't let the Soviet team out of their defensive zone. All they did was pass the puck back and forth. All we did was play five against five, and the Soviets were only saved by luck. Fifty two seconds before

And the 1988 Poldi Kladno team.

the finish, we finally managed get the puck behind Tkachenko's back, but the referee refused to count the goal. The Swedish Kent Frederikson had refereed the entire game extremely well, but at that moment he was being a little hard on us. Reichel couldn't believe the referee's decision and protested so vehemently, that the judges sent him to the locker room because he threw his hockey stick into the stands. We still had all six men on the ice, but we lost the face-off. Kozlov passed to Bure who sealed the Soviet team's victory with an empty net goal. While the Soviets hugged each other, we went into the locker room with tears in our eyes.

The Kiev Championship was an important experience for me. For the first time, I had the opportunity to compare my hockey skills with the best players in the world, who were a year older than me. I didn't disappoint anyone, even though I didn't make it onto the All-Star roster. Those who did were Tkachenko (USSR), Sergei Selimanov (USSR), Christer Olsson (Sweden), Holik (Czechoslovakia), Reichel (Czechoslovakia) and Bure (USSR). I really like recalling that championship — we were an outstanding bunch of players with excellent coaches, Florian Strída and Josef Giblák. After that, I longed to put on the Czechoslovakian uniform to represent our country again. I was soon able to fulfill that longing.

The surprise was waiting for me at the end of June in the mailbox. It took the form of an invitation to play with the Czechoslovakian team at a training camp and to play in some scrimmage games in Germany. Invited along with me were the other youngsters — Holik, Reichel and Jiri Vykoukal. I was totally thrilled about it, as I was still only seventeen years old. I was extremely happy, even though I knew they had only invited me to try out.

I played in my first representational game, albeit an unofficial one, in August in Rosenheim against the Federal Republic of Germany (West Germany). We won 6-1, but it was clear that the coaches were counting on me for the Under 20 team. In the summer, we had already begun training for the World Championship in Finland. In August, we took part in the traditional Tournament of Four in Piestany, where we beat the USSR 5-1 but lost to Sweden, finishing second.

In the middle of September there was a big holiday for the entire hockey public. Czechoslovakian hockey celebrated the eightieth anniversary of its founding, and it couldn't have wished for a better gift. That year's Stanley Cup champs, the Calgary Flames, played two games in Prague. Everyone was mainly interested in two players — Sergei Makarov and Jiri Hrdina.

Makarov, a member of the legendary Soviet offensive trio of Sergei Makarov-Igor Larionov-Slava Krutov, didn't disappoint anyone during his first year overseas and garnered sixty-six points. But in Prague, he was merely playing at the level of his teammates. And Jiri Hrdina was coming home. He knew every corner of the Prague Sports Arena and wanted to show the home crowd that he belonged.

However, the Canadians as a whole didn't show off very much and lost twice 4-1.

In the second game, I played on the front line with Reichel and Holik. We even got a goal during a power play against us, when Reichel's shot on goal was deflected and Holik sent it into the net. I didn't finish the game because I injured my kneecap and had to sit out.

I didn't really get the chance to enjoy myself with Hrdina. That was to come a little later. However, I do remember that he swore in English during the game.

Two days after the test of strength with the Canadians, the season started with Václav Sykora and Frantisek Kaberle coaching us. But the season opener didn't say much for them. We lost the first game at home. Then we went to Ceské Budejovice, where things came together. We won 4-2. I got a goal and was also named our team's MVP.

I took hockey very seriously, so I was that much more upset when I didn't do well. I had serious problems with coaches who continually wanted to tie me down to set plays. I wasn't too big on that. Apart from my dad, I didn't listen to any coaches, not even those who meant well. And now they were trying to make a puppet out of me who played according to the way they pulled the strings. I needed freedom and space. But practices were no paradise, either. They called me "junior," so I had to take care of the pucks and equipment. And then my older teammates let me have it during scrimmage games. Apparently, so that I'd get used to it. Physically, I was relatively well equipped to handle it. I had strong legs and, thanks to the frequent work in the fields, strong hands. But my thoughts were still those of a child. After all, the majority of my teammates had children of their own, and I wasn't even an adult. I mostly hung out with my peers — David Cermak, Martin Bakula, Pavel Bares or Mirek Mach.

The best players in the league at that time were Robert Reichel and Ota Janecky. I liked Janecky from the time I was a little boy. He had an amazing technique, and I found myself watching him during our games. I still didn't play that much. The coach sent me onto the ice twice per period, which gave me more of an opportunity to observe the individual players.

Once we scored about twelve goals against Pardubice when we were playing at home, and Janecky scored at least four of them himself. Our fans were so turned off by the scene that they started rooting for Pardubice.

When I think back on those years, I realize that the world off the ice didn't exist for me. My friends went to dance classes, flirted with girls, had teenage fun, and I went to the stadium. My dad often rode with me to games and practices and took me home right afterward. To be perfectly honest, I was so tired I usually wasn't interested in going anywhere. Besides, there was always homework waiting for me. I definitely was not a disco king.

After the sixteenth round of the league season, I took some time off to represent

Czechoslovakia because the A team was playing three practice games against the Soviet Union. I was invited to the Under 20 training camp, but they indicated that they would only let me play with Reichel and Holik in the third game against the Soviet Sborna.

And they stuck to their word. After we'd lost two games 4-2 and 6-3, I played in my first official game in an official Czechoslovakian uniform for the A team in Prague on November 2, 1989. And the game went pretty well for me. We lost, but the assistant coach of the Sborna, Igor Dmitriyev spoke very highly of us. "Both teams are looking to the future, and from this perspective, your young offensive team of Jagr, Reichel and Holik really shone," he said after the game.

On November 21, I made it into the Czechoslovakian media. I found myself on the last sports page of what was at that time a very popular weekly magazine, *Stadion..* I answered six questions in my first big interview. I was seventeen years old.

Four days before that, something happened to me which influenced my life greatly. From that day on, my later hockey career began to come together — in the best league in the world, the North American National Hockey League. Not that I was thinking about it so much at the time, but certain barriers which might have prevented me from entering the NHL in the future were removed.

On November 17, 1989, the Velvet Revolution began — and it affected all the citizens of Czechoslovakia, including us hockey players. In Prague on Národní trída (National Avenue), a procession of students was brutally attacked by the police, an act which set our country on the path toward democracy. Several days later, there were strikes and about half a million people collected on Wenceslas Square every day. The communist regime crumbled like a house of cards, and by the end of the year we had our new president, Václav Havel.

When the revolution began, we refused to play for several games in support of the striking students. In Ceské Budejovice, we agreed that Ceské Budejovice's players and coaches, along with ours, would go to Ziska Square, where the captains of both teams read a joint declaration. Other hockey players were doing the same thing in other cities across Czechoslovakia.

During the communist regime, only veteran players could play abroad. There existed a set of criteria, which applied from the moment you donned Czechoslovakia's colors, which meant that you couldn't leave to play abroad until your career was almost over. That was also the case with hockey players from the former Soviet Union. If someone like Slava Fetisov had had the chance to go play in the NHL in his twenties, he'd have definitely had fewer problems getting recognized and would have surely become one of the best defensemen in the NHL.

Fortunately for my generation, the revolution changed all that, and we could leave when we were young. So while November brought democracy to the people of Czechoslovakia, in my case, it allowed for my future in hockey.

The league started playing again after November 17, and I was already thinking about putting on the colors of another team someday, somewhere else. Under the direction of coaches Josef Vimmer and Stanislav Berger, we started training for the Under 20 World Championship, which was to take place in Finland over New Year's. We wanted at least a medal. We had a relatively good team. In addition to the tried-and-true Roberts — Holik and Reichel — there were others on the team: Jirka Slegr, Milos Holán, Jirí Vykoukal, Petr Kuchyna, Richard Smehlík and others.

We began the tournament wonderfully. We beat both Finland and the USA 7-1. I scored two goals in the game against the Americans. In one outstanding performance after another, we defused Poland 11-1, Norway 13-2 and even Sweden 7-2, right after we arrived from a game in Turku, completely frozen after a two and a half hour trip in an unheated bus. After five games, we already had nine points, enough to assure us a bronze medal, and we were itching to sink our teeth into a game against a real opponent.

The only problem was that we ran into a roadblock. The Soviet Union once again showed us how to play, and we found ourselves losing by five goals. Ultimately, we got away with a respectable score of 8-3, but even that was a big disappointment.

The ones who taught us a lesson were our old friends Slava Kozlov, Pavel Bure and Andrei Kovalenko. But because Sborna had lost to Canada 6-4, we still had some hope of beating them. Beating the extremely tough Canadian team would mean we could finally rejoice over a world championship. In fact, it wasn't that unrealistic a thought. In a scrimmage game with players from the land of maple leaves, we won 3-1. But history didn't repeat itself.

We dominated the first part of the game, and in the final minute of the first period we took the lead thanks to a goal by Reichel. But then the Canadians upped the stakes and started putting the pressure on us. In the twenty-ninth minute, Mike Craig tied the score, and three minutes before the end of the second period, Ducayne Norris scored the decisive goal for a close victory. Canada became the world champions. After tying with Sweden in their last game, the Soviet Union took second place. We got the bronze. It was clear that after the first half of the tournament, we had probably been a little too optimistic and had underestimated the most important games.

In the seven games, I scored five goals and had thirteen assists. In the final rankings, according to Canadian points, I placed second — right behind Robert Reichel (twenty-one points) and in front of Canadian David Chyzovski (thirteen points). I made it onto the All-Star team, along with goalie Stephane Fiset, defensemen Jiri Slegr and Alexander Godynyuk and Reichel and David Chyzowski on offense.

We were also represented on the B All-Star team by Jiri Vykoukal and Holik, who were joined by Tom Eskelin, Zubov, Roman Oksiuta and Kozlov.

I wasn't lost in the crowd of All-Stars, and the scouts probably made a few remarks about me in their notebooks. There was already talk that I would be drafted the following year in 1990. Scouts from several NHL teams even contacted me. The first ones who got in touch with me were the Hartford Whalers. In an interview for a Slovak magazine, my father actually insisted that Hartford would be the best because I could study management or something at the local university there. I don't know if my dad actually thought that seriously. I would have liked it in Hartford, particularly because Ivan Lendl is one of the shareholders in the club.

However, I wasn't thinking too much about the NHL at the time. I had an entire season in our league ahead of me, and only after that could I actually sit down and contemplate what I should do next. At the same time, my father made certain that my successes wouldn't go to my head. He constantly went over with me everything I did. No little mistake escaped him. I even reached the point where it was uncomfortable to sit in the car with him when he drove me home from games. After a while my mom asked us both to limit the after game discussions.

I often think back on those moments when I go home after a game from the Civic Arena and imagine what my dad would say if he were there. He was, and still is, my harshest critic, and he has always been very direct. And when a game doesn't go well for me, I imagine him there, waiting in the car. When he sees me, he says sarcastically, "There you are. I was afraid something had happened to you. For the entire sixty minutes I didn't even notice you on the ice. Where were you?"

Jagr Smokes Sparta

Even though I was in only my second season as a professional in Czechoslovakia, my desire to try out for the NHL was growing stronger and stronger. I knew that I was lucky in one big way already to be playing professionally, and that whatever happened with my career would be up to me. No one was going to prevent me from going abroad as long as an agreement with Kladno could be reached, and the team was already beginning to come to terms with my eventual departure. Milan Novy confided to me that he envied me a little because the players of his generation had to stay and represent the Czechoslovak Socialist Republic for propaganda purposes, and it was only after they were past their primes that the Players' Union would grant them leave to try playing somewhere else.

Still, I didn't know whether I had what it took to play in the NHL during the next season. My skating was above par certainly, but my shooting was causing me nothing but problems. I didn't yet have the confidence that would be necessary.

Because we were late in getting back from Finland, I didn't begin playing in the new year until the game against Ceské Budejovice. I had again been named our team's MVP, and in my seventeenth game of the league season, I scored my fourteenth and fifteenth goals. But then we went to Jihlava and got blown away 7-0, the worst loss I had suffered yet in my career.

At the beginning of February we lost again, 6-2, to Sparta in Prague. Sitting in the crowd of 9,000 that day were two North American hockey experts, Paul Geller from the U.S. and Farrel Miller, an agent from Canada. The Prague evening paper quoted Miller as saying, "That No. 15 [Jagr] is physically ready for Canadian hockey. If he's really only seventeen, then he should definitely be the dark horse of this year's draft."

The "dark horse" next played in front of the scouts in Kosice, all the way at the eastern end of Czechoslovakia, although it was the home team's forward Peter Bondra that they were there to see, not me. We ended up winning the game, but I didn't score any goals. Neither, I think, did Peter.

Our last game of the regular season was in Zlín, and the players on both teams were wearing black armbands. The new year had begun tragically. In a game against Kosice on January 5, Zlín's Ludek Cajka, a 26-year-old Czechoslovakian national team player and veteran of 297 league games, raced for the puck at top speed when he collided with an opposing linesman and flew headfirst into the boards. He lay unconscious in the hospital with a severe spinal cord injury for forty days before passing away on Saturday, February 17.

I remember that game in Zlín very well. Nobody really wanted to play, and we couldn't care less who won. The game ended up a 5-5 tie, and I think one goal was scored by seventeen-year-old Roman Hamrlik, who was drafted number one by Tampa Bay two years later.

Kladno finished seventh overall in the regular season, and our first-round play-off opponent, in a best-of-three series, was the number two team, VSZ Kosice. So back we traveled to the other end of the country for Game One.

Kosice's hockey rink is something like the old Chicago Stadium in that the stands are very close to the ice and the fans can make so much noise that you can't hear yourself think. Because we really had nothing to lose, we played fast and loose, and at the beginning of the third period, we managed to take the lead. The home team then pushed forward with an all-out attack and tied the score with nine minutes left to go in regulation. At that moment, I thought the stadium was going to collapse, the fans were going so wild.

Things quieted down in a hurry a moment later, though, when I caught a pass on the fly, slipped past Kosice's defenseman and scored the winning goal. In the locker room after the game, we were unbelievably psyched because we had just negated the home team advantage and felt we had a chance to pull off an upset in the tournament.

But first we had to get out of the stadium alive. A mob of angry Kosice fans was waiting outside for us or, more specifically, for me. The thing is throughout the game I had been responding to the crowd's abuse with different, well, gestures, and now they wanted to make me pay. The police had to protect me all the way to the bus.

Game Two versus Kosice is one I'll remember for a long time because I was sweating from beginning to end. Actually, I had a fever, and so did most of the other guys on the team. We had all fallen victim to a flu epidemic, and we were battling with our own bodies, nevermind our opponents. Just one day before the game, we were all lying in bed with high temperatures. We didn't publicize this information, though, because we didn't want the other team to know how weak we were feeling. Right before game time, the local sportswriters had received only the visiting team's lineup because coaches Sykora and Kaberle were waiting to find out how each player was feeling. Some of the guys on the team suited up and played, even though they really should have been lying in bed in their pajamas, and a few, including our goalie Vladimir Kames, went back and did just that after

"Jagr smokes Sparta" (with no. 15 on my back — I scored three goals)

the first period. He couldn't even stand up and had the chills so badly he was shivering. In the second period, he had to be replaced by Milan Hnilicka, who was only sixteen years old. At that point, the fans must have realized something was wrong. All in all we had only four players who weren't suffering flu symptoms, and I wasn't one of them. I had a fever, and during the game I was thinking I wouldn't make it through to the end. Right afterward, my temperature was measured at almost 100 degrees Fahrenheit.

The game did not start off well for us, and we fell behind in the fifteenth minute when Peter Bondra lifted his stick back to shoot, and Kames didn't see the puck until it hit the back of the net. Fortunately, we managed to even the score before the end of the first period, and early in the second we actually moved ahead. Kosice was an excellent attacking team, though, and started scoring again. It looked like they were going to go back to the dressing room leading by one until Drahomir Kadlec tied it up just fourteen seconds before the buzzer. That goal was so important because if we had been trailing at that point, as we literally crawled off the ice, we probably would not have turned it around.

My goal five minutes into the final period, though, finally gave us the lead for good, and Pavel Matula provided insurance with eight minutes left to go. At that moment, we knew we were going to make it even if we all had to just sit in front of the goal. That game was a real triumph of will for us, which Coach Sykora acknowledged afterward in his statement to the press, saying that he "took off his hat before the superhuman effort of this team. Only four players took to the ice not suffering symptoms of the flu. I thought it was over when we went down by a goal halfway through the game. These boys deserve more credit today than any other time this season. I'll tell you, some of those players out there had temperatures above 100 degrees."

Back in the locker room, we were literally on our hands and knees. If we had lost this game, the team probably wouldn't have even gone back to Kosice for Game Three. There wouldn't have been anyone left to play.

Even after our win, we had only three days to put ourselves back together for the semifinal series against Sparta Prague, a best-of-fiver with the first two games at their rink. The Kladno-Sparta matchup attracted huge interest, and we would definitely have drawn 15,000 to the main Prague arena. An exhibition tennis match between Ivan Lendl and Milos Mecir had already been scheduled for that venue, however, so we had to play in the smaller Eden Stadium, with only two-thirds the capacity of the bigger hall.

Because the flu afflicting our team didn't go away as fast as we had hoped, we had to go to Prague without seven of our players, and we played accordingly. Although we did score first in the fourth minute of the game, that was all we managed that day against Sparta, who tied the score later in the period and ended up routing us 5-1.

Game Two began with a big surprise in the sold-out arena, where all eyes turned toward the arrival of two great sports legends, Bobby Orr and Ivan Lendl. Both were in Czechoslovakia to convince Robert Holík, who the Hartford Whalers had drafted in 1989, to come to the NHL. After the game, Lendl, a part owner of the Whalers, said that he was impressed with my play and that Hartford was also very interested in me. Later on, though, he told my father that I wouldn't end up playing for them because he was sure some other team would draft me first.

Kladno was almost back at full strength for the game, and we were still feeling good even when we fell behind 2-0 after nine minutes of play. We got one goal back before the end of the period and evened it up with Zdenek Eichenmann's goal early in the second. We came out attacking to start the final session, and when our third goal came on my assist to Mirek Mach, we knew this one was ours. Eichenmann widened the lead on another goal with seven minutes left to play, and even though Sparta scored again in the last minute, the game ended 4-3 in our favor.

Sometimes in hockey there's nothing like a big win to make a team slack off in the next game, and unfortunately that's what happened to us in Game Three. Whatever self-confidence we had picked up in Prague disappeared back on our home ice. The 7,000 fans in Kladno's sold-out arena erupted five minutes into the game when I faked out Sparta's goalie in front of the net on a power play to score the first goal. That was the high point of the day for us, though, as Sparta retaliated with a goal later on in the period. They never let us back in the game as they went on to win 5-2. Down two to one in the series, we faced elimination if we didn't win the next game.

That next game, though, is one that I will never forget as long as I live. It was the best I've ever played. The funny thing is I almost didn't play at all. I had been tired and frustrated and had not been playing well, and the coaches were all over me. I had also just announced that I was going to do my military service after the season was over, which didn't endear me to the club management very much. All in all, I was in miserable spirits, and to make things worse, my knee was killing me. So I said that I couldn't play, and on game day I decided to stay home. That afternoon, my father came home from work at just about the time that I would ordinarily be about to leave for the arena. When he saw me lying in bed, he couldn't believe his eyes. "What do you think you're doing?" he asked me. "Staying home," I answered. "My knee hurts."

My father, who was not in the mood to be challenged, frowned and said to me, "You had really better be kidding. Get your clothes on and get your butt to the arena. I don't want to see you here." Hearing the tone in his voice, I was dressed and out the door in a minute. I was the last player to arrive in the dressing room, and I said I would try to play. The doctor gave me an injection in my knee, and I went out onto the ice.

The game began the same way as the one before, with me scoring on a power play, this time on a rebound off the goalie after our defenseman's shot from the blue line. And again Sparta tied the game shortly before the period ended.

We played the next period like we were out to lunch somewhere, and Sparta scored to take a 2-1 lead. After that, our coaches read us the riot act, and they got us so fired up that it was a totally different Kladno team that returned to the ice for the final period. After we blew past the Spartans to tie the score in the first minute of the session, the stage was set for my two big moments.

With Kladno a man up in the twelfth minute of the period, I got the puck and moved into perfect position between the circles, where I fired it past Czechoslovakian national team goalie Peetr Bríza, who could only look back helplessly at the puck resting in the goal. And I wasn't finished yet. In the final minute Martin Procházka went on a break down the left side and passed the puck to me in front of the goal, where I backhanded it in.

It was the game of my life. I mean, who would have thought that an eighteen-year-old kid could dominate a key playoff game like that? The atmosphere in the locker room was festive, and everyone congratulated me. The whole thing was like a dream to me, and I hardly remember any of it. What I do remember was seeing my name in all the headlines in the sports pages the next day. My favorite was in the paper *Ceskoslovensky Sport,* whose headline played on the use of the Sparta name for a popular brand of Czech cigarettes and came up with "Jagr Smokes Sparta."

That great 5-2 victory turned out to be our swan song, however, as both our strength and our luck ran out when we went back to Prague for the decisive fifth game. Already up 2-0 after two periods, Sparta finished us off with Josef Tlacil's goal in the final session. After we managed to close the gap to 3-1, I put another one in the net, but the referee had already blown the whistle and the goal wasn't counted. Sparta got the last laugh by beating us 4-1 and moving on to the finals, while we were left to play for third place.

Before the start of the season, we would have probably sold our souls for the chance to take the bronze, but our attitude was different after the series with Sparta. We had disappointed our fans and lost our motivation. Our opponent in the best-of-three consolation series was Litvínov, which had just been swept by Trencín. Their first game had been decided on a penalty shot by "Hugo" Beránek, now with Vancouver, who had scored to beat the team then being coached by his own father.

Litvínov played the opening game in Kladno so well that we were lucky to lose only 3-1. Not surprisingly, given our performance, the fans had already filed out of the stands well before the final siren. We did a little better on Litvínov's ice in the second game, in which we led most of the way before finally being overwhelmed by their talented young players, three of whom — Martin Rucínsky, Jiri

Rest during preparation in Piestany before the 1988 World Championships in Bern.

Slégr and Robert Reichel — I now play against in the NHL. Indeed it was none other than "Alby" Reichel who shifted into high gear and scored their winning fifth goal just before the end of regulation time.

So we finished in fourth place, which, despite the disappointment of the loss to Sparta, was better than anyone had expected of us before the season. I was our team's top scorer with thirty goals and twenty-nine assists in fifty-one games, good enough for seventh in the league and twenty-four points behind MVP Robert Reichel. I finished fourth in the voting for the Golden Stick award, only four points behind third-place candidate Jirí Dolezal. The clear winner was Dominik Hasek, followed by Reichel. I was also put on the All-Star team, which meant that I would get to play in the World Championship tournament.

I started feeling a little anxious when the season ended, and I made no secret of my desire to try out for the NHL the following year, although a lot of people tried to dissuade me from doing so. Kladno of course wanted to keep me there as long as they could, and Coach Sykora suggested that with one more year at home I could really make a name for myself and have an easier time breaking into the NHL after that. They were also ready to offer me a new and improved contract. But my mind was made up, and I was determined to use the World Championship in Switzerland to see if I really had the right stuff.

We started practicing for the tournament in Piestany. There were a couple of tune-up games against Finland, as well as one in Zlín against a team of select players from the Czechoslovak League in memory of Ludek Cajka, with the proceeds going to his family.

Then right before the World Championship got underway, we had a game against Canada — my first encounter with the NHL stars. I had heard a lot about their reputation for tough, brutal play, and everyone remembered the shameful 1977 incident with Phil Esposito in Vienna. The media was making them out to be a bunch of killers, and the younger players on our team were a little scared. I was even afraid of running into these guys off the ice, and one time when I went into a men's room at the tournament in Switzerland and saw Tim Hunter, I was so intimidated I turned and ran out.

Canada beat us 5-3 in that warm-up game led mainly by Rick Tocchet, Mark Recchi, and Greg Adams, who scored two goals. We had lost every game we played going into the championship tournament, but that didn't seem to bother us too much. The team was in a really good mood, and we knew that everything could turn around once the real competition began. We were looking forward to the start of the main event in Switzerland.

The tournament started out well. Our first game was against the Americans, who looked tired and didn't put up any fight whatsoever. Their one fluke goal came after they were already down 6-0. Chris Dahlquist found himself all alone with the puck upon leaving the penalty box and scored on an unassisted breakaway. The final score was 7-1. During the game, Kevin Stevens and Jergus Baca collided several times, and Kevin is still mad at Baca about it to this day. In the Pittsburgh locker room, he always looks at me like he's going to punch me, muttering "Baca, Baca."

Our hot streak continued with a 4-2 victory over the always dangerous Finns, in which I scored a second period goal, followed by a 9-1 thrashing of Norway and a win against Germany to give us a perfect record after four games.

Then came Canada. I only recognized a couple of the most famous players on their team, but it was not long before I got to know most of the others. Theoren Fleury and I became "good friends" immediately. A small but skillful player for Calgary, Fleury apparently got it into his head to start teaching me English during the game. He wasn't too creative, though, and the only word he said the whole time was the "F-word." Whenever we got together on the ice, he began harassing me with his stick and cursing me out to try and keep me in my place. Fleury took such a liking to me that he continued these lessons when I got to the NHL, although he has added a few words over the years. He still says mostly the "F-word," though.

Fleury was the worst but not the only Canadian player to give me problems. I later found out from Paul Coffey that the players from Pittsburgh had been given a special assignment — to test me. Their head coach, Bob Johnson, even came to Bern for the game. The Penguins were thinking about drafting me so Bob told his players to step on me a bit, although I never had the feeling that any of them were coming after me especially hard. Coffey was checking me out, though, and he thought that Pittsburgh was crazy to want to draft such a little kid. Once I was on the team, Coff even told me that when he had seen me and Reichel kicking around a football in the hall before the game, he just shook his head.

Of all my future colleagues, however, the one I recall most vividly from that time is Ulf Samuelsson, who was walking out of the locker room with a Hartford jacket when Holík pointed him out to me. I still remember Hollie's voice perfectly as he said, "That's the guy I'm playing with next year."

Canada took it to us right from the opening face-off and put us away in the first period with three unanswered goals. Even though Reichel scored first following the intermission, there was no way we were going to make a comeback. Canada won 5-2 with two goals by Brian Bellows and one apiece by Rick Tocchet, Steve Yzerman, and Adams.

After that we kind of collapsed and blew our remaining first-round games, losing 4-1 to the Soviet Union (their goals were scored by Vladimir Konstantinov, Alexander Semak, Sergei Gusarov and Valery Kamensky) and 5-1 to Sweden. I scored our goal in that last game when I snuck up in front of the Swedish goalie and directed Robert Reichel's shot into the net. Finishing fourth in the standings turned out to be good enough, though, to allow us to advance to the final round robin. Our first opponent was Canada. Again.

We had learned enough from that previous game not to let them get off to a big start, and we led after one period on goals by Frantisek Kucera and Zdeno Cíger. When Holík scored our third goal, our lead was big enough to stave off the comeback attempt mounted by Canada. Despite giving up goals to Adams and Doug Lidster, we won the game by a final score of 3-2, virtually ensuring us a medal for the tournament. Beating Canada meant a lot to us, especially the younger players. All through the tournament we had been talking about the NHL and what playing there must be like, and we really didn't know if we were good enough for that level of competition. Now we had actually beaten a team with real NHL stars.

To be honest, before that tournament I didn't have a clue as to how things worked "over there" in the NHL or even how the league was set up. It was Robert Holík who filled me in. We spent all our free time together in our room, and Hollie explained to me how the teams were broken up into divisions, how the schedule was put together, how many teams made the playoffs and so on. He had already been drafted by Hartford, and I had happened to be there when the call came from Ivan Lendl in Australia during the Under 20 World Championship to negotiate his move to the NHL. The two of them then met personally in Prague when Lendl came for an exhibition, and Robert was signed up for the next year in America. Compared to me, he was already an expert on the league.

When I look back at the surprises and twists of fate that life had in store for me, I can only shake my head in wonder. Who knew then, when Hollie was teaching me about the mysterious ways of the NHL, that five years later we would be playing against each other in the Stanley Cup conference finals — me with two Cup championships already behind me and finishing up a season as the league's leading scorer, and Hollie himself soon about to hold the Cup above his head in victory along with his fellow Devils.

At that time, the two of us were focused on victory in the World Championship, and our next game, against Sweden, turned out to be a real thriller. Because Dominik Hasek was injured, Bríza was in goal for us, and less than two minutes into the game, before he could even get his bearings, Ulf Samuelsson had already scored on him. Anders Eldebrink then scored again immediately, and after five minutes, we allowed another goal and were down 3-0. It already seemed like time for us to throw in the towel. Our hopes revived a bit later in the period when Eldebrink accidentally rebounded a shot by Procházka into his own goal, but Sweden increased its lead back to three at the beginning of the second session. Even after Procházka scored for us again, it still didn't look good for us as we went into the locker room down 4-2 with one period remaining.

In the Czechoslovak uniform against Sweden.

I've always considered being a representative to be a great honor.

That final period was a wild one, starting off with me scoring off a feed from Holík to narrow their lead to one. Right after my goal, though, Sweden's Hakan Loob took control of the puck and widened the gap back again. Two minutes later, however, I passed off to Reichel for another goal. Feeling like we had a chance to complete the comeback, we went on an all-out attack, literally falling on our faces trying to score one more time. Our efforts paid off five minutes before the end, when Hascák tied the game on a perfect shot, and we managed to avoid the all-but-certain defeat.

Before our last game, against the Soviet Union, we found out that the Swedes had beaten Canada by two goals. That meant that we had to either tie or just barely lose in order to gain the silver medal.

We were very nervous in the locker room before the game. Coach Stanislav Nevesely gave us our final instructions. "Gentlemen," he said, "whenever you see that someone on the other team is about to shoot, you always fall down onto the ice and stay down. You don't get up. Please, boys, don't lie down."

We actually managed to follow these instructions for the whole first period. After that, the Russians unleashed a hurricane on us, and we were caught napping by Viacheslav Bykov, Evgeny Davydov, Sergei Makarov and twice by Valery Kamensky. Thoroughly chastened, we disappointedly left the ice with only the bronze medal.

The World Championship was a real eyeopener for me, though. First of all, I got a good feel for how exhausting high-level play really is. Even though the national team had four lines and I played significantly fewer minutes each game than I averaged during the league season, I was wiped out after every one. I also discovered that I still didn't know how to shoot at all, especially when I watched the phenomenal Steve Yzerman, who scored nineteen points over the course of the tournament. He was joined on the tournament All-Star team by the Soviet players Viacheslav Chomutov, Slava Fetisov and Igor Tatarinov and our own Reichel and Hasek.

It was also at that tournament that I first met a tall, swaggering man who looked to me like a cowboy who had just gotten off his horse. But he was no cowboy. Donald Meehan was one of the hockey agents who had come to the tournament to check out the upcoming bunch of NHL recruits. A number of general managers were also there looking, among them Craig Patrick of Pittsburgh and Eddie Johnston, who was then still with Hartford. All three of these men were to be a part of my future. It was Meehan, though, who came to Kladno and invited me and my parents to attend the NHL draft in Vancouver.

I Become a Penguin

I knew I was going to be drafted in 1990, and I was already thinking about how I would rather play in America than Canada and especially in either Philadelphia or Pittsburgh. The order of the team selection itself seemed to favor my going to one of those two places.

Every year, the NHL scouts and general managers put together a list of the world's best junior players, and I was ranked seventh. Pavel Bure, who had already been drafted by Vancouver, was first. Robert Holík (taken by Hartford) was number two, followed by Vyacheslav Kozlov, Mike Ricci and Teemu Selanne (Winnipeg). Robert Reichel, whom Calgary had already drafted, was sixth, and after me came Stephane Fiset and Mats Sundin (both at Quebec). Eric Lindros and Petr Nedved were tied for tenth.

Nothing seemed to be standing in the way of my going to the NHL, although I expected that a few matters would have to be taken care of after the draft. Kladno was already causing some trouble, waving around the "statutory contract" I had signed when I was sixteen. They were going to try to do anything to hold on to me for one more year, which was understandable from their perspective.

There was also a decision to be made about when exactly I was going to make the move overseas. The Czechoslovakian national team was going to be playing the Goodwill Games in Seattle, and I was supposed to go with them, but I thought that I should settle in America as soon as possible and start learning the language. And more than anything else, I was wondering where my new business address would be.

That was decided in Vancouver, at the NHL draft which I attended at the beginning of June. Vancouver is a beautiful city, but I didn't get much of a look at the place on my first visit there because I was too busy living out a dream. With the negotiations with team representatives, fan interest and media attention, I was in a state of shock. Once I got to Vancouver, I knew that I would be taken by either Philadelphia or Pittsburgh. Quebec had also expressed a good deal of interest in me, with team representatives even coming to see me in Kladno before I left. Peter Stastny provided assistance in our discussions. The Nordiques did make some pretty incredible promises, saying they'd speak with President Havel about getting me a military exemption and offering me a fairy tale contract. But I really didn't want to go to Quebec, even though it is a nice city, because the Nordiques weren't a playoff team. A year later Lindros would feel the same way. Of course if they had drafted me, I would have gone there, but I was glad when they decided to pick someone else.

The day before the draft, I had a meeting with Pittsburgh GM Craig Patrick and Coach Bob Johnson. I have to admit I was pretty scared at the beginning, first of all because the whole affair felt like some sort of secret mafia gathering. As we waited for them on the twelfth floor of our hotel, everything seemed so mysterious. Finally the elevator doors opened and out stepped Patrick, Johnson, and a few other people, including a translator. Patrick had an aloof air about him and didn't say very much. He explained a couple of things to me and said that he mainly wanted to know if I would be ready to come for the upcoming season. Johnson, who had already gotten to know me at the World Championship, acted completely different, smiling and joking that he would learn Czech to make everything easier for me. The next morning, Patrick approached my father and asked for a handshake agreement that I would really come that year. I later learned that Pittsburgh had also had its sights set on two other players, and it did not want to risk letting them go for nothing.

When we arrived at the draft later that day, I could not believe what a big show the whole thing was. First of all, the fans were behaving like there was an actual game going on. What really impressed me, however, was how well the agents already knew us, how perfectly organized they had been in finding out every detail about not only my hockey career but even my personal life, such as what kind of relationship I had with my parents, all my personality traits and everything. I realized at that moment that they had been spying on me, and the other draftees as well, for quite a while.

Finally it was time for the main event. A lot of guys breathed a sigh of relief when Quebec chose Owen Nolan with the first pick. Vancouver was up next and chose Petr Nedved, with whom I had been having a lot of conversations. Petr is a only a few months older than I am, but he had defected from Czechoslovakia before the revolution and already had been playing in Seattle as a junior. Detroit had the third pick, but they weren't interested in any Czech or even European players that year and so chose Keith Primeau. And then my heart began to pound — the fourth pick belonged to the Philadelphia Flyers.

I knew they were interested in me, and later I found out that their scout, Inge Hammarstrom, had even come to watch me play in Kladno. I have spoken with him a number of times since the draft, and like a lot of the Swedes, he is quite a nice guy — not to mention he was an excellent player in his day. My father had also liked him when we'd had dinner with him and other team representatives, and to be honest I thought I was going to be moving to Philadelphia. But it was not to be. Instead of me, the Flyers chose Mike Ricci. Inge apparently began to cry when the team's other scouts outvoted him. He kept trying to convince them to choose me, but ultimately, he was without success. No one in Philadelphia believed that I would really be ready to play in three months.

That meant that Pittsburgh now had its big chance. And so, of course, did I.

Craig Patrick mispronounced my name a bit when he announced the team's choice, but I jumped for joy and kissed my mother and hugged my father. I quickly put on my jersey with that smiling Penguin on it and ran up to the podium. I was in the NHL!

After the draft, Craig Patrick brought us down to see the city of Pittsburgh. I still remember how during the whole trip, I kept thanking him for drafting me and promising that he wouldn't regret it. When we got there, Craig drove us to a point above the city from which we had a beautiful view of the whole downtown area, including the Civic Arena, where my future in hockey was waiting for me.

And then it hit me. Looking down at that big city with its skyscrapers and highways, I suddenly realized that I was leaving home. I would be moving to a completely new environment where I knew no one, had no friends and didn't even speak the language. At that moment I started to cry, and my parents immediately felt it, too. I had lived with my family my whole life and had hardly ever gone anywhere except for school and hockey practice. And now I would be in a completely different world.

I didn't even have a place to live yet, but Craig came up with a very nice idea to ease the relocation process for me. He threw a small party in his own apartment and invited a number of Pittsburgh citizens, including some local Czechs. "Have a good time," he told my parents and me, "and talk to the people here. Then tell me who you'd like to live with." My family had already figured that the best thing for me would be to live with a Czech family who could explain to me how things worked in my new hometown. When this got announced in the local paper, about twenty families came to offer their help. The family we chose were the Nemecs.

Stefan Nemec was in his sixties and had worked for many years in the steel mills. He definitely knew his way around Pittsburgh. After we told Patrick that he had impressed us, the two men met and began making arrangements. When I came back a month later, everything was ready for me. I still remember it like it was yesterday. My mother and I arrived at his house, and I sat down on the stairs and announced, "Well, here I am." They had no idea what kind of bird had just landed in their nest.

The other players and their wives were also invited to that party at Craig's, and some of them were nice enough to actually come and welcome me. After a while, there was suddenly a commotion with the arrival of one unexpected guest. Mario Lemieux. I was pleasantly surprised when I saw Mario and his then-fiancée Nathalie, but the people who knew better were beside themselves. Mario, I later learned, doesn't go anywhere, shuns all publicity and spends almost all of his time at home with Nathalie. What was he doing at a little party to welcome some eighteen-year-old kid from Czechoslovakia?

And then something happened that I will never forget. Mario came up to me, extended his hand and said, "If you need anything, you can always come to me. I was in the exact same situation as you are now when I came to Pittsburgh speaking only French, and I still remember how hard it was. So don't worry, I know the problems you'll be having, and I know how you're feeling. I'm ready to help you at any time."

I had my picture taken with Mario that night, and to this day, whenever I look at that photograph, I remember what Mario said to me.

The one other thing that Craig and I had to talk about was when exactly I would come back to the States. There were a few possibilities. Craig would have liked me to move in right away. Another option would have been for me to come back in a month, after the Goodwill Games. The final possibility was for me to play in the World Junior Championship and come back after that. Craig made it perfectly clear, though, that I would have a hard time cracking the lineup if I missed any of the training camp because my teammates weren't going to just accept me automatically. My father wanted me to wait awhile, but I decided to be back in Pittsburgh the next month and to sign a contract immediately.

Donald Meehan was my agent, and during negotiations, Craig told me it would be better to accept a smaller basic salary, which would be announced, with the potential for higher bonuses. In that way, no one would envy me starting out. And here I had thought there was no envy in America.

I ended up signing a $200,000 contract for three years with a one-year option, meaning that other teams could bid for me in my fourth year, but the Penguins had the opportunity to match any offer. I was careful to ensure I had a "one-way" agreement because a "two-way" agreement would mean that if I wasn't playing well or had a slump, they could ship me out to their farm team, where I had no desire to go.

We also agreed that I would arrive on July 21 and begin learning English before camp started. For that reason, I had to withdraw from the Goodwill Games, which aroused a good deal of ill will toward me back home. The newspapers wrote that I didn't want to play for my country and that I had violated a legal agreement with my Czech team by signing a foreign contract. What they seemed to forget was that I had signed my Czech contract as a minor. There had already been a number of problems surrounding my departure, but the biggest ones were still to come.

Kladno was not going to let me go for nothing, and for a while it looked as if the two sides wouldn't be able to reach a settlement.

Pittsburgh offered to buy me out for $250,000, but Kladno said that was too little and then they started to go overboard with their demands. First Kladno called Pittsburgh asking for $500,000, then $750,000 and then changed that demand to 300,000 Swiss francs. Where they came up with francs I still have no idea.

With only three days to go before the start of judicial proceedings, Craig Patrick came to Prague and met with a group of Kladno representatives, including my father, in the Hotel Intercontinental.

"Seven hundred fifty thousand dollars," they said to Craig, "or we can just let the local judge here decide where he's going to play." Craig smiled calmly and assured them that he would be happy to simply pay $50,000 in court costs. The group then haggled on until the Pittsburgh GM simply stood up and asked if that $750,000 was the Kladno side's final offer. When the Kladno team chairman answered yes, Craig politely thanked them and said that his visit was over. And then my father gave them a lecture.

He said that Kladno should be ashamed to ask for that kind of money when they had never done a thing for me. The little league and junior teams at SONP (now Poldi) got all their equipment for free and even some meal money as well. PZ, where I had played, gave me nothing. Ever since I was a kid, no one had ever done anything for me except my father, who had taken me everywhere, advised me, raised me. And then I joined this team that had contributed virtually nothing to my development as a player, and they were asking this kind of money for me after just two seasons? I had signed that statutory agreement for a salary of 2,500 Czechoslovakian crowns (then about eighty dollars) a month. And now they wanted thousands for me.

Dad left the room, and the two sides continued their negotiations until they finally agreed that Kladno would get $200,000, which was not a bad deal at all, especially considering that the league's top scorer, Peter Bondra, had gone to Washington for a mere $40,000.

I was very relieved when I heard that a settlement had been reached. I grew up in Kladno, I have a lot of friends there and I did not want to leave with any bad feelings. My father had a few problems after that episode, but a new committee was named shortly after that and everything calmed down. Eduard Novák was named the team's new coach, and he likes me, so I have always been able to practice with the team during my summers home.

I had already signed my contract with Pittsburgh before that whole business, although it was awhile before the news was actually announced. In the meantime, I was interested to know how much Kladno thought I was worth. So when Pavel Holman, the team president, called me to see if I wanted to play for Kladno, I

Before the Vancouver draft with Dad and Mr. Jandra (center).

After the Vancouver draft. Next to me sits the general manager of Pittsburgh, Craig Patrick.

After the draft, general manager C. Patrick took me to Pittsburgh to the place with the prettiest view of the skyline and confluence of the three rivers — with Dad, Mr. Jandra and C. Patrick.

June 19, 1990 — during the post-draft visit to Pittsburgh, a tour of the Civic Arena.

decided out of curiosity to find out how much they were offering. When I went to his office, he handed me a piece of paper and said, "Here's the contract we're offering you. I hope you'll be happy with it." The paper said that they were giving me 6,000 crowns (then just under $200) a month. Now in 1990 Czechoslovakia, that was no small amount of money, but I was still a little disappointed. I thought they were going to offer me twice that.

"That doesn't seem like quite enough," I told him. "What kind of highway robbery are you trying to pull?" Holman responded agitatedly. "You know we don't have any money." "Well, I'm sorry," I said, "but it really doesn't seem like very much to me. I can't sign. See you later." And I was out the door. Two days later, I was in America.

My arrival in Pittsburgh was magnificent. As it happened, a new Frankfurt-Pittsburgh plane route was being inaugurated that very day, so everybody joked that it was all because of me. People there knew me already because Paul Steigerwald of local television station KDKA 2 had already taken footage for a documentary about me on my first visit. I hadn't said too much because the only word I knew was the one Fleury had taught me, and that one wasn't too appropriate for television.

And then I began undergoing a torturous experience — eight hours a day, for six weeks, of English lessons. A few years later, Craig Patrick now admits that he overdid it a bit, but I still don't think he knows what I went through.

I mean, it was just a nightmare. I had never been able to sit still in school for even half an hour at a time, and now I was stuck to a chair for eight hours every day. I would go home exhausted and not feel like doing a thing. At least my mother was there with me; I think otherwise I would have gone insane. I made it through one whole week, and then I started playing hooky a bit. I always tried to find an excuse to avoid at least some lessons. They finally lightened my schedule, and I only had class a few days a week, so I felt a little better. But still it was worse than any summer training I had ever had to do.

After that I started going to high school. I had to dig up all my school transcripts from back home, with the courses I had taken and the grades I had gotten, and have them translated into English. I took five subjects, and I struggled with my homework every evening. I usually had to write something about my family or what I had done that day, and it was absolutely horrible. It was tough enough having to try and write it in Czech, but in English? Forget about it.

Nevertheless, I did manage to hang in there for a whole year, and I have to say there were times when I even kind of liked it. I had one really good teacher who did help me an awful lot. His name was James Warren, and he'd had experience with cases like mine because he mainly taught foreign students. He knew he had to talk slowly to me, so I could understand almost everything he said. I was happy to listen to him because he was such a great storyteller. He talked about everything, especially history, and I often found myself even looking forward to school. But then Warren left the school, and soon after that, so did I. It wasn't fun anymore without him.

I was well received by my teammates at the beginning, partly I suppose because I was something of a novelty — the first European hockey player ever to play in Pittsburgh. Also, because I had been skating in Monroeville before camp started, I had already met some of them there. Basically, I just showed up at camp with my eyes wide open and waited to see what would happen.

And everything went perfectly. Mario gave me a pat on the back and told me everything would be OK. Then some of the other stars began arriving, including Paul Coffey, whom I liked as soon as I met him. The best players were the friendliest to me, which is understandable because they had nothing to be afraid of. The others treated me more or less normally, although some of them glared at me a little. Those were the ones who felt threatened.

There was definitely a difference between my entry into the Czechoslovakian league and my start in the NHL. Sure, I was in a foreign country, which was tough for the first half of the year especially, but there was also something else.

In Kladno only a few people had already known who I was. Sure, there had been talk about some kid named Jagr who was scoring a lot of goals as a junior, but that didn't necessarily mean I would amount to anything in the big league. Numerous talented young players had not been able to make the transition. There's a big difference between the juniors and the pros, and it's always some time before even the best players can help their teams. In Kladno, therefore, I had always been looked on as a player with potential who had the chance to grow into a good hockey player at some point in the future.

It's different in the NHL because, especially if you're a first-round draft pick, everybody already knows about you. *The Hockey News* profiles draft prospects months before the selection is even made, and coaches and general managers count on young players to make a strong contribution by their second year. After all, these players are chosen every year from among hundreds of young Canadian, American and European talents. So even when you haven't played a single NHL game yet, you're already a name. It wasn't always true then, but top picks now are already signing for almost a million dollars without a single game under their belts.

All these changes were getting to me a little, and it took me some time to get my bearings. Fortunately, some of my teammates helped me tremendously. The first one to take me under his wing was Bryan Trottier. We lived together in camp, and he also had experience with kids like me, including David Volek with the Islanders.

I was starting to get fed up with myself for not yet being able to speak and

*Before flying off
to the U.S. I went
to church with
Dad, with
Grandma and
Grandpa.*

*I arrive in Pittsburgh
on July 22, 1990.
I put my suitcases on
the ground and say
— "Well here I am."*

*One of my dearest photographs. After my arrival, Mario Lemieux
came to welcome me at a private party.*

understand English properly. Trots was perfect, though, and he tried to explain everything to me. Looking back, I think I got on his nerves at least a little bit because, really, I couldn't understand him at all. He's so laid back, though, that he never showed it.

When we watched TV, I would just bug him nonstop. When hockey was on and there was a closeup of one player, I'd cry out, "Who's he?" and Trots would answer, "That's Player X." "And why's he good?" "He's got excellent moves and turns every scoring opportunity into a goal." "How does he do that?" I really hounded him. "Intuition," my teacher calmly responded, "and knowledge of the game." "And how do you get that?" I persisted. And so it went, over and over again.

Trots also helped me on the ice. He told me what I should be looking for and who I should be paying attention to. He also explained a number of basic tactics, such as when and how to change lines.

My family loved Bryan. When my father came over in November, Trots said to him, "Now that Jaromir's here, we're definitely going to win the Stanley Cup. I'm doing everything I can to help him, but he has to help me out, too. I'm a bit slower than I used to be, so I need those passes to be right on the money."

When I was feeling disappointed about my lack of playing time early in the season, it was Trots who caught on and told me, "You just need to have one thing: patience. Don't worry, your time will come." Whenever I spent most of a game on the bench and felt like the world had done me wrong, Trots would shoot me a glance and mutter, "Patience." It got to the point where to make fun of him, I would interrupt him whenever he started saying anything to me and blurt out, "I know. Patience."

I was always hungry during camp. Back home, I was used to good-sized portions, but what we got here was definitely not enough for me. We were living in a hotel, and my mother was always bringing me food, mainly homemade pastries. Trots especially liked the Czech specialty called *buchty,* and he was happy whenever my mother came over with a new batch of goodies.

Trots was having terrible back problems during camp, and he had to lie on a hard board. He didn't practice with us very much, and he traveled with us even less, so after a while it became time for another veteran to adopt me.

Paul Coffey was a different kind of guy from Trots altogether — a real hotshot, always dressed in black and always out on the town. He knew many interesting, cultured people in the arts. He introduced me to a number of them, but mainly he instructed me in social behavior.

When he took me to a restaurant, he showed me how to talk to the waiters, how to order and how much to tip, and he showed me where to go to buy different things and so on. He always paid for everything, simply saying, "Next time, you'll pay for me. That's how it works here." But when it was my turn, he always chose an inexpensive restaurant and usually only let me invite him to breakfast. He really helped me so much because he knew I was all alone and didn't know anybody in town. I couldn't even go to bars, what with the drinking age in America being twenty-one.

Some of the other younger players were jealous that I was getting that kind of attention from such a star, and when Coff got injured, they put notes up on his locker saying things like "Jaromir's waiting for you" and "Jaromir's asking where you are."

Out on the ice I was unable to take my eyes off him. He did not skate, he flew, and his style was fantastic. When I happened to get my hands on his skates one time, I couldn't believe what I saw. They were completely flat, without any grooves, because Coff didn't brake. When he had to stop, he just turned a little and skated around in a circle. And, man, was he fast. When I came to America, he was absolutely the fastest skater in the league, and even today he's still one of the top five. In practice he would weigh down his skates to make them heavier, but he still blew by everybody with ease.

When I actually tried his skates on, I couldn't even control my own feet. Those skates pulled me in different directions so suddenly I almost strained a groin muscle. Coff laughed so hard I thought he was going to be sick.

He was an inspiration to me, on the ice and off. I would gape in wonder at how, even after a tough day's workout on the ice, he would still hit the exercise bicycle for half an hour. Such a big star and still working so hard! I've never loved the training room, but the sight of Coff plugging away kept me there that extra time. There was no way I could go home while he was still at it. He wasn't the only one who worked late, I should say, and I remember that Jay Caufield used to be there after hours as well.

I had no problems during training camp. I was so happy that I didn't have to go to school anymore and also, mainly, that I was getting a lot of ice time. I knew the competition would be tough because only twenty-five out of the seventy players there would actually make the cut, with the rest being sent to the organization's farm teams. As the fifth pick in the draft, I kind of figured that probably wouldn't happen to me. However, I have no idea where some of the guys, like Jock Callander who I was on the ice with a great deal, ended up.

Our season opened on October 5 against the Capitals in Washington, D.C. Although rookies in the NHL are never on the ice for the season-opening face-off, there I was, at eighteen, the youngest player in the whole league. Michal Pivonka told me to appreciate the honor in a big way because it really is very unusual.

My debut went pretty well. I was on the ice when Kevin Stevens scored our first goal of the season, and I even had a scoring opportunity myself. Kevin got the puck to me from behind the goal, but when I took too long to decide what to do,

Paul Coffey flew by from out of nowhere and put it home. I realized I had fallen asleep out there and let my first chance get away. Still, we won that game 7-4, and I was looking forward to our home opener.

I remember that first game in the Civic Arena against the New Jersey Devils very well, especially the instant when Stevens passed the puck off to Jim Johnson, who fired off a shot from the blue line. Fortunately, I had been hanging around in front of the goal, and when the shot deflected off the goalkeeper, I kind of awkwardly put it back in the net for the first goal of my NHL career.

The fans rose to their feet and erupted in a roar, chanting my name and halting play for three minutes. What a feeling! The referee even brought the puck over to the bench for me to keep as a souvenir, and I still have it to this day.

My next goal came in our fifth game, against the New York Islanders, when Mark Recchi brought the puck around from behind the goal and found me with a perfect pass that allowed me to easily backhand it in. Against the Islanders again at the end of the month, I scored twice. One of my goals was kind of strange, coming when the two Islander defensemen and the goalie all waited for each other to take control of the puck. I noticed their confusion and came around from behind the net to move in between them and score again.

My honeymoon ended when we went to Winnipeg. First of all, I made a complete fool of myself on the way there because I had forgotten that we were going to Canada — you know, a different country — and left my passport at home. This caused a commotion when we got to the border, and I was so stupid I thought I could use my bank ATM card as an ID. The other guys on the team could not control themselves they were laughing so hard, and they didn't let me forget about that incident for a long time. Somehow the border guards were persuaded to let me through.

Worse, though, was that my goal off a pass from Coff in that game was my last one for an extended period. In the fifteen games after that, I didn't score once and had only a single, measly assist.

The View from the Bench

The main reason I wasn't scoring was that I was playing only a few minutes each game. My self-confidence was completely deserting me, and I didn't know what to do. There was one game in Boston, for example, when I didn't even touch the puck. I just skated around mindlessly, afraid of messing up. I was used to a lot of playing time in Kladno, but now I felt like a spectator, which was all the more frustrating because I had no idea why I was being benched.

There were some games when it made sense, like when we played in Los Angeles and the line that had practiced specifically to counter Gretzky stayed on the ice almost the entire game. But even when we opened up a commanding lead, I was still only out there once a period.

Bob Johnson was renowned as one of the world's best hockey coaches, and at the beginning of training camp, he had taken me aside and reviewed the ABCs of hockey with me. He explained to me how the game is played in the NHL on offense and defense, how rotations are executed, how power plays are used. And he did put me on the ice for at least a few minutes in every game. That was his specialty, giving everybody at least a little playing time. Almost nobody had to sit for all sixty minutes.

Bob was intentionally being conservative with my playing time, and I didn't understand why. I started playing so tentatively when I did get in that I made numerous mistakes, but I really wanted to be out there. I think now that Bob was afraid that the goons were going to come after me and beat me up a little, and he didn't want me to lose my appetite for playing. He was careful not to rush things, to let everything proceed step by step.

Because I had so little playing time, I felt like I had to go all out to prove myself on the ice. But wanting to do everything too much made me reckless, and I started playing so stupidly that my teammates stopped passing me the puck. I don't blame them. I mean, I was making the mistakes of a beginner, like trying risky cross passes when our defensive alignment was out of position. The harder I tried, the worse I played.

To make matters worse, Coach Johnson wasn't able to explain anything to me because he didn't speak Czech and I couldn't understand English. I would sit in the corner during our pregame sessions and listen to him while he talked, but I had no idea what he was saying. I just kept looking at him.

Finally, either he or Barry Smith or Rick Kehoe or one of the other guys on the team sat me down in front of a big blackboard like I was a child and drew diagrams of where I was supposed to go. "You," they said, pointing a finger first at me and then at the spot on the diagram where I was supposed to be. "Here. OK?" "Yes," I was able to respond.

That's how we communicated. Coach Johnson had a great way of inspiring optimism in the team and motivating every individual player on it, but with me he mainly went over the basics without filling me in on the big picture. He was also the only person with the team who didn't seem to get it that I couldn't understand a word of English. He just sat down with me and rattled away while I could hardly figure out where one word ended and the next one began, let alone understand any of them. It didn't occur to him that he might as well have been talking to the wall.

Another problem was that except for Coff and Trots, I didn't have any real friends on the team. There was a completely different atmosphere with the Penguins than there had been with Kladno, and guys didn't talk with each other very much. I guess it's hard to make friends with someone who's preparing to take over your job.

I couldn't help but think back to when I was playing in the little league for Pracovní Zálohy against SONP, and the reserve players would be openly rooting for the other team. Maybe that's just a normal human reaction; in any case I'm always aware that some of the subs loudly rooting for their team from the bench are actually hoping that the player ahead of them makes some mistake that would justify his being pulled. In Pittsburgh, I noticed that the benchwarmers were so pissed off by their status that they wouldn't even be watching the games. They would work out and go to the training room to lift weights or ride the bicycle, but their minds would be elsewhere come game time. It's a little different in the playoffs, when the team has to come together, but during the regular season it can get really bad.

The best friends on any team are those who don't feel threatened by each other. That's why, after Trots and Coff, the player who helped me the most was Mario Lemieux.

Mario was out for a good part of the season, but when he came back I felt like he was rooting for me. I have to admit that at first I was so in awe of Mario I could hardly play with him. I was so nervous I would tremble and pray to heaven that I didn't do anything wrong. I was so afraid of making a mistake that I almost didn't even want the puck. On a number of occasions, I couldn't even take a pass.

I was not afraid that Mario would yell at me — I knew he never did that — but I didn't want him to think I was a stiff. It didn't take him too long to realize, however, that I was in need of some calming down, and he began coming over and sitting next to me during games, pointing at the ice and saying, "Look how this guy shoots" or "Have you noticed how that guy is always open?" Sometimes just before he went on, he'd advise me, "Watch how I play this guy and then try it yourself."

A number of players on the team could have cared less about me, and there were three or four who acted like I wasn't there. These guys didn't want to let me play at all. During rotations, they would come off the ice last, so that by the time the rest of my unit had been on for well over a full minute, I was out there sometimes only twenty or thirty seconds before it was time to change over again. Or, vice versa, as soon as my unit was on the ice, these guys would already be calling out, "Jags, switch!"

I always had to fight for the puck because no one ever passed it to me. Or when someone did send it my way, the pass was so bad I couldn't get to it. Then they would yell at me so much during the games that I started to feel like an idiot. Sometimes they would make jokes in the locker room, and everyone would start to laugh. I wondered if the jokes were about me.

The problem, of course, was the language barrier, which was partly my own fault. I always felt so stupid whenever I started speaking my version of "English" that I preferred not to speak at all. The Nemecs, the family I was living with, were telling me not to "make a big deal out of it. Those jerks wouldn't be able to learn Czech in twenty years." But I was still embarrassed so I kept my mouth shut, which prevented me from making contact with any of the other players. Instead of becoming one of the guys, I was just widening the gap between me and them.

As if I wasn't having problems with everything else already, I then found out that my teammates wanted to cut my hair, a tradition on NHL teams that rookies are supposed to have no choice but to submit to. Bobby Holík had his whole head shaved. Even Mario had short hair when he joined the team. Naturally, I did not want my hair cut and protested that I would not agree to let them do it, which of course didn't mean anything to them. At that moment I felt like I just wanted to go home. There was only thing to do — buy my way out. I think Coff was the one who came up with the idea.

Together with Paul Stanton, who was in the same predicament, we took the entire team out to dinner, which cost a total of about four thousand dollars. Tom Barrasso bought a single bottle of wine for three hundred dollars. I thought that was that, of course, until a short time later my "friends" on the team showed up again and said that the dinner didn't count, and I still had to get my hair cut. And they weren't kidding. Mario came to our defense and said we'd made a deal, and Craig Patrick got annoyed enough when he heard about the whole affair to ensure that there would be no more talk of haircuts.

There has never been a time in my life more draining than my first season in the NHL. When I wasn't playing, I spent all my time at home listening to my mother and watching television. My mother I understood, the TV I did not. I just stared at the screen and tried to understand what was going on from watching the people move around until I fell asleep.

Socially, I was limited also. I couldn't go out at night because I was only eighteen and not allowed into any of the bars. And anyway, I didn't even have a car to go anywhere in. The team didn't want me driving, so Craig assigned George Kirk, the head of the team's Youth Development Department, to drive me everywhere.

George didn't have an easy task because the only things I knew how to say in English were still just "hello" and "thank you." He bought an English-Czech dictionary at the University of Pittsburgh and learned a few basic phrases, but for the most part we just gestured to each other until our hands hurt.

My "chauffeur" took care of me like I was his own child. In the morning, he picked me up and took me to school, and in the afternoon, he came and took me home. If I wanted to go skating in Monroeville, I just picked up the telephone and George was there in five minutes. Sometimes he brought along his own skates, too, and we'd pass the puck around.

The first album I bought in Pittsburgh was the Dr. Feelgood cassette by Motley Crue. George almost went crazy when we put it on, and to this day, he still says it destroyed his car stereo. George wasn't the only victim of my musical tastes. Whenever I came home to the Nemecs, the first thing I did was put on some heavy metal tape to rock the house. They put up with it for a little while, but they soon got sick of having to hear my music all the time and lost patience. One day, Mrs. Nemec came home with a small box. Inside it was a Walkman. "Put this on and listen to whatever you want," she told me. "By yourself." From that moment on, I always used a Walkman when they were home.

I will always be grateful to George for the way he took care of me. He was incredibly nice to me, even though I could be a real pain in the neck. One time, I got on his case for being late when he came to pick me up five minutes after the time we had agreed on. I think I was feeling frustrated about having to be chauffeured around while all the other players were driving to the arena in their own fancy cars. George knew how to handle me, though, and simply answered, "If you don't like it, take the bus." I shut up.

The communication between us was somewhere around the nursery school level. It got to the point where George himself once forgot how to speak English and just began sputtering. I think if he'd had to spend one more year with me, he would have lost it.

On our rides to and from the rink, I would look at the other cars on the road and ask George about them. No matter what he answered, my reaction was always,

"I'm gonna buy one of those." One time, as a joke, I got into his car and announced that it was a "piece of s — ." My English was really progressing.

Eventually I asked if I could drive his car myself. George protested at first, but I was able to convince him. After one skating session in Monroeville, I resolutely declared, "I'm driving home." George consented, I got behind the wheel and off we went.

But not very far. The car had a stick shift, which I didn't know how to use, and I just couldn't get the thing started. I was letting up on the clutch too fast or too slow or something. The car kept dying on me, and I began to lose patience. I decided to give it one more try. The engine made such a big noise when I pushed down on the gas that I got scared and jammed on the clutch. I don't know who jumped farther then, the car or George, but he jumped in front of it and screamed at me, "Stop! Stop!" like he thought I was going to take off without him. Humiliated, I surrendered the steering wheel and sulked all the way home. After that, I restricted my motoring to the ice for a while.

Around that time, it started to look like I was going to leave my skates there, too. I began telling the Nemecs that I couldn't take it anymore. My parents had long since gone back home to Czechoslovakia, and I felt really unhappy. I had no real friends in Pittsburgh, and I didn't understand the people whom I did meet. The main problem was still the language barrier, of course, but everybody seemed strange to me in other ways, too. The Nemecs helped me immeasurably and took care of me like their own son, but you can't replace your real parents, after all. And I started saying that I wanted to go home.

Mr. Nemec eventually got fed up enough with me that he answered, "OK, just tell me when you're leaving, and I'll drive you to the airport."

Craig Patrick came to visit us one time, and I instructed Mr. Nemec to "tell him I'm going home. Translate it for him." Mr. Nemec laughed and told him that I was "just kidding."

My scoreless fifteen-game nightmare began in Los Angeles, almost two weeks after my parents went home, and I couldn't handle it. By the end of December, I had essentially reached a crisis point, and things came to a head after one game against New Jersey. Although we had won by a large margin, I'd failed to score yet again and my output for the season fell into the minus category.

That was my rock bottom. Back in October, my mother had caught me sobbing in my room, but now I burst into tears right there at my locker. I simply couldn't control myself. George was waiting for me, as usual, when I left the stadium, but I just kept crying. At that moment I no longer gave a damn. I was unhappy about not playing, I was homesick and, on top of it, I had now embarrassed myself in front of the whole team. I felt like I couldn't go back to them now.

When I got home, I locked myself in my room and lay in bed. For the first —

September 1991
Issue #11

U.S. $2.95 /
Canada $3.95

On the cover of a hockey monthly, besides a "live" shot of me, a collector's card reproduction.

Left: 1990-91 season.

and actually the only — time, at that moment, I really thought I was not going to make it in America.

Of course my crisis did eventually pass. But ever since then, whenever something goes well for me here, I always think back to that night after the New Jersey game. The legendary Czechoslovakian hockey player Vladimír Martinec had a famous motto: "Even if they knock you down a hundred times, then rise up a hundred times and move on." I think my own motto has come to be something like: "Never make an important decision when you've hit bottom and feel weak." If I'd gone home then, when I said I would, I'd never have gotten to find out what it's like to drink out of the Stanley Cup. But I'm getting ahead of myself here.

Things started turning around for me when Craig Patrick brought another Czech player, Jiri Hrdina, to Pittsburgh. That was a really smart move on Craig's part, and it did a lot to pull me out of my slump.

Hrdina was a blast and kept me in stitches. Even though he had a family with him and was a lot older than me, we went out together a fair amount. Finally, I had somebody I could talk to! And to make things even better, Jiri and I also played very well together, and for a while the two of us with Bryan Trottier made up the most effective line on the team. The most important thing at the beginning, though, was that I was happy again.

Jiri was able to gain the acceptance of the guys on the team pretty quickly, and then, largely through him, so was I. The two of us spent time traveling and playing tennis and going to bars. He always managed to fix it so that I could get in, which was great, except for two unfortunate incidents.

The first was with the Nemecs, who tried to keep me at home. Early on, I didn't even have any desire to go anywhere, but now I was starting to feel bored staying around the house. The Nemecs, however, did not want to let me go out. Whenever they talked with my parents on the phone, they would assure them that they had everything under control. We started getting into arguments. One time I said that I felt like I was in prison, and they answered, "We don't care. You're staying home. We're responsible for you."

This got me pretty pissed off, and I yelled at Mr. Nemec, "You can't tell me what to do. You're not my father!" To which he replied with icy calm: "Be glad."

The Nemecs were not the only ones who didn't like it that I was going out to bars even though I was still well under twenty-one. There were two bars in Pittsburgh that I usually went to and where they knew me and normally let me in. Things got complicated, though, when one woman got mad at the staff of the Sports Garden for not admitting her underaged daughter while I was allowed to enter. The next time she saw me hanging out there, she called the police. The bouncers got in trouble and I was kept out for about three weeks after that, but eventually everything calmed down.

Jiri joined the Penguins on the lucky thirteenth of December, and I began scoring again one week later, registering goals against Minnesota, the Islanders and Washington. I even allowed myself a bit of showing off against the Capitals when I got control of the puck and broke out of a crowd of players Gretzky-style. I moved around the defenseman to the other side of the goal and into a good shooting position. Even though my backhand hit the far post, it deflected back in front of the goal, where it waited for Zarley Zalapski to fire it home.

I am proud of the goals I score unassisted, and I managed to register one of these in Toronto, one of the real great hockey towns of North America. Taking off from our own end of the ice, I picked up speed until I soon found myself at the Maple Leafs' blue line and saw two big guys ahead of me who didn't look like they were going to step aside and let me through. So I faked a pass but kept rushing forward just fast enough to slide in between them toward the goal, finishing off the play with a little backhand trick for the score.

Against New Jersey I took a pass from behind the goal and skated past Slava Fetisov before beating Chris Terreri for yet another point, and I was set for the month. Everything was better. I was getting more playing time, Hrdina was babysitting me, and our team got a big boost from an old friend.

The "Man" returned. After missing the first fifty games due to a back operation, Mario Lemieux came onto the ice and immediately began playing like he was from a superior planet.

Mario began his comeback in Quebec on January 26, and I could not believe it was possible for anyone to play like he did after a half-year layoff. Once when he got the puck near the goal with Joe Sakic — only one of the best players in the NHL, mind you — coming right at him, Mario pushed it through the defenseman's legs like it was nothing and found himself alone in front of the goal, his normal position. His legs were still trailing him, but with his mile-long arms he got his stick on the puck and went for the score.

I was almost relieved when his shot went wide, otherwise it would have been difficult to believe this guy was human.

Mario did score, though. It was in the next game, back in Pittsburgh, against the Capitals, and I felt privileged to be a part of it. Taking a pass from Al Iafrate, Mario sent it on to me. The goaltender deflected but did not catch my shot, and as always, Mario was there to bang it in for the goal. Paul Stanton scored another one to give us the margin of victory, and the perfect homecoming was complete.

After that, my own big day was not long in coming, either. In the Boston Garden at the beginning of February, I scored my first NHL hat trick! My first goal came on a break when Larry Murphy took a shot from the blue line. Murph's shots aren't usually missiles, but they are almost always on the money. So I snuck up in front of the goal and waited for the puck, which flew just above the ice. I got my stick on it and finished it off.

And then Coff set me up twice. He was such a joy to play with. Once he got moving, watching the other team try to catch up to him was like watching leaves blowing in the wind, the way they just scattered in his wake.

Coff took the puck behind our own goal and took off down the rink in his inimitably elegant style. And half a second later, he was already on the other side of the Bruins' blue line. After dishing it off to me, he skated to the right side and drew their defense with him. With the left side of the net exposed, I had a clear opening and swept the puck past the frozen goaltender for goal number two.

My third goal resembled a textbook play. Before going out on the ice, Coff had said to me, "You have a chance for a hat trick today. Wait for the puck at the red line." And so I did, following the action from the boards to see what would develop. Coff took the puck in the corner behind the goal and began moving across to the other side, which I took as my cue to move toward the center. Oh man, it's as if it happened just this morning. Coff waited with the puck while I picked up speed and calmly fed it to me just as I approached the red line. It was like he was drawing a diagram. I was already going too fast for anyone to catch me, and I faked a regular shot before switching to my backhand and sending the puck into the net.

I was so excited, I jumped for joy. A hat trick and in a big game, no less! Phil Bourque picked up the puck and brought it back to me on the bench as a souvenir.

I scored several more times before the regular season came to an end. One goal in particular comes to mind because it came on exactly the kind of play I had been working on in practice — the quick shot off the pass — as if someone was trying to show me that focused training pays off. In a game against the Oilers, Mario sent me a cross pass from the left, and I immediately swept it in. It was actually a pretty nice goal, but it didn't count for much since we lost that game.

Nevertheless, we wrapped up the regular season in good shape, finishing first in the Patrick Division, ahead of the New York Rangers and Washington. I was one of only two players on our team to play in all eighty games that season, although my appearances had been largely symbolic early on. I finished third in the league among rookies in goals scored with twenty-seven, and I had a total of fifty-seven points, thirty-seven of which came in the second half.

My troubles were behind me. Thanks to Jiri, I had been able to make friends with several of my teammates, especially Paul Stanton (to whom I even managed to teach a few Czech phrases that he should definitely not use if he ever visits Prague) and the mammoth Jay Caufield. Assistant Coach Rick Kehoe devoted a lot of time to me in practice and helped me with my shooting a great deal.

I ran up quite a phone bill calling my parents in Czechoslovakia that year. Dad and I were able to go over my individual games together because Josef Nemec,

Stefan's brother, recorded them on video and sent them to my father every two weeks. Dad bought a dual-system VCR so that he could watch the NTSC tapes from America. And mom bought all the newspapers every morning so that she could tell me what they were writing about the NHL as well as what was going on in the Czechoslovakian league.

I was adjusting to the city of Pittsburgh. The fans were really great, recognizing me on the street or waving at me in George's car, not to mention coming up to me for autographs after games. That kind of thing really helps me. I was still a little shy and didn't talk much to anybody, but such a warm welcome pleased me. And at the time it was something absolutely new to me. People are a little less spontaneous back where I'm from and would certainly never wait such a long time after a game for me to come out and sign a baseball cap.

On my birthday, I found myself overwhelmed with presents, and scores of people even sent me packages filled with different cakes and pastries, including real Czech-style buchty. And after sending me sweets, some girls themselves came after me.

From the very beginning, they tried to find out where I lived, and one time I announced that our house was in Monroeville, which was only partly true. (Well, I went to Monroeville a lot.) A couple of times, George and I got into some real Hollywood-style car chases, as vehicles started following us as we drove away from practice. We always managed to shake them, though, and nobody found out where I lived.

Nobody, that is, until Ron Cook, a sportswriter for the *Pittsburgh Gazette,* let the cat out of the bag in a published interview with me that took place in my house. A blind man could have figured out where I lived from his article. And after that, the deluge began. Fans started coming up to the house night and day until I thought the Nemecs were going to totally freak out.

Being older people, they have earned the right to a little peace and quiet, but what they actually had on their hands was a circus. There were so many cars driving back and forth outside, you'd have thought that their quiet residential street was a freeway. Sometimes these nuts would actually park facing our house and turn on their brights. This even happened late at night, and then the Nemecs weren't able to go to sleep.

Girls would come up to the door and keep pushing the doorbell until one of us opened the door. Or they'd pound away until I thought they would break the door in. Occasionally, the Nemecs would even call the police, although sometimes the cops just came anyway because the neighbors had called or they had noticed something was going on.

My host family must have breathed a huge sigh of relief when they finally got me out of their hair. I think they aged about five years during my one-year stay in their home, but they were always incredibly nice to me and helped me out with everything, right down to my financial accounts. My parents were overjoyed to see how thorough Mrs. Nemec was in this regard.

There were a great many things I needed to have taken care of, from setting up a bank account to filling out my income tax form. All that kind of stuff was foreign to me, and I just told the Nemecs I wasn't going to do it. Boy, did they go crazy then. "They'll put you in jail!" they told me. "Everybody has to pay taxes."

In the end we got it done, but without their help I would have been completely lost.

My English at that time was still far from perfect. All this only meant more work for the Nemecs.

I didn't want all that much from my agent Don Meehan, just some help with a few basic things that I had no idea how to do myself. Sure, I realize that because of my meager English I was more difficult to handle than some other foreign players, but Meehan was not as responsive to me as I would have liked. We never got into any real conflict with each other, but he was obviously not the right person to represent me. I stayed with him for about a year until I got a new agent, Mike Barnett.

Anyway, the Penguins managed to clinch the division title a few games before the end of the regular season and began to get psyched up for our first-round play-off opponent, the New Jersey Devils.

"We're Gonna Cut
That Finger Right Off!"

The difference between the regular season and the playoffs is enormous, and the "second season" is especially difficult for European players. We simply come from another world, and even when we put our hearts and souls into it, it is a major challenge to match the intensity of the players who grew up in North America.

I had already been surprised earlier in the season by how tough things got at the end of every game. For instance, there was the time when I was sent out onto the ice in the final minute, during a power play. The struggle began as soon as the ref dropped the puck, and I found myself in the middle of such a whirlwind I didn't know what was going on. I'd been doing OK all game until, all of a sudden, the new, increased energy level was more than I could handle, and I was lost out there. After a while, of course, I got used it, but at the beginning, I was absolutely shocked by this change in tempo.

But that increased tempo, I soon found out, is the norm in the playoffs from the first minute of play. The rink suddenly gets smaller, the puck moves faster, and players are a lot more hesitant to make the riskier passes that they would usually make during the regular season. The style of play is also much less physical, and fights are less common because every power play might potentially decide not only the game, but the whole series.

As the regular season came to an end, I didn't yet understand the essential difference between the contests to come and the eighty games we'd just completed. One look at Mario was enough to give me the idea that something was up. He had undergone a transformation. The Stanley Cup championship represented the only major goal he had not yet achieved in his career, and he still had to win it in order to ensure his legendary status. He wanted that trophy with all his heart. And the change that came over him when the playoffs began was unbelievable.

Mario has a very modest, almost shy personality. He usually doesn't say a word in the locker room, preferring to listen to what everybody else is saying. It doesn't matter if he goes scoreless or if he picks up a hat trick — after the game he's always the same. He's happy to let his play speak for itself and justifiably so. But that's just during the regular season. In the playoffs, Mario comes alive.

It's almost like he becomes someone else. He gets into conversations and starts psyching up the rest of the team. All of a sudden, he's everywhere. And as the ultimate goal got closer and closer, Mario grew zealous, rousing every teammate and hammering it into our heads that we were going to do it. One of the other guys characterized him as a man who had been wandering through the desert and suddenly sensed that water was not far away. That's Mario in the playoffs.

But at the beginning, I still didn't get the whole picture. Of course, by now I'm well aware of the difference, but green as I still was at the time, I didn't think of changing my style for the playoffs. I started out taking the same chances I always did, zigzagging in front of our own goal and the like, figuring hey, if we give one up we'll get it back. I've grown wiser since then.

I couldn't help but be overwhelmed by the magical atmosphere in the locker room before the first playoff game. We got together with all our scouts, who gave us their analyses of the other team in the most incredible detail. They told us everything: who comes on for their power play and for the opponents' power play, who on their forward line plays defense and how they execute their line changes. We were even informed about the strengths and weaknesses of each individual player. And I don't mean just the three or four best ones, but the whole first and second units. By the end I felt like the only thing they hadn't told us was what the Devils liked for dinner and what their favorite TV shows were. Before that I couldn't have told you every player's name, but now I was ready to anticipate their every move.

Also unbelievable were the laser shows before each game, when the players were introduced. The arena darkens, and each player is announced individually over the PA before skating out to the blue line with the spotlight on him. And of course, there's music to complete the effect. The house lights finally come back on when everybody's lined up, and the crowd rises to its feet. The show begins.

My first NHL playoff game was on April 3, 1991, in the sold-out Civic Arena. It was the Devils, led by Peter Stastny, who taught us a lesson that night. Although Mario scored the first goal of the game on a power play in the second period, five minutes later Stastny got to a loose puck and tied it up.

That was our first warning. The second came at the beginning of the final period, when Stastny slyly crept out unnoticed from behind our goal and scored again. Less than a minute later, Laurie Boschman gave the Devils an insurance goal, and it was time for us to pack it in. We left the ice in a state of shock. After all, we were the division champions and had finished nine points ahead of New Jersey in the regular season.

Depression reigned in the locker room after the game, and no one dared say a word. Even Mario was silent. But when Bob Johnson came in and saw us moping, he improved our mood a bit by asking, "Hey, what's going on? Come on, we could lose the first three games, and we still wouldn't be out of it. Let's just get ready for Friday." That was Bob. Never one to succumb to pessimism, he knew exactly the words to get us back on our feet.

Game Two of that series is one I'll never forget. Two days after our opening loss, we were back in the Civic Arena looking to tie up the series. We didn't get off to an ideal start, though, as New Jersey's John MacLean struck first, and even after Kevin Stevens evened it up for us, MacLean scored to put them in the lead again. The pattern continued in the second period when Coff tied it 2-2, only to see Brendan Shanahan slip past our defense to put the Devils in the driver's seat once again. Things looked bad for a while until Phil Bourque scored to give us life one more time.

It was a really well-played game, and the fans must have enjoyed it tremendously. I can't say the same for us, however, because we were too nervous about the outcome. Two home losses in a row, and we would most likely have removed ourselves from contention before we even got going.

Troy Loney opened the period for us with a seeing-eye goal that gave us our first lead of the game and got us so excited you'd have thought we were insurmountable. But we weren't. The Devils were already an excellent team even then, and Alexei Kasatonov brought them back with one more goal to tie it at the end of regulation.

We actually did get one last chance to finish the game before the final siren, when Mark Recchi and I made one final assault on the Devils' goal, but we didn't put it in.

We were both exhausted and tense as we made our way back to the locker room after that third period — exhausted from the all-out effort we had put forth and tense over what might happen in OT. One freak goal by the Devils and we were screwed. At moments like these, there's not much talk going on in the locker room. Everybody just lies on the benches for a quick rest and prays for a happy ending. The coaches do try to fire up the team one more time, but even they don't talk tactics at this point, they just say a lot of "It's now or never!" and "Let's do it!" inspirational stuff.

Now, I don't know if Coach Johnson had a feeling based on my performance at the end of the season or if he was just relying on that legendary intuition of his, but one thing the old "Badger" had was the uncanny ability to say the right thing at the right time. Right before we went back out onto the ice, he leaned toward me, slapped me on the back and said to me, "You're going to win this one for us today."

My moment came in the ninth minute of the sudden death overtime. Jiri Hrdina started the play on the right side and passed it to Bourque in the middle. Phil then saw me darting forward back down the right side and passed it back to me there. At that point, the whole thing still looked just like a normal back and forth that could be broken up at any moment. I was all the way over by the boards when I reached the blue line, but I had control of the puck and looked around to see who was nearby.

When I saw MacLean was covering me, I played the puck against the boards and tried to push him aside a little, which I was able to do because I had come up on him pretty fast. By the time I got past MacLean, the puck had gotten away from me and I barely managed to get my stick back on it, but once I did, I was suddenly faced with two possibilities.

My first option was to keep moving in the same direction I was already going and skate back behind the goal, where I could look for someone in front to pass to. But Bourque sort of made my decision for me by trailing behind me after giving me the puck. He was assuming that if Tommy Albelin, the Devils' Swedish defenseman came at me, I would dump it back to him, and he would have a clear shot at the goal. Albelin realized what we were up to, though, and moved toward Bourque in anticipation of just such a play. By doing that, he offered me the second possibility without even making me think about it: Head straight for the goal.

Ever since I was five years old, my father has been telling me over and over again that I always have to push through to the area in front of the goal because that's the only place where natural scoring opportunities are created. "Fight your way there as soon as you get the chance," he instructed, before adding, "Of course, you have to have the strength."

That advice has always served me well and has proved to be especially appropriate to the game in North America, where the rinks are somewhat narrower than in Europe. At least over there you have more space to sort of trace an arc before ending up back in front of the net.

By moving toward Bourque, Albelin opened up a space for me in front of the goal. So even though I was skating at full speed along the boards, I rerouted myself and did as my father told me to. And before Chris Terreri knew it, I was suddenly there in front of him.

What we had then was the classic hockey one-on-one confrontation — shooter versus goalie. The only problem for me was that Terreri was in a good position to stop my shot as I flew in from the right. Fortunately, I was skating fast enough to get to the other side of him before he could move across which is exactly what I did. And once he had fallen down trying to turn around, it wasn't too hard to flip the puck just under his extended glove. The game was over, and the Civic Arena exploded.

Of course I was overjoyed, and so was the rest of the team. Coff jumped into my arms, and the two of us danced together for a second until my other teammates also came and started hugging me. It took a little while for it to sink in that I had really won the game for us.

Unfortunately for me, in the euphoria of the moment I also managed to commit a real no-no that I would pay for dearly — for the rest of the series. You see, after

I scored that goal I took off my glove and, almost without realizing it, turned toward the Devils' players and raised my finger in celebration. No, not the one that means "We're number one," but the one next to it. Yeah, the middle one. I had often done the same thing in Kladno, but I've really never meant it as an insult or any kind of mockery directed toward the guys on the other team. It was just kind of a spontaneous joyful reaction to scoring such a big goal. I didn't know what it really meant.

I would have thought that it was worse to actually talk trash to the other team at such a moment. But I was wrong. There is an unofficial but strictly enforced punishment in the NHL for the specific offense that I committed.

In the meantime, I was still basking in the glory of the victory when we got back to the locker room. I was mobbed by sportswriters wanting to talk to me, but they probably weren't too happy that I was the one who scored that winning goal for us because I was literally speechless. Some of the articles the next day even included apologies for being unable to print my "comment" in the absence of anyone to translate for me. Naturally, though, my teammates could offer their praise of my performance, and Coach Johnson was quoted as saying, "Luck usually plays a big role in overtime games, but that wasn't the case tonight. This game was decided by talent. That goal was a demonstration of real talent."

That night I invited the Nemecs out on the town for the first time. Before the game, I had told them that if I scored either three goals or at least one really important goal, I'd take them out to celebrate. So the three of us went to the Sports Garden, which did not turn out to be the best idea. First of all, the bar was totally packed, and then as soon as we got inside, I was descended on by about two dozen girls. The Nemecs' jaws just dropped, but thankfully there was such a racket inside there that they couldn't say anything to me. In the end we decided to take a rain check on our evening out and went home. I had to get up the next day for the team's flight to New Jersey.

The euphoria of Game Two naturally did not last very long because, after all, the series was still only tied 1-1, and if we wanted to advance we were going to have to win at least one game at the Devils' home rink. Given how the first two games had gone, that did not seem like too easy a task. Even in the second game, which we won, they had been the better team, outshooting us forty to twenty-five overall and even seven to two in OT. Of course that second shot of ours was the one that counted.

New Jersey was out for blood in Game Three, and it wasn't too difficult to figure out whose blood they had in mind. The Devils began shadowing me in the pregame skate, and several of their players were already telling me, "Just wait, we're gonna cut that finger right off!" And once the game started, they started putting their talk into action.

The first one to take a crack at me was Brendan Shanahan, who right from the start of the game began to hit me with his hockey stick so often that I was soon covered with bruises. Soon afterward, Laurie Boschman joined in. He threatened me throughout the game and during one break in the action smacked my hand with his stick five times in a row. Even Claude Lemieux got a piece of the action when he came up and hit me in the face with the butt end of his stick as we were getting into position for another face-off. My mouth filled with blood, and I had to go to the bench before the referee even dropped the puck. The Devils kept up their assault on me for the full sixty minutes, and I didn't have a big game that day.

What mattered, of course, was that we won anyway. The score was tied after each of the first two periods. Although we did take the lead twice, on shots by Recchi in the first and Bob Errey in the second, both of our goals were answered by Shanahan when he took time out from what seemed to be his principal task of beating me to a pulp.

When our third lead of the game, which came on Joe Mullen's goal to open the third period, was once again erased by Doug Brown, it began to look like we were headed for another overtime session. But in the last minute of regulation, we got some unintended help from the Devils' defenseman Eric Weinrich, who was unable to clear the puck off a difficult bounce in front of the New Jersey net. After Weinrich's second failed attempt at contact, the puck spun back toward the goal and all Recchi had to do was tap it in to give us a 2-1 lead in the series and put us back in the driver's seat.

Despite this position, however, the Devils managed to blow us out in Game Four. Claude Lemieux started things rolling for them off a pass from Zdeno Ciger, and Stastny widened the gap by the end of the first session. After a scoreless second period, Mario scored in the third to make it 2-1, but then New Jersey turned it on again, scoring two more times to finish us off.

As if losing the game wasn't bad enough in itself, we also lost Coff when Fetisov sticked Paul in the eye at the beginning of the third period. For a brief moment, he couldn't even see. It would be hard to say that the Devils' famed Russian defender injured him intentionally. I mean, I've been whistled for high-sticking a number of times myself, so I know that these things happen. Coff had to leave the game and nobody knew when he'd be able to play again.

The fifth game of the series was like a carbon copy of the first. Once again we couldn't find a way to handle the Devils' tough defensive play, and once again we lost at home, this time by a score of 4-2, their last goal coming after we removed our goalie just before time expired.

Our spirits were pretty low as we traveled back to New Jersey for the sixth and potentially final game of the series. We were losing 3-2 in the series, and in order to keep our season alive, we were going to have to win, not only without Coff, but

Paul Coffey helped me out a lot. he must be saying something
interesting if Jirka Hrdina watches us with such interest.

also without our top goalie, Tom Barrasso, who was also injured. Fortunately for us, his replacement, Frank Pietrangelo, came up with the game of his life.

The Devils got the jump on us when MacLean scored the first goal of the game. Fortunately, Kevin Stevens then rose to the occasion and turned things around with two goals that put us back in the lead.

And then came the moment that decided the game for us, a moment when we could only be thankful that fate, and Frank, were on our side. The score was still 2-1 in our favor, and we were really buckling down on defense, when the Devils had control of the puck in our end of the ice. I was watching the action from the bench when all of a sudden the puck somehow shot out from the corner of the rink and ricocheted off the goal right on to the blade of Peter Stastny's stick in front of the half-open net. At that instant the blood of every Penguin froze, and the fans in New Jersey's Brendan Byrne Arena rose to their feet with the assumption that the score would now be tied and the Devils would be just one goal away from advancing to the second round.

I've never asked him about it, but I imagine that Peter will have that moment ingrained in his mind for the rest of his life. I know I would. The puck was practically past the goal line already before he even took his shot, which he did without a split second's hesitation. But then something happened that no one could have anticipated. As the puck flew toward the net about ten inches above the ice, there in a flash came Pietrangelo's glove out of nowhere to stop it just before it reached its destination!

Pietrangelo had been standing all the way on the other side of the goal when Stastny got the puck, and if he had tried to move back into position, the scoreboard would have already read 2-2 by the time he got there. Nothing but pure instinct led him to react the way he did in that nanosecond, and thus, he preserved our precious lead. The Devils' fans and players alike seemed to be deflated by Frank's presence of mind. And by our luck. I believe that was the play that won the series for us.

Right after that incredible moment, I scored for us again when Mario's slap shot — off a pass from Ronnie Francis — rebounded off of Terreri right to me. Francis then scored yet another goal to increase our lead to three, and even though Eric Weinrich and Claude Lemieux brought the Devils back with goals in the final minutes, we managed to hold on for the victory and bring the series back to the Civic Arena for the seventh and deciding game.

At that point, I knew we couldn't lose. We had survived everything the Devils had thrown at us, and now we even had Coff back with us, which inspired me to no end. The doctor had actually warned him that he risked permanent blindness in the injured eye if anything else happened to it. But on the morning of the game, when the eye specialist told him that his condition had improved, his decision was made, and he announced to everyone: "Tonight I am going back out on the ice." I, myself, would have probably sat it out if I had been told that I risked losing my vision in one eye by playing again so soon. But no one's tougher than Coff, and just the sight of him back in the locker room was enough to fire us up.

Pietrangelo had another great outing in Game Seven, but this time so did Jiri Hrdina, who scored our first goal when Fetisov thoughtlessly brought the puck out right in front of his own goal and lost it when it brushed against Alexei Kasatonov's skate. Jiri raced to the circle where the loose puck had ended up and fired it past Terreri. After Mario put us up 2-0, Jiri struck again off a pass from Bourque, who had made an excellent move to get past Ken Daneyko. The first period ended with us leading 3-0, and it was left to Coff to put the icing on the cake with one of his trademark coast-to-coast rushes to score our fourth and final goal.

We had survived. As for me, I was exhausted and not only physically, but psychologically as well. One bad break and we would have been eliminated. In the end, though, all that mattered was that we had advanced, although the Washington Capitals, our next opponent, were not going to roll over for us either.

The series against Washington started out exactly the same as the one against the Devils had: We lost the first game, won the second in OT and then won number three in our opponents' arena.

After that the pattern broke, as we managed to win yet again in Game Four to take a 3-1 lead in the series. Tim Bergland opened the scoring for the home team, but Recchi came right back out of nowhere to even it up. Stevens beat the Caps' defenseman Rod Langway in the third period to give us the lead, and Bourque closed the books with an empty net goal in the final moments. Washington was a good team, no question, but they weren't quite as hard-hitting as the Devils, so we felt pretty good about our chances going back to the Civic Arena.

While we hardly lacked for motivation in any case, given the atmosphere of the playoffs and our prospects for advancing, our resolve intensified for Game Five because we were devoting our efforts to Coff — who had suffered a broken jaw in Game Two and was out for the series — as well as Ulf Samuelsson, whose father had just passed away in Sweden.

Our first goal came after fifteen minutes, when Jiri Hrdina stole the puck from Dale Hunter and gave me the puck behind the Washington net. I then spotted Joe Mullen out in front, and he fired it past a helpless Don Beaupre to put us ahead.

My next contribution came when we were up 2-1 in the third, and I picked up a loose puck at the red line. Turning on the jets, I reached Beaupre in no time and beat him with a backhand fake. Recchi added one more with a minute left to go, and our thoughts turned to the Adams Division champions from Boston.

The Bruins had finished the regular season with more points than us and therefore enjoyed the home ice advantage for the series. I probably didn't mind that as much as I was supposed to, though, because I loved the atmosphere of the decrepit old Boston Garden and felt practically at home there. The place didn't seat more than 15,000 fans, but they sure managed to turn up the heat in there. Even the seats in the uppermost decks afforded a good view of the action, and once the crowd got going, you couldn't hear anything else.

The series opener jinx that had been plaguing us in the postseason reared its ugly head again in Boston, as the home team pushed us around in exactly the way our scouts had told us they would try to do. We started out OK, jumping out to leads of 1-0 and 2-1, before Cam Neely's goal tied it up again for the Bruins just before the first period came to a close. But after that it was all Bruins. First, Tommy Barrasso misfired when trying to clear the puck, and his pass went straight to Boston's Ray Bourque at our blue line. Bourque passed it off to Vladimir Ruzicka, who then found Bob Sweeney in front of the goal with a sweet pass of his own and that was it for us. I didn't help things any with my own mis-play at the blue line, practically handing Neely yet another goal. Although Errey then cut their lead to one, Dave Christian and Bourque scored again for the Bruins to complete the rout.

It was obvious after that loss that we were going to have to change our game plan somewhat if we were going to have any chance of winning the series. Bob Johnson saw that better than anybody and began spending a great deal of time talking to Ulf alone. I think we all knew what he was telling him, though. Ulf was given the task of "neutralizing" Cam Neely, the Bruins' most dangerous player, who we were going to have to handle somehow.

Neely stands well over six feet tall and has to weigh something over 220. Mixing it up with him is like taking on a steamroller. He is particularly dangerous in front of the goal where, because of his size, speed and genuine hockey smarts, he is especially good at clearing the space of anyone wearing a jersey colored differently from his. Neely's career was at its peak around that time, and there was no way he could have expected that the injuries he was about to sustain would slow him down for good. Although he's still one of the best players in the NHL today, the knee problems that arose from his merciless battles with Ulf in that series prevent him from being everything that he was before.

Ulf wouldn't back down from an opponent even if the other guy was three feet taller and 200 pounds heavier than he was. I still shudder when I think of how those two guys went at each other. Unfortunately, one particularly intense clash ended up with Neely laid out on the ice with his knee out of joint. It took him two years to recover from that on-ice accident (and I should emphasize it was an accident), and he's never really fully returned to form.

Game Two was closer than the first one, but the outcome wasn't much different. Neely struck first for the Bruins by clearing out the area in front of the net and scoring his third goal in four periods. Stevens answered back for us with a goal of his own, but Boston soon took the lead again. Now it was Mario's turn to perform some of his special magic. I think Mario's probably the only player in the world who can actually score from behind the net, and it was almost comical to see him standing there in back with those long arms of his out in front of the goal pushing the puck with his stick past Boston's bewildered goalie, Andy Moog. Mario gets the job done.

The defensive battle continued, but we did manage to take the lead, which lasted until we got whistled for a double penalty with less than four minutes left in the third period. Playing with a two-man advantage, Boston worked the puck around until someone took a slap shot on Barrasso from the blue line. Tommy blocked that one, but Vladimir Ruzicka was there laying in wait when the puck bounced back in front of the goal. Vladimir then did the smart thing, and instead of trying to fire it right back into the net immediately, he calmly passed the puck back to Craig Janney on the other side of the goal, who had a wide open shot in front of him. We then lost the game in overtime on a fluke goal by Ruzicka off an incredibly unlucky bounce of the puck that went right to him in front of the net.

It's funny, but we really weren't feeling as down-and-out at that point as you'd expect of a team that had lost the first two games of a playoff series. Maybe it was just Bob "the Badger" Johnson's infectious optimism or something, but I still remember very well how we were all just saying to ourselves that Moog wasn't going to be able to maintain the miraculous level of play he had been demonstrating, and that all we had to do was keep the pressure up.

And we were right. Ulf didn't give Neely an inch of breathing space and Moog was brought back down to earth, as we won two games in a row back in Pittsburgh by identical scores of 4-1. Our first win of the series got under way with Stevens's long-distance goal, and Francis followed with another to put us up 2-0. I think it's fair to say that we were in control from beginning to end that day, and it was Mario again who sealed things for us when he pried the puck away from Garry Galley at the blue line and scored his fourth goal in three games. Game Four went pretty much the same way, and we went back to Boston with the series tied at two apiece.

Game Five is traditionally put-up-or-shut-up time in an NHL playoff series, and we rose to the occasion in a big way. Kevin and Mario in particular were just fantastic, turning a 2-2 tie after one period into a 7-2 drubbing by game's end, and the Bruins really never had a chance. Ulf closed out the exhibition by scoring our last goal himself to punctuate his triumph over the hapless Cam Neely.

The fans came to the Civic Arena for Game Six in a mood to celebrate, and we gave them their money's worth, although it wasn't as easy as I'm making it sound. Actually, the score was still tied at three with four minutes remaining in the third, when Recchi took a pass in the circle and beat Moog with a wrist shot for the game-winner. Mario's empty-net goal in the final moments provided all the insurance we needed, and suddenly we found ourselves in the Stanley Cup finals!

The NHL championship series is the dream of every hockey player in the world, but I didn't have much time to stop and reflect on how fortunate I was to be there in my rookie season. There were only a few days before the series started, and the Minnesota North Stars were not an opponent to look forward to. What they lacked in pure hockey skill, they more than made up for in toughness. Their defensemen were a bunch of bashers, and I had to get ready for the prospect of being sent flying every time I stepped out onto the rink.

But we had a lot going for us, too: Barrasso was absolutely bulletproof, almost no one got past Ulf alive and Mario was at the peak of his career. What's more, Kevin Stevens and Mark Recchi were playing for their future because both were in their option year and therefore had special motivation to perform in the series. Of course, the Stanley Cup itself is the greatest motivation there is.

My parents flew in to Pittsburgh for the series. When they were going home in November, Craig Patrick asked them when they would be coming back again, and dad had actually answered, "For the finals." No one could have guessed so early on that we were really going to get so far, but Craig felt that my father's clairvoyance deserved some reward, and he sent them two plane tickets.

We didn't get off to too great a start in the finals, however. Ulf did a great job of clearing our forward's paths to the goal, but we were still trailing when the first period came to an end. We went all out to try and turn it around in the second, with Mario constantly inciting us to rise to the occasion before showing us how to do it himself. With a nice move off a pass from Francis, he tied the score when we were playing a man down. Minnesota scored again after that, though, and this time we didn't come up with an answer, losing the first game 5-4 at home. The North Stars were a team of real enforcers, and we hadn't figured out how to counter them yet.

The second game differed from Game One right from the beginning in two respects. First of all, Coff was back after a layoff of almost an entire month, which provided not only a huge edge for us psychologically, but also improved our play immensely. Very few players are able to move the puck from one end of the rink to the other by themselves as effortlessly as Coff, and maybe none of them are then able to set up the scoring opportunity as intelligently as he does.

The other difference was that we were the ones to jump out to the early lead. Bob Errey beat the North Stars' excellent goalie Jon Casey to open the scoring before Kevin and Mario teamed up for a picture perfect goal. Kevin got the puck right in front of Casey and immediately passed it off to Mario, who pushed it into shooting position with his skate. Instead of taking the shot, however, he passed the puck back to Kevin, who had the open net in front of him.

Mike Modano cut our lead to 2-1 on a power play early in the second period, but this goal was followed by the highlight play of the whole series. Mario got the puck in our end of the rink and took off down the ice. Reaching full speed somewhere around the red line, he still had both Minnesota defensemen in front of him. One moved back to cut off the left side while the other, Shawn Chambers, positioned himself to stop Mario directly. Without breaking stride, however, Mario let Chambers come at him before making his move, and what a move it was, shifting the puck to his backhand side and sticking it between the defenseman's legs while skating around him to the other side. The whole thing played itself out so fast that poor Chambers didn't even have a chance to react. With Casey waiting for him, Mario zoomed in toward the right side of the goal. Just as he looked like he was about to shoot, he surprised everybody in the house by pulling up and switching over to the backhand side, totally befuddling Casey and giving himself a wide open net to shoot into. It was simply an incredible play, and the crowd stayed on its feet a full five minutes to applaud the master's work.

Stevens scored another one to put us ahead 4-1, and we traveled to Bloomington, Minnesota, in a good mood. Little did we know how things would start to unravel once we got there.

The first blow came before Game Three even started. Mario developed back pains, and the team doctors told him he had to sit this one out. Then by the end of the game, we were all more or less wounded as the North Stars rolled right over us for a 3-1 victory. That I had a part in our one goal was small consolation. I had the puck behind the net and managed to make a falling down pass in front to Phil Bourque, who beat Casey to avoid the shutout.

Fortunately, we were able to turn things around in Game Four with Mario back and in command from the outset. Taking a three-goal lead, we were able to stave off Minnesota's comeback drive even when Troy Loney was ejected and the North Stars enjoyed a five-minute power play. Bourque sealed the victory for us with an empty-net goal in the dwindling moments of the game.

Back in control, we came out scoring again two days later in the Civic Arena, opening up a comfortable 4-0 lead. We did manage to turn an easy rout into something of a nail-biter as Minnesota came back to reduce our lead to one. Loney scored for us again, however, and we held on for the win. We then flew back to Minnesota one more time determined to end the series there.

Throughout Game Six, we just played inspired, unstoppable hockey. Less than two minutes into the game, Ulf got us started with a goal from the blue line, and Mario and Joe Mullen extended our lead before the period was out. I had a chance to contribute when I came out from behind the goal early in the second, but I let the puck get away from me. Fate was on our side that day, however, as even my slip-up translated into goal number four when Errey reached the loose puck and

We win the Stanley Cup. In the locker-room after the match with my parents and Jirka Hrdina.

sent it home. The game turned into a mere exhibition well before the final siren, with even backup defenseman Jim Paek scoring for us before Larry Murphy finally ended the barrage. The final score was 8-0 and the Stanley Cup was ours.

I had never in my life seen a celebration like the one that ensued after that game ended, with everyone jumping up and down like madmen. But this was the Pittsburgh Penguins' first Stanley Cup ever, and we were the heroes of the day. The locker room filled up with well-wishers and sportswriters, and the players' wives and girlfriends came in. And somehow alone at the center of the whirlpool sat Mario.

Everybody came up to pat him on the back, but Mario more or less kept staring at the ground and was still sitting there when the room began to empty out. Only after almost everybody else had left did he slowly rise and begin to get dressed. I saw that there were tears in his eyes.

The long trip home that night culminated when we arrived at the Pittsburgh airport at three o'clock in the morning. Never in a million years would I have guessed that a crowd of 40,000 people would be there to greet us at that early hour. But there they were. A sort of aisle had been cleared out for us to walk through the airport, and as we walked down it the fans were reaching out to touch us, pat us on the back and shake hands. There was such a big crowd there that night that the players couldn't even get to their cars to drive home.

We all hopped aboard a school bus and drove to Tommy Barrasso's place to wait for the report that the crowd at the airport had dispersed and we could go back to the parking lot for our cars. Then, as if some unknown force was trying to keep the night alive, our bus ran out of gas on the way back to the airport! So there we were, the newly crowned Stanley Cup champions, spread out along the highway in the dead of night with our thumbs in the air, trying to get back to the airport we had just flown into. It was already daylight by the time we finally reached our beds.

The celebration continued over the next four days and nights. Eighty thousand people gathered in Pittsburgh's biggest park to thank us for bringing them the Cup. I even saw a number of Czechoslovakian flags flying in the crowd there, which gave me a wonderful feeling.

The sheer joy of holding that legendary trophy was immense. I even got to take it home to the Nemecs, and we took about a million pictures of ourselves standing with it. The team also carted it from one bar to another around the city, where it took its fair share of licks. By the end of that 100-hour victory party, we could barely remember one another's names.

I was as happy as could be, but I was also looking forward to going home. Ever since my parents had arrived at the beginning of the Cup championship series, I had been struck by a strange sort of feeling. I realized that the person they had come back to see was someone different from the boy they had left behind. After all, they could now find Jaromir Jagr jerseys, posters, towels and drinking glasses for sale all over the city of Pittsburgh. Seeing them again made me realize that I had not let my parents down. I felt that everything they had invested in me had paid off for them in the form of pride and joy in their son.

I realized that my father had not gotten up before dawn every morning to drive me to practice for nothing; that mom, who had devoted all that time to helping me with my homework and filling up my notebooks so that I could focus solely on hockey and still keep up in school, now also knew that it was all for a purpose. I had wanted to show my parents that I could achieve something. And then they saw me win the Stanley Cup.

So eager was I to get home that my parents and I flew back even before the team's meeting with President Bush. While the rest of the guys were on their way to the White House, I was heading for Kladno.

When I got back, I was a little nervous about how the people I grew up with were going to react to me. I imagined that some of them would act envious, while others would avoid me because they thought I would have changed. The first time I went into the local discotheque and saw my friends from school, their first reaction was like "Oh, the big man's back. We thought you wouldn't even remember we existed any more." I was pretty annoyed by that and felt like walking out. But for the most part, the people I knew were glad to see me, and I spent the summer kicking the soccer ball around on the old lot by the church and playing tennis just as I'd always done before.

I also had a beautiful summer romance with a girl named Denisa. While the Penguins were playing in the Stanley Cup finals, Denisa was being crowned Czechoslovakia's Miss Fitness 1992. In an interview with *Czechoslovak Sport* magazine, she declared that her favorite athlete was none other than Jaromir Jagr. She said that she used to go to all the Kladno games just to watch me play.

When I got back from America, the magazine invited me to do a call-in question-and-answer session with the fans. A few days before the event took place, they published the specific time when people could call in with their questions for me, and selected excerpts were published in the next issue. That day, one of the *Sport* editors, Pavel Lonek, who I have known for a long time, brought Denisa into the magazine's office. I was nineteen, she was twenty, and we ended up spending a lot of time together that summer.

Denisa was very charming and pretty, and both of my parents liked her very much. The two of us took trips to Prague together and walked around the winding streets, visiting the monuments and historic sites of the capital city, and I could hardly believe my reactions. Imagine me interested in culture! That was not a transformation fated to last for very long, but it was nice while it lasted.

With Mom at the party — Celebration of my first Stanley Cup victory (5/29/1991).

Below: After winning the Stanley Cup we couldn't make it home. We hitch-hiked, it was a perfect mood. Me, Frank Pietrangelo, and Jirka Hrdina.

*The Nemec fami-
lies still help me
out in the U.S.*

*Celebrating with Joe
Nemec, Mrs. Olga and
Mr. Stefan Nemec.*

I invited Denisa to the wedding of my Kladno teammate Jan Krulis with my father acting as our chaperone. This was right after she won her Miss Fitness title, and her parents were afraid that she might be kidnapped or something like that. So dad and I went to pick her up at Prague's extravagant Hotel Diplomat and promised her father, who had taken her there, that we would take good care of her that evening. We had a great time together.

I helped dad around the house that summer, but I didn't enjoy the work as much as I used to. I went out with my friends and also did a lot of interviews. I had no idea that so many newspapers and magazines even existed in Czechoslovakia. Things were especially complicated because we still didn't have a phone at that time, and people had to call dad at work to reach me. He kept a big notebook at his desk in which he wrote everything down and then just told me who was coming and when. I think I met with people from every single newspaper in the country that summer. After making coffee, mom would go out into the garden because she couldn't stand to listen to me anymore. I couldn't stand listening to myself, either. I must have said the exact same things to over fifty different interviewers.

The Kladno coach, Eda Novák, allowed me to train with the team to keep in shape, and I also made regular trips to Germany to work out on the ergometer. That September was the Canada Cup tournament, and I wanted both myself and the Czechoslovakian national team to come through with a shining performance during the competition. Unfortunately, that's not what ended up happening.

I had really been looking forward to the Canada Cup, but I left thoroughly disappointed. We had a good team, but we just didn't click. Some of the players were definitely trying to show off for the North American hockey establishment, and their style of play became forced. And then there was the tension between players from the different NHL teams as well as between the NHL players and the players from the Czechoslovakian league. In addition to myself, the players with NHL experience included Dominik Hasek, Frantisek Kucera, Frank Musil, Robert Reichel, Michal Pivonka, Robert Kron, Jergus Baca, Zdien Cíger and Jiri Látal (who left early). There were also some other players who had just been drafted. Basically, we lacked cohesion and did not play with much of a common purpose.

I was as disappointed with myself after the tournament as I was with anybody else, even though I was far from the worst player on the team. My play was uncreative and I was frustrated by the lack of communication on the lines, even though we all spoke the same language. Coach Ivan Hlinka kept putting me on the same unit with Reichel and Robert Kastak. Now, Robert is without question an excellent hockey player, but our individual styles of play are too similar to each other. Robert likes to finish what he starts himself and often takes the shot when he might be better off passing. I have to say that we just did not play very well together. The combination had worked fine the summer before in Switzerland, but one year in the NHL had rendered us incompatible and the spark was gone.

I approached Hlinka twice during the course of the tournament with the suggestion that it would be better for the team if he split us up, but he didn't want to hear it. Because we had opened up with a win against the Soviet Union, he felt like there was nothing that needed changing. Only against the Americans did he play with the lineup, teaming me with Josef Beránek and Martin Rucinsky, which I found to be a much more effective line. But after that one game, he went back to the original line.

We did have a great first game, jumping out to a 3-0 lead against the USSR in the first period with Zigmund Palffy increasing our lead at the beginning of the second. We never let them get near us, and even though Alexei Zhamnov and Sergei Fedorov did register goals, the game ended 5-2 and we felt good about our chances going into the next game, against Finland.

That game was such a heartbreaker, though, that it haunted us for the rest of the tournament. I remember that terrible decisive moment perfectly because I was on the ice at the time. Both teams were scoreless going into the final minute of play, when Christian Ruutu got the puck from Teemu Selanne and drove toward Hasek from the left side. Hasek came out to meet him while at the same time keeping an eye on Striko coming in from the other side. When Ruutu made the expected pass, Rucinsky moved in to intercept it, but the puck deflected off his hockey stick right toward the goal. Because Hasek had moved out in front a bit to cut off Striko's angle, there was no one in front of the net to stop the puck from dribbling off poor Rucinsky's stick and crossing the line into the goal with only a few seconds remaining on the scoreboard.

That fluke goal seemed to break us. Although our next opponent was the beatable U.S. team, we were not the ones who could beat them. We didn't even get our bearings before goals by Pat LaFontaine and Jeremy Roenick put them up 2-0. Tomas Jelinek cut their lead in half for a little while, but the Americans then scored two more times to put the game out of reach. I picked up one goal on a wrist shot past Mike Richter, whose view was blocked by Chris Chelios, but that wasn't anywhere near enough.

The Americans were definitely a down-and-dirty team. During the game I was taken down with a cross-check to the face. I was a little shaken up for a moment, and my lip was bleeding, but I finished the game.

Because of the lineup change, that game against the U.S. was my best of the tournament, but after that Hlinka put me back on the same line with Reichel. It was a shame, really, because Rucinsky, Beránek and I did play well together, effectively moving the puck up the ice and making the right passes on the offensive end. But Hlinka separated us again for the Canada game.

I had been especially looking forward to the matchup against Gretzky and company, as well as playing against Coff. He and I started laughing at each other as soon as we got on the ice and kept it up even after the game started. I was no longer smiling by the end, however, because Canada had no problem breezing past us, scoring the first three goals of the game and finally winning 6-2.

My main feeling was that I just wanted to get out of there. I called my dad a few times and told him this, but he reminded me that I had an obligation to play and that it would by considered a break of promise. The atmosphere on the team was lousy. We didn't get into real arguments with one another, but we just kind of sulked the whole time. I was also getting pretty sick of Jelinek riding me for not being more vocal in my moral support of the other guys when I was on the bench. He had started bugging me about this at the World Championship the year before and seemed to have gotten pretty angry about it by now. But that's simply not the kind of player I am. I do better by focusing and keeping my concentration on myself. I guess it seems to Jelinek like I just don't give a damn, but he should know that's not the case.

The Swedes finally put us out of our misery by eliminating us from the tournament in yet another game in which we scored only two goals (by Reichel and Leo Gudas). I always like playing for my country, but I was thoroughly disappointed by this experience. Maybe I had expected too much, but in any case I was glad it was over. I was looking forward to going back to camp and starting my second season in the NHL.

Among the Stars

I didn't go back to Czechoslovakia after the Canada Cup ended, but headed straight for Pittsburgh, where I was moving. I was leaving the Nemecs and moving in with a non-Czech speaking American family, mainly in order to learn better English and also to get a better sense of the typical American lifestyle. I also needed a little more freedom. I had finally gotten my own car and gained a degree of independence.

The car I bought was a black Camaro, and I thought it would be a nice idea to take George Kirk out for a ride. I don't think he enjoyed it very much, though, because I noticed he started trembling when I went up to ninety miles per hour on the Boulevard of the Allies. After he got out of the car, he told me I shouldn't drive without a crash helmet.

Another change was my new agent, Michael Barnett, whom I hired to replace Don Meehan. It was Jirí Crha, the former goalie for Pardubice and then the Toronto Maple Leafs, who I have to thank for helping me make that decision. Jirí had taken a liking to me and my play all the way back to my junior league days, and he always used to send me Christian hockey sticks, and sometimes even gloves, without asking for anything in return. When his daughter became a professional tennis player and started looking for an agent, Mike was the one they turned to for help.

Mike wanted to be my agent and asked Jirí to set up a meeting with me. So one day we all got together — on the telephone. I have no idea how these things work, but with Mike in Los Angeles, Jirí in Germany, dad in Kladno and me in Canada (this all happened during the Canada Cup tournament), we were all able to talk to one another and come to an agreement.

Mike wanted to start getting me some endorsements, and from the way he talked about it, I was convinced it was a good idea. Mike became my new agent before I went into my second NHL season, and he took perfect care of me from the beginning. The first thing he did was buy two new fax machines, one for me and one that Jirí Crha brought over to my parents, so that all of us could stay up to date about everything that was going on.

When my family came over for Christmas, Mike bought them plane tickets to Washington and gave them a tour of the city. He also took them to New York and brought them to his office. I was on the phone with Mike almost every day, and he would always ask if I needed anything and how he could help me.

I also started getting a lot of deals to do advertisements, and in the course of shooting these I got to know some of the other members of Mike's flock, such as Wayne Gretzky and Brett Hull. I went out to dinner with Wayne and Brett and their wives a few times and became friends with them, as well as with such other players as Sergei Fedorov. Mike gave me the introduction I needed into hockey's society, helping me out in much the same way as Paul Coffey had the year before.

The beginning of my second season in the NHL was not at all a happy one, however, marked as it was by the loss of our beloved coach, Bob Johnson. I had a very hard time coming to terms with it, and I don't think anyone on the team could believe that our eternal optimist was never going to come in and infect us with his contagious good mood again.

The tragic series of events began to unfold a few days before the start of the Canada Cup, in which Bob was supposed to coach the U.S. team. He flew to Pittsburgh from Saskatchewan for the team's first game, which was to be played at the Civic Arena against Sweden, with a severe toothache. These pains were not so unusual for him though — he had been suffering from them intermittently throughout the past season — and he went to see his dentist that afternoon. Unable to determine the source of the problem himself, the dentist scheduled an appointment for Bob to undergo a more complete examination at Mercy Hospital the next day.

In the evening, Bob suffered a stroke and had to be taken immediately to the hospital, where the terrible truth was discovered: He had been afflicted with a widespread cancerous brain tumor.

After an immediate operation, Bob was able to give his team some final pregame instructions the next day, but everyone with the Penguins knew that he was not going to come back to the bench for us. On September 12, he was taken to Colorado Springs, where we visited him later that month and saw him for the last time.

I will never forget the moment on November 26 when Craig Patrick came into our dressing room and told us that Bob Johnson had died. The entire team fell silent, and tears rolled down the cheeks of several players. We had already been made to understand that he was not likely to win this final battle, but the cruel news of Bob's passing devastated us nonetheless. The phrase with which many of us had come to identify with him, "It's a great day for hockey," was certainly not appropriate on that particular day.

Scotty Bowman was named our new head coach right before the start of the new season. Bowman had already been with the team as a tactician but had not taken

Bob Johnson — my first trainer in Pittsburgh.

an active part in our actual practices. At the same time he knew the team very well and was the logical choice for the position. His subdued temperament was almost the opposite of Coach Johnson's, and he maintained something of a distance from the players, never calling us by our first names, for example. The important thing, though, is that he's an absolute expert on the game of hockey, and his years of experience as a student of the sport were recognized immediately.

I missed the beginning of training camp due to my participation in the Canada Cup tournament, along with Ulf, Murph, Coff and Joey Mullen. Nevertheless, I managed to get the season off to a good start, with three assists in our opening-day victory over Buffalo. A short time after that, I even came up with a coast-to-coast breakaway goal against the Islanders, although the most interesting thing about that particular game was that the team turned in the biggest comeback in the Penguins' history. Down 6-2 at the beginning of the third period, we began our scoring barrage on a goal by Mark Recchi, followed by two from Mario and finally my own goal in the twelfth minute of the session. Then it was not long after the overtime period began that Phil Bourque quickly completed the turnaround with our fifth unanswered goal for the win.

All in all, however, the team's season start was pretty sluggish, reaching something like a crisis point in mid-October with a home loss to the New York Rangers, a tie against Chicago, further losses in New Jersey and Montreal and the ultimate embarrassment: an 8-0 loss to the Washington Capitals in the Civic Arena, without a doubt the worst loss I've ever been a part of.

The team was surviving more than progressing as Christmas rolled around, although I have to say that personally I was feeling much better than I had felt at the same time the previous year. I was still glad to see my parents when they came over to visit me for the holidays, even though they did not seem as happy at their first sight of me, as my mother cried out, "Oh, my God, you're so thin! Aren't you eating anything? The Nemecs told us you're not eating properly and that the backseat of your car is covered with hamburger wrappers."

The Casanovas weren't as fastidious about cooking for me as the Nemecs had been, but then again no one could have been. At my first home all I had to do was mention that I was hungry and boom — food on the table. My new status was more or less that of a regular member of the family who sat down to dinner with everybody else. I guess I was a bit shy about asking for anything to eat at more unusual times, even though I know they would have been willing to fix something for me, and the refrigerator itself wasn't as full of off-hour snacking opportunities as the one at the Nemecs had been.

My year with the Casanova family was really a great time, though. They had a son who played football (American football, that is) and explained to me how the rules of the sport worked. We even went to a couple of games in Pittsburgh together. And most importantly, I was finally learning how to speak English properly, although I did occasionally miss having someone to speak Czech with.

My principal passion off the ice was my car, even though I did have an unfortunate accident the day after I got it. I was driving home from practice, when all of a sudden a deer ran right out in front of me. I slammed on the brakes, but it was too late for the deer and my Camaro got bent out of shape a bit as well.

The police were not exactly thrilled by my fast driving, either. Things were cool at the beginning, as the police were good about not giving me tickets. They just warned me that I had to slow down, but with me, that advice went in one ear and out the other. I was especially inclined to step on the gas when driving home from the airport when we got back from away games. Since the highway was usually empty, I liked to race my way home just for fun. At other times, though, I had to drive in a hurry because I was running late, often due to my oversleeping. That hadn't been so much a problem before because Mrs. Nemec knew that I always had to be woken up at least four times before I would finally drag myself out of bed. The Casanovas, on the other hand, only came to wake me up one time. Since I was used to falling back asleep after only the first warning, it was often later than I thought when I opened my eyes again, and I had to hightail it out of the house to get to the game on time.

Every year in the middle of January comes the NHL's All-Star weekend, and as the votes began to be counted, I suddenly realized that I might be invited to attend this meeting of the "lords" of hockey. The way it works is that ballot cards are distributed at all the hockey rinks in the league, and fans can vote for their favorite players. The top vote-getters in each position (goalie, defensemen, centers and wings) then make up the starting lineup for the two conferences in the All-Star game itself, with the rest of each team selected by the coaches from the previous year's Stanley Cup finalists.

The partial returns from this fan balloting were regularly printed in the newspapers, and as time progressed it became clear that I was going to be selected to the first team. In the end, I actually received a total of about 226,000 votes, so along with Mario, Kevin, Coff and Trots, off I went to Philadelphia for my first mid-season exhibition.

I suppose I've gotten a little used to receiving this honor by now — the fans have put me on the All-Star starting lineup three times already — but that first meeting of the "hockey aces" was something unbelievable to me and, except for the Penguins' Stanley Cup victories, the absolute highlight of my career.

It's not the game itself that's so exciting, but everything surrounding it. I had never seen players from opposing teams socializing with one another that way before. I'd been surprised my first season by how little contact there was between the members of the different clubs, as even former teammates would just mutter a little "Hey, how ya doing?" when they ran into each other before moving on. There's simply no time for anything else during the season. But the All-Star weekend is different. Everybody loosens up, and even players who'd been banging away at each other the day before sit and talk like old friends.

I found it hard to believe that I belonged there. I pretty much played the wallflower at the beginning, and along with Alex Mogilny, who also felt a bit out of place, just sat and watched the show.

In comes Mark Messier, for example, wearing a long black coat and looking like some kind of mysterious big shot. He spots Coff and the two of them sit down together and talk about the old days when they were teammates back in Edmonton, obviously enjoying their reunion. Then Mario walks by, and even though he and Messier barely know each other, having played together only briefly on the Canadian national team, they shake hands like old friends, too — just a couple of all-time hockey greats glad to have the chance to say hello. Over in a corner sit the goalies, who seem to be having a secret conference among themselves. Who knows, maybe they're discussing the tricks of the trade and comparing notes on the other players in the room.

Then the sportswriters are let in, and they begin to swarm around each of the players in the room. The flash bulbs pop away incessantly, and the TV cameras purr. The crush of people really raises the temperature in the dressing room, and everybody starts to get covered in sweat. I myself was not exactly the center of attention that day, first of all because I still didn't have too much to say in English yet and, secondly, because there were a lot of bigger stars than me to talk to. The players are always relieved when the announcement for the press to leave the room finally comes because there's barely any space to move around with them in there.

There are two parts to All-Star weekend. On Saturday are the so-called "skills competitions," in which various players dressed in their own team uniforms go up against one another in different categories.

I was one of eight entered in the "fastest skater" competition, in which players are paired up and race each other one time around the rink. The players with the two fastest times then go head to head in the final round. Unfortunately, I got a bit overanxious and faltered somewhat at the start of my heat. I finished in fifth place, although the actual time difference between me and the two eventual finalists, Sergei Fedorov and Alexander Mogilny, was not very much. The final round itself between these two players was quite exciting, with Fedorov finishing just a hair ahead of his fellow Russian for the victory. Little did I know then that Sergei and I would take each other on in a different kind of battle in Madison Square Garden two years later.

The next competition entailed players on each team taking the puck for one-on-

Going to the test of skill at the All-Stars game. In front Kevin Stevens, behind me Mario Lemieux.

Greeting future stars before the game itself.

ones against the opposing goalie three times each. The team whose players scored the most goals won. I managed to score on two out of my three attempts, which put me in a tight spot because the overall score was tied and one player from each team had to be selected for the shootout.

Steve Yzerman was selected for the Campbell Conference and easily beat Patrick Roy for the potentially winning goal. Now we had to pick somebody, but I didn't like the tone of the discussion in our Prince of Wales war council one bit, nor the conspiratorial smile that snuck across the faces of Coff and Mario. Then, just as I feared, the two of them pointed to me and said, "You're up, Jags. You're the one who scored two out of three, after all."

"No way," I said, trying to protest. If I missed, then we'd lose, and I didn't feel like I needed that kind of pressure. But then the rest of my All-Star teammates joined in, telling me I was the one and there was no way I could miss. God knows how I let them talk me into it, but there I stood with Chicago's Eddie Belfour, one of the best goalies in the NHL, staring right at me. My knees were shaking as I set up at the red line, preparing for the national embarrassment of my impending failure.

So I started up, still not knowing when I got to the blue line what move I was going to try. I knew that Belfour was fast and smart and by no means likely to fall for a fake, so I decided to try my luck with an ordinary slap shot. As I waited for Eddie to move in one direction or the other before firing away, I felt a huge weight lifted from my shoulders as I watched the puck fly past his pad and into the net.

After that, I was surrounded by my Prince of Wales teammates, who slapped me on the back and said, "Good job, Jags." Later, Mario ended up winning the competition for us. That night was the big "President's Party," but I was too tired to stay long. I chatted only with Mike Barnett for a little while before going back to my room and falling asleep. The All-Star game was the next day.

I was in the starting lineup for the Prince of Wales' side, along with Montreal's Patrick Roy in goal, Ray Bourque of Boston and Coff behind me and Kevin Stevens and (of course) Mario Lemieux on the line with me. Facing us were Wayne Gretzky at center, Brett Hull of St. Louis and my future teammate Luc Robitaille, then with Los Angeles, on the wings. The Campbell Conference's defensemen were Chris Chelios of Chicago and Al MacInnis of St. Louis, who has one of the hardest shots in the NHL. Eddie Belfour was in goal.

Trevor Linden scored the first goal of the game for the other team, but Mario evened it up halfway through the first period on my assist. That was my first-ever All-Star point scored, but it didn't make much of a difference as the Campbell Conference won the game 10-6. Ultimately, no one gets that excited about who wins and who loses these events.

The game was pretty fun at the beginning, but the excitement wore off after a while, and by the end I was kind of bored. The whole thing is really little more than a glorified skatearound for the fans, and almost no one plays the boards or gets physical at all. As if by unspoken agreement, no personal scores are settled during the All-Star game. Kevin even told me that the year before Rob Brown and Cam Neely had practically sworn to kill each other during one regular-season game and ended up on the ice together as teammates a week later at the All-Star game.

After the game ended, we all went back to the locker room, and I thought to myself that it was fun, but in a few days we'd all go back to hammering one another. I think the other players had something like the same feeling, judging by how slowly everybody was in getting ready to leave. It was as if they all wanted to extend the happy, comfortable, yet necessarily short-lived, atmosphere of the weekend as long as they could. Mogilny's locker was next to mine, and he smiled at me with that shaved head of is (he actually looks more like a prisoner than a hockey player). I get the impression Mogilny doesn't let too much bother him and just goes through life with kind of a blissful, carefree attitude. Ray Bourque, on the other hand, has something of a natural air of authority about him, and when he suggested that we take up a collection for the boys who looked after our equipment and stuff for two days, we all sort of grumbled but gave in.

The final event of All-Star weekend, that everybody looks forward to, is the closing dinner. This is always a fun party. Not only is there a huge buffet table laid out for everybody, but the organizers always come up with some interesting attractions, which always fascinate me.

Table hockey, for instance. The players in the game are dressed up and made to look like the actual starting lineup of the All-Star teams themselves, except that each one is wearing his regular team uniform. And then if, say, Jagr makes a bad play, you can take him out and substitute Messier. Another event is a big cage with a goalie standing in front of it, and the guests can line up to take shots against him. It's fun if you're one of the guests, but when I saw the goalie taking a breather, I saw how worn out he was. I don't think it was too much of a blast for him.

The longest line is for the opportunity to have a head shot photo taken and then either superimposed on the uniform of some star player like Gretzky or Mario or printed onto an official game puck with the All-Star logo on the other side. I toyed with the idea of getting one of those pucks with my picture on it, but was dissuaded by the long line of people wanting the same thing. I had to laugh, however, when as I turned away I saw a smiling Scotty Bowman standing at the very back of the line waiting his own turn to be photographed.

For the most part I just walked around the room and mingled with various players. We would give each other a smile, exchange a few words and move on. After a while, Mario's wife, Nathalie, came up to me and exclaimed, "There you are! Mario sent me to find you. I think he was afraid you'd get lost somewhere." She then led me back to the table where they were sitting.

All in all, I had a very nice time in Philadelphia that weekend, and I still remem-

All-Stars game in Philadelphia.
With Kevin Stevens, Mario Lemieux,
Paul Coffey and Bryan Trottier.

ber my first All-Star game quite fondly. Unfortunately, I got myself into real trouble right after that.

One week after the All-Star game, the Penguins arrived in Washington for a game in the Capital Center, now called the USAir Arena. The place was packed to the rafters, as our games usually are wherever we play. The team was in an upbeat mood, having just the day before beaten the Islanders in New York in a game in which I scored one goal and assisted on another that even the Islanders' fans applauded.

After Mario had gotten the puck on our blue line, he and I just took off down the ice for a two-on-one. We passed it back and forth one time before reaching the Islanders' blue line, where he pulled up in order to draw the defender to him. Having done so, he sent the puck back across to me as I was charging down the left side and heading toward the goal. Mario's pass was right on target, and I moved back in toward the middle with plenty of room to take the shot. Both the New York goalie and the defenseman came out to try and stop me, but I completely surprised them by passing it back to Mario once again, and he easily put it in the net to finish the play. And that was to be the last game I had to be happy about for a while.

I remember Sunday, January 26, in Washington too well. It was freezing cold outside, but the sun was shining, and the Caps and Penguins played a good game. The home team jumped out to a two-goal lead, but we stayed alive when Coff took the puck from end to end, and then from behind the net found Erry, who scored our first goal.

Washington increased its lead by two right after that. Washington's defenseman Al Iafrate cross-checked Kevin Stevens and held him down on the ice for about half a minute while Michal Pivonka began holding on to Mario and Calle Johansson did the same to Mullen. Iafrate finally let Kevin go when he saw a chance to head to our goal. He was in full flight when the puck came to him, and Tommy never had a chance to stop him. To add insult to injury, Kevin got two minutes in the box for unsportsmanlike conduct, and we were feeling wronged.

Early in the second period Mario had the puck and drew the defensive coverage toward him before finding Recchi with a picture perfect pass to create our second goal. Then I tied it up a few minutes later when Mario passed me the puck from behind the goal, and I got past Washington's Dimitri Khristich before beating their goalie Don Beaupre with a backhand shot. Murph scored to put us ahead 4-3, but Randy Burridge evened the score for Washington just before the end of the period.

And then came the all-too-exciting conclusion that I'm afraid I'll never forget, much as I'd like to. With a minute and a half remaining in the third period, Kevin Stevens came skating down the left side and passed me the puck near the goal. I fell down before I could get my stick on it, however, because Washington's Kevin Hatcher floored me with a solid hack and followed it up by knocking me against the boards. Then when Mario had control and made a sweet move to get past Mike Ridley, he too was tripped up from behind before he could complete the play. The game ended when Kelly Miller scored for the Capitals just before time ran out.

At that moment Ron Hoggarth, the referee, was standing behind the goal, when Stevens came up to him and began arguing with him. I had been trailing the play when Miller scored, and even after the action came to a halt my momentum carried me back around the goal where Hoggarth was standing. I didn't see him until the last moment. I was upset with him because the Caps had been wrapping their sticks around me all game, without a penalty being called.

Still, I didn't actually intend to cause a collision with him, and nothing would have happened if Hoggarth had moved a little bit to the side. But because he happened to be standing right in my path, I unthinkingly barreled right into him at something close to full speed, and he tottered for a moment before falling down against the boards. It didn't immediately dawn on me what kind of problem I had just created for myself, and if I had had my wits more about me, I would have at least come back to help him up. As it was, however, I got called for an intentional attack against an official and soon came to the realization that I would be penalized more than two minutes for what I had done.

Three of us got sent off to an early shower at that point — Kevin, Mario and me.

Back in the dressing room, I began to think about what I had done and realized that I had gotten myself knee-deep in trouble. I was so scared that I called my parents as soon as I got home and started repeating myself as if I'd been hypnotized: "Oh, dad, I did something terrible. I mean, I did something really, really terrible." His first thought was that I'd run somebody over in my car, so he must have been a little relieved to hear I'd only run over an official on the ice. I gave him the whole story, and he told me I'd probably be reprimanded by the league.

And he was right. The TV announcers had already been saying during their postgame wrap-up that I'd probably be hit with a ten-game suspension, and they were not mistaken, either. I got the "big ten," all right, and was given more than enough time to think about who I was and who I was not allowed to ram into during a hockey game.

I was distraught over this string of events. Never having missed a single game before that, never having been injured or anything, I felt terrible at not being allowed to play. I was even forbidden to practice with the Penguins, but I still went out on the ice and worked out alone every day, probably training harder during those two weeks than I ever have before or since. Convinced that I had let down the whole team, I resolved to atone for my sin when I returned.

Not only was I embarrassed by my suspension, but I was also terribly bored. I therefore welcomed the offer from the WDVE-FM station in Pittsburgh to read the

In competition with my future team-mate Luc Robitaille.

weather report as a gimmick during my enforced absence from the ice. I went there every day to say that tomorrow it would be "fair to partly cloudy" or "overcast with a chance of showers" or whatever they wrote down for me to say. It was actually pretty funny, and at least it gave me the chance to think about something else for a while.

When I think back now on that fateful game, I have to admit that Hoggarth didn't even do such a terrible job of officiating that game. His job was definitely pretty tough that day and was not made any easier by what he was able to overhear going on between the Penguins during the course of the game. The newspapers the following day quoted him as saying, "I already had a feeling early on that the final minutes of the game were going to be tense. The Pittsburgh players had been yelling at each other throughout and often getting on my case as well, especially Stevens. Maybe I should have called the Capitals for holding or hooking at the end, but I only had a split second to make my decision and it was a borderline call. As for Jagr's allegation, all I can say is that he must not have understood me."

Hoggarth was no more able to escape the consequences of that unfortunate game than I was. His next appearance at the Civic Arena was greeted by an almost deafening collective groan of disapproval from the spectators. But before that, he received several anonymous phone calls threatening revenge for my ejection. I think, in the end, the poor guy had more sleepless nights than I did after the incident.

The affair also brought out a sense of humor in a number of fans. One particularly inspired gift I received was a cloth doll wearing a referee's uniform with Hoggarth's name on it and with tearaway arms, legs, nose and head. The doll is still whole to this day.

The funny thing is that Hoggarth and I eventually became friends. Some time later I ran into him in a bar after a game in Winnipeg and bought him a beer. We had a good talk about the whole thing and have been on quite good terms ever since. At the 1993 All-Star game in Montreal, he even introduced me to his wife. When he saw me walking down the corridor at one point during the weekend, he called out to me, "Jaromir, wait up!" He then brought his wife over to meet me with the words, "Well, this is the guy."

Hoggarth was definitely the first referee I ever got into a conversation with off the ice. He's retired now, but after things settled down, I always used to look forward to his officiating the games I was in because we would get into some pretty funny exchanges. Once he yelled at me while I was skating by him, "Hey, you just stay away from me," and I answered, "You mess with me, I'll knock you down again." Without taking his eyes off the action, Hoggarth smiled and said, "You do that and you'll get twenty years this time."

I had never thought too much one way or the other about the referees and their job before that incident, but I then began to realize that they don't have it easy at all. The officials have to make their decisions in a split second and then stand behind them, while the fans get to watch a play ten times over in a slow-motion replay. What is also interesting is how some of the players subtly cooperate with them, especially at tense moments when they have to calm things down. Of my teammates, Murph and Ronnie Francis are especially inclined to provide the refs with this kind of assistance.

For the most part I have not had any problems with the officials, other than that one time. Sometimes in the heat of the moment I'll yell something at one of them, but otherwise I tend to keep my distance on the ice. Incidences with the officials are very rare and in general I have the utmost respect for them. I have only had 2 brushes with them in the six years I have been in the NHL.

Little did I know as I took the ice for that fateful game in Washington that it would be the last time I played on the same team with Paul Coffey. The Penguins were going through a bad period, registering only one win in ten games, and facing the possibility of not even making the playoffs. The Islanders were coming up fast. So Craig Patrick made a radical move. He decided to trade two of our most skilled players, Coff and Recchi, for defenseman Kjell Samuelsson, right wing Rick Tocchet and goalie Ken Wregget. It was actually kind of a complicated deal, involving three teams — us, Philadelphia and Los Angeles — and its purpose was clear: to strengthen our defense and increase our toughness.

Coff already had a feeling that his days in Pittsburgh were numbered, and he wasn't too surprised when he learned about the trade. He came into the locker room and calmly said his farewell.

Recchi took it much worse. He couldn't believe what had happened to him. Some months before, Mark had turned down an excellent offer from the Flyers in order to stay in Pittsburgh. Now he was on his way to our cross-state rivals anyway, but at half the salary he could have had, and he burst out crying as he said his goodbyes to us.

Although I was pretty sad to see Coff go, I had to admit that the trade made sense. Opposing teams were beginning to pick up more and more goals when he was in the game, and even though he scored a lot himself, the balance was turning against us. Kjell Samuelsson was a defensive defenseman, and he knew how to play tough. And Tocchet, well, he's just about the toughest man on ice a team could ever hope for. I don't think I've ever seen him lose a fight. His role was clear. Intimidate, score, and protect Mario. Craig Patrick knew what he was doing.

My return from the ten-game exile, in a game against Quebec, was a success, as I scored one of the more unusual goals of my career. I had once managed something similar against Sweden in the European Under 18 championships and later repeated the feat against Boston in the playoffs as well as in the Montreal All-Star game. Carrying the puck to the goal from the left side, I saw the Quebec goalie come out to cut down the angle. Then as I cut left, I shifted the puck to my backhand side and one-handed it past the goalie into the net.

After we opened up the final quarter of the season with a home loss to Hartford, we then found ourselves in a game where the Islanders trailed us by a mere point. Fortunately, with that game, we began turning things around, enjoying three consecutive wins, including one in Chicago, where visiting players easily begin to tremble even before stepping out onto the rink.

The hero of that game in Chicago was none other than our new acquisition, Dicky Tocchet, who demonstrated just how fierce a competitor he actually is. Going into the third period, we were trailing 3-1, due largely to the stellar performance in goal of Chicago's Dominik Hasek. In the final session, however, we finally discovered the right formula to beat him, and it was Tocchet who led the charge.

During the second period, Dicky had gotten hit in the face by a flying puck and suffered a fractured jawbone. After receiving treatment from the team doctor, he refused to sit out the rest of the game and came on for the final session in the same bloodstained jersey he'd been wearing, even though he was in great pain. He proceeded to score in the eighth minute of the period to cut the Blackhawks' lead to one. Then seven minutes later, he tied it up. We were about ready to carry him off the ice on our shoulders at that point. A minute later, Larry Murphy beat Hasek one more time for the winner, and we had completed the comeback with this much-needed win.

That was the game that put us back on track. Two days later, we beat Edmonton and after that, Quebec. I scored a strange sort of goal in that second game after stealing the puck at our blue line and heading straight for the Nordiques' goal unaccompanied. On my way, though, I lost control of the puck and it spurted out in front of me, where it looked like the Nordiques' goaltender would be able to get to it first. But oddly enough, when he did get to the puck, he somehow missed it entirely, and the thing just kept on floating back until it entered the goal. Still going full speed, I tripped over the goalie and slid on my belly all the way back to the end of the rink, where they practically had to peel me off the boards before I could get up.

Then came the players' strike, which began on April 1 and lasted almost two weeks. When the strike started it looked for a while like the season was not going to be resumed. Therefore, my thoughts turned toward that spring's World Championship tournament in Prague. With all our equipment locked up, the team went out to Monroeville for informal practices wearing only sweat suits. As I skated around, I began reminiscing about the previous year, when my American career began, and how it was right there on the Monroeville ice that I had first met Coff, Cullen and Recchi. Now all three were gone. That's life in the National Hockey League for you.

I began talking on the phone a lot with Frank Musil and "Alby" Reichel, who had

I get more and more popular in Pittsburgh…

Raggedy Hogarth. I still haven't torn anything off him, not even his head…

actually gone back to Prague during the break. We discussed how we were keeping in shape and when we thought we were going to start playing again. They didn't have their equipment either, and Vladimir Ruzicka had to buy it. In the end, though, it wasn't at the World Championship that I ran into Ruza again, but in the playoffs.

After a two-week halt, the players and the owners reached some sort of agreement, and we played our final three games of the regular season. Not only had we left the Islanders behind, but we even managed to come on strong enough at the end to pass New Jersey and finish in third place in the division.

I finished the regular season with thirty-two goals, five more than my total the previous year. I also picked up ten more assists than I had in my rookie year, and all this in spite of my missing ten games in the middle of the season this time around. Of course in the NHL, the only thing that really matters is the playoffs. It was that time again, and our first challenger was the Washington Capitals.

The Caps were a good team and getting better. Michal Pivonka and Peter Bondra were a formidable offensive threat, and their defense was excellent as well, led by the unpassable giant Kevin Hatcher and the formidable Al Iafrate. The Washington rink is also well known around the league for its bad ice and stifling humidity. Although we were pretty glad not to have to open up the postseason against the big, bad Rangers, the playoffs are always a trial by fire no matter who you're playing against. We were also well aware that Washington had been the better team during the regular season.

All our fears were confirmed during the first two games of the series. After those two losses, our dream of a successful title defense began to fade. Our run of bad luck began less than four minutes into Game One, when Peter Bondra scored off a pass from Michal Pivonka. Although Loney tied it up for us immediately, John Druce put the Caps back up by the end of the period, and the score stayed 2-1 until just before the end of the game, when Iafrate broke loose down the left side and found Bondra with a cross pass in front of the goal. I did manage to get the end of my stick on the puck, but ultimately I couldn't break up the pass, and Bondra had an easy shot to seal the victory for the home team.

After missing the series opener, Mario returned to the ice for Game Two and picked up a couple of early assists on goals by Murph and Stevens. Those were our only goals of the game, however, while Pivonka's line registered three in the first period alone before we ended up losing 6-2. Things looked bad for us at this point with the Capitals in firm control and Bondra boasting to the press about having figured us out since last year. We headed back to Pittsburgh as if we were going to a funeral, the only optimistic voice on our team being that of Jiri Hrdina. "So what if we lost the first two?" he challenged us. "We can win them back at home now. This series is going to be ours because we have the better offense." And, indeed, our spirits were lifted by the results of Game Three, which we won largely thanks to one player. Mario, of course.

Trailing 2-1 going into the second period, we tied the score on Mullen's goal off a pass from Mario. Not much later, he sent me a perfect feed as I was skating down the ice, and I fired the puck past Don Beaupré to put us ahead. Then the man, Mario, took over himself scoring two more by the end of the period and completing the hat trick at the start of the third. The final score was 6-4, and we felt much better.

Our joy was short-lived, however, as we got hit with a real cold shower two days later, losing 7-2 at home in Game Four. Before we knew it, we had fallen behind 3-0, and we didn't score at all until Mario's goal in the third period. We were now only sixty minutes away from potential elimination, and we knew that it was going to be no easy feat to pull off a comeback at this point. We had to win in Washington, then at home, and then in Washington again. That sounded close to impossible.

When Bowman brought the team together for a strategy session before Game Five, he asked the players if they had anything to contribute. No one said anything until Mario stood up and began to lecture the rest of the players, who listened with rapt attention to one of the most intense people any of us had ever encountered. "We can't play the way we've been playing," his speech began. And as he continued over the next several minutes, it dawned on us that despite the present situation, we were going to prevail.

"We're playing naively," he continued, "opening things up without even then getting good shots off. That has to change. Our only chance is to fall back on defense and concentrate on taking away their opportunities, while not letting a single one of ours get away. One of our guys will stay forward and attack, while the rest wait at the blue line. The main thing is to hang back. We're not playing to win a beauty contest here. We're playing to win the Cup again." We listened to him like he was a god, and we realized that there was no way we could lose with him on our side. Mario concluded: "If we just keep attacking without thinking, we're through."

Newly inspired, we played exactly as he had told us to, cutting off the Capitals' chances and waiting for our own to develop. And although Iafrate scored first in Game Five, Errey tied it up and Murph gave us the lead. Then in the third period it was my turn.

Up by a goal, we were focusing all our efforts on defense and playing mostly in our own end of the rink. But when the Capitals' Sylvain Cote lost control of the puck at the blue line for a moment, I saw my opportunity and went for it. I stole the puck from Cote with the tip of my stick and took off alone toward the goal. The Capitals' defenseman, Brad Schlegel, came across to try and get in my way, but I was already going too fast for him to catch me, and I honed in on Beaupré. Because the Washington ice is so bad, the puck wasn't sliding along with me as fast as it normally would, and I almost skated past it. Fortunately recovering in time, I got it back in front of me and moved it to my forehand before flicking it over the goalie's stick and into the net to widen our lead. The win was punctuated in the closing moments by Errey's open-net goal, and we were still alive. Our next task was to win at home.

Nothing came easy for the Penguins that year, and Game Six was no exception. Even after Kevin Stevens got things going for us with two goals in the first five minutes, the Capitals came roaring back as Bondra scored twice and Dale Hunter and Iafrate scored once apiece to take the lead by two early in the second period.

At this point, a funereal silence overtook the Civic Arena. I called out to a team-mate — they could hear it all the way in the upper deck. The mood remained dark for several minutes until Mullen revived our hopes with a goal, and we were back in it. Bourque then tied it up for us, and with Hatcher in the penalty box just before the period expired, I found Mario in front of the goal with a cross pass from the right side. Mario then did one of his patented fake outs, and though his legs and body went behind the net, his seemingly twenty-foot arms extended out in front to bury the puck in the goal, giving us back the lead. He then scored an insurance goal in the final session for his fifth point of the game, and he had once again pulled us out of the grave.

Somehow the tension did not feel as thick back in Washington for the seventh and final contest of the series as it had in earlier games. The Caps' body language spoke volumes about their lost self-confidence. Even my ever-ebullient country-man Michal Pivonka, who in earlier matchups had approached me during the course of the game and challenged me with comments like, "Haven't we embar-rassed you enough already?" and "Time for you guys to go home," had gotten real quiet all of a sudden. I understood their demoralization. Having had the series all but wrapped up, they failed to finish the job, and the momentum had switched to our side in a big way. There was no stopping us now.

Mario scored first for us off a rebound shot by Francis when we were playing a man down. Iafrate tied it up for Washington at the beginning of the second, but then came the moment of truth. Todd Krygier was in the box for the Capitals, giv-ing us the power play. Mario had the puck behind the Washington goal, and it looked like he was going to wait with it there until the rest of us got into position to set up a play. He was forced to make a quick decision, though, when he saw Hatcher coming at him with Kevin being covered by Calle Johansson on the other side. That left me open in front of the net, and of course Mario saw me there and passed the puck to me immediately. When I got it, I was standing less than four feet away from Beaupré, who went down immediately, allowing me to flick it over him with a backhand for the deciding goal of the series.

I think everyone in the house could see that the home team did not have it in them to come back at that point, and Joey Mullen even scored an empty-net goal

at the end to finish it off. It must have broken the Capitals' hearts to watch us all head toward Barrasso to celebrate our big win. Actually, I heard later that the team stayed in the locker room for a long time after the game and many players had tears in their eyes. I heard that Dino Ciccarelli was so deeply affected by the loss that he sobbed uncontrollably. I can understand how they felt. To lose to a team that's simply much better doesn't sting so much, but that's not what had happened to them. Washington's tears welled in frustration and regret at having given us the series after they had outplayed us for so long. As I said, I sympathize with them. But I'm glad the series unfolded the way it did.

We only had one night to be happy about that series, however, because our next opponent was the toughest team in the league: the New York Rangers. I was not looking forward to playing the Rangers at all. The ice in Madison Square Garden is even worse than in Washington, and unless your pass is absolutely perfect, the soft rink will take it wherever it wants. Not to mention that New York traditionally plays some of the toughest hockey in the world and gives opponents a lot less space to maneuver than anybody else.

The Rangers' best was Mark Messier, but in that series their formidable lineup also included Adam Graves, Mike Gartner, defensemen James Patrick and Jeff Beukeboom and goalies Mike Richter and John Vanbiesbrouck.

Things got off to a good start for the Penguins when we pulled off a surprise win in New York to open the series. Loney and Murphy scored for us in the first period, and Stevens made it 3-0 early in the second. Although they did finally score, the Rangers were still never in contention, and Francis's goal kept it from even being close.

Game Two also began well when Stevens scored from the left side less than two minutes in, and we got the power play right after that when Joe Cirella was ejected. We kept the pressure up effectively until, with 5:05 showing on the clock, something happened that would be the subject of heated discussion for weeks.

Mario got the puck on the blue line and was setting up a play when all of a sudden Graves swung his stick at him like a baseball bat. It was several minutes before we could finally get Mario up off the ice and over to the bench. His hand was completely swollen, and it was clear that he would not be able to play the rest of the game, which we ended up losing. It was not too long before the X-ray confirmed our worst fears — the bone in Mario's wrist was completely broken. If we wanted to win the series, we were going to have to do it without him.

A war then began. The Rangers' coach, Roger Neilson, poured oil on the fire in the press the next day with his comment about it being "so nice not to have to worry about Lemieux." Nothing could have angered us more. The controversy as to whether Graves had wounded Mario intentionally continued even after the league later suspended him for four games. The atmosphere for the rest of the series was tense, and we were without two key players. In addition to Mario, Joey Mullen was out with a serious knee ailment.

The series returned to Pittsburgh for Game Three. As you might expect, Adam Graves was greeted with overwhelming disapproval, and the Civic Arena echoed with whistles and threatening chants. Anti-Graves banners hung from every rafter. It's kind of ironic that he scored the game's first goal.

We ended up losing in OT when Kris King's shot deflected off Barrasso into the goal. Our chances didn't look too good at that point. True, Washington had had us even more on the ropes in the previous series, but Mario had been with us then. Still, we had no intention of giving up.

Game Four started off disastrously as Randy Gilhen and Tony Amonte gave the Rangers a 2-0 lead before we knew what hit us. Mike Needham's goal cut their lead temporarily, but by the time Messier scored their fourth goal at the beginning of the final period, we looked gone for sure. But then Mike Richter suffered a momentary collapse, as Francis breathed life back into us with one of the longest scoring shots I've ever seen. Right after that, I got the puck on the right side and took it down the ice until I ran into the one-man crowd, Jeff Beukeboom. Somehow I managed to get the pass off to Troy Loney in front of the goal, where he scored to tie the game at four. John Vanbiesbrouck replaced Richter who was forced to leave the game.

There was another overtime, but this one was much shorter, ending after less than three minutes when Messier dangerously took the puck right in front of his own goal, where Murphy stole it from him. Murph quickly dished it off to Francis, who beat Vanbiesbrouck to complete our impossible comeback victory and, indeed, turn the series around.

Luck was on our side, but we had won by playing our game. Bowman had urged us not to get caught up in an emotional battle but just to concentrate on getting the job done in the workmanlike fashion that had gotten us this far. He knew that the tough but less skilled Rangers were going to try to provoke and intimidate us, and so he drove it into our heads that we should not respond in kind to even the most egregiously aggressive tactics that New York might use to try and shake us up. Let the Rangers commit the penalties, he told us, and they did.

Twelve minutes into Game Five, the Rangers' Joey Kocur got sent to the penalty box and Tocchet scored a goal off a pass from Francis. Then, finally, it was my turn. Taking the puck all the way from our end of the rink, I got past Beukeboom and took off toward the Rangers' goal. No sooner had I reached our blue line than I noticed Brian Leetch crossing over to cover me. Leetch is an excellent skater, and I knew that my only chance was to be in front of him by the time he got over to my side or he'd be able to stop me. The thing about Leetch is that he's not only fast, but he knows how to use his small, heavyset body as an obstacle. The two of us ended up in a horse race from one blue line to the other, but I was just one step ahead of him the whole way. Because I didn't have enough time to try anything fancy, I decided to pull up and shoot. Before I got my shot off, however, I felt Leetch's arms around me. I lost my balance and both of us fell to the ice, knocking over Vanbiesbrouck as well.

I immediately looked up at the official, thinking he'd better send Leetch off this time. And indeed the ref was signaling something, so I felt satisfied as I skated back to the bench assuming that we would now have the power play. Imagine my surprise, then, when I was summoned back onto the ice. I didn't realize it initially, but what the ref had actually called was for me to take a penalty shot.

My knees literally began to knock, and my heart was pounding like a bass drum. Understanding that this moment could make or break us for the whole series, and therefore the whole season, was enough to make my hands shake. But as I approached the puck, my thoughts began to turn away from the weight of the situation and toward the question of what I was going to try.

The first thing I ruled out was any kind of attempt at an elaborate fake-out move. I had been on the ice a lot of minutes that game and, what's more, had just been in a wrestling match with Leetch. The combination of being so winded and the terrible ice at Madison Square Garden was nothing to inspire confidence in the possible success of a trick play. All I needed was to let the puck get away from me before I could even take a shot, and I would be humiliated for life. No, thank you. As I took off toward the goal, I decided that I was going to challenge Vanbiesbrouck with an ordinary shot. I just didn't know where I was going to shoot yet.

Gaining speed as I crossed the blue line, I began twirling the puck around a little to make sure I knew exactly where it was. I moved a little to the right in order to pull the goalie over to the side and decided to aim my shot right at his weak point: his stick hand. Vanbiesbrouck made my job a little easier by remaining deep in the net, and when I reached the goal I was able to sweep the puck just above his glove and in. What a relief. We were up 2-0.

My work for the day was not done yet, though, because the Rangers came back and tied the score on Gartner's goal at the beginning of the third period. So with about five minutes left in regulation, I turned in the play that ended up earning me the nickname, "Mario Junior." More importantly, it was also the play that won the game for us.

As I skated down the right side of the rink from center ice, Gord Roberts rebounded a pass off the boards right onto the tip of my stick. Crossing the blue line, I saw that only Beukeboom stood between me and the goal. This is the classic situation that I have found myself in at least a thousand times since my earliest games in Czechoslovakia, and by now, I think I've learned a thing or two about getting by defensemen.

Because he didn't know which way I was going to go, Beukeboom came right at me, which helped my decision-making process considerably. I made as if I was going to move toward the center before sliding past him on the right. Now only Vanbiesbrouck was left to try and stop me, but at least he had made things more difficult for me by coming way out in front of the goal, which meant I could not shoot yet. I had to make a move to get by him. The smart move was to go past him up the middle because that gave me the whole goal to shoot into. If I had gone around him on the backhand side, I would have had to shoot at an angle and the target would have been smaller.

The way I describe these things makes it sound like I had forever to calculate the pros and cons of each option. In reality, the whole sequence I'm talking about took place in only two seconds, and I didn't actually think about anything at all. It's just intuition. I made my move past Vanbiesbrouck up the middle and shot the puck into the net. Simple as that.

I was overjoyed at that moment and began literally dancing on my skates. The first teammate to jump in my arms was Roberts, followed by Murphy, and then everybody else was on top of me, too. I was named player of the game, but at that moment that didn't matter at all. As I emerged out of Madison Square Garden into the New York night, I bought a hot dog for the bus and thought all the way to the airport about how we were only one game away from advancing to the Prince of Wales Conference finals.

And Game Six in the Civic Arena was the clincher. Neither team scored in the first period. Dicky Tocchet scored for us five minutes into the second, but Doug Weight tied it up almost immediately. It was 1-1.

It was time for me to do my thing again. Kevin Stevens's pass from the face-off flew up over Beukeboom's stick and came down right where I was standing. I knocked it down with my glove and waited for Vanbiesbrouck to lie down. Finding a crack between his pads and the post, I put my shot right there and watched it hit the back of the net for my sixth playoff goal and our second lead of the game.

It was all we needed that day, as two minutes later Shawn McEachern came out from behind the goal like a man on a mission and provided us all the insurance we needed. I think we began celebrating that game a little earlier than a team really should, but we knew we weren't going to relinquish that lead.

After we won the Stanley Cup again, a video cassette of our 1992-93 season was released with the commercial title *Against all Odds*. Without a doubt, it was the series against the Rangers that justified that name more than anything else.

Another Garden Party,
Another Cup Party

On May 17, we opened the conference finals against Boston in the Civic Arena. Mario was still out, but on the other hand, so was the Bruins' best player, Ray Bourque. It was a tough, ugly game, and we were definitely not the better team that day. But we kept playing tough, and our hard-hitting style caused the Bruins real problems. The fact that they outshot us 41-31 for the game gives some indication of how they outplayed us. But we were lucky.

For the third game in a row I scored the winning goal, and the way it happened was not unlike my last goal against the Rangers. Don Sweeney took a pass from Kjel Samuelsson at the center line, and when he realized he was not in a position to move the puck up the ice, he fed it back to me. Using Sweeney as a screen, I went back around to the right side and raced toward the goal. This time it wasn't Beukeboom in front of me, but Matt Hervey. No matter. Hervey didn't come at me but moved back, which meant I couldn't get past him by moving to the side. Instead, I surprised him by looping back to the center, again around Sweeney, and swiping the puck past Andy Moog, whose view of the action, I made sure, was blocked.

After the game, even the other team was praising my play. Apparently even the Bruins' coach, Rick Bownes, complimented me in the press, which was the second time I had received favorable notice from an opponent. After the previous series, Beukeboom had said that I was impossible to play against.

The fans in Civic Arena began going wild before Game Two even began. Mario Lemieux had returned. At the beginning Mario came on mostly for the power plays, but as the game progressed, he took the ice more often until by the end he had won the game for us, scoring two goals and beautifully assisting Tocchet on another in our 5-2 victory. Mario was named player of the game, and I was runner-up with one goal and two assists.

The next two games were played in the steam bath of Boston Garden, where the temperature was over eighty-five degrees. The Bruins had set up Ulf as their primary target because Cam Neely was still unable to skate up to full speed, and the Bruins had revenge on their minds. Bowman didn't think they would go too far in risking penalties, though, so only our second defenseman was assigned to protect him.

It was in Boston that we played our best hockey of the entire playoffs. The first game was sort of a homecoming for Kevin Stevens, who had grown up in Massachusetts and played quite a few games in the Garden. With so many of his friends and family members in the stands, Kevin obviously wanted to have a big day. And did he ever.

It took him only six minutes to register the first playoff hat trick of his career, and he even added a fourth goal when we managed to break down the Bruins' defense in the game's final moments. I had gotten past the Bruins' line and darted a cross pass to Mario, who, instead of shooting, looked for Kevin and found him open near the goal one more time. The final score was 5-1, and we were pretty sure that we were going to end the series the next game.

And Game Four was just like a carbon copy of Game One. We spent most of the time playing back before exploding into fast breaks. We were already up 2-0 when I scored a goal exactly like the one against Quebec. Taking a pass from Francis at the center line, I drove down the left side toward Moog. Just before reaching the goal, however, I flipped the puck to my backhand side and sent it past him with a one-handed shot.

Right after that goal, it was Mario's turn to show not only how smart and skilled he is but also how fast he is, with just about the most beautiful play I have ever seen in my life. Mario actually looks a little slow when you're watching a game from the stands, but looks can be deceiving as Ray Bourque, one of the best defensemen in the NHL, found out the hard way.

With Paul Stanton in the penalty box, we were down a man, and the Bruins were doing a pretty good job of keeping the puck in our third of the rink. But when Mario intercepted an attempted setup pass from Joe Juneau at the blue line, he took off. Only the retreating Bourque stood between him and the goal, and Mario was absolutely brilliant. Moving at full speed Mario pushed the puck between his skates and waited for Bourque to come toward him at the blue line, which he did. At that moment Mario suddenly shifted the puck forward past Bourque on one side and skated around him on the other side. Now alone in front of Moog, he actually faked twice before shooting a bulls-eye just below the crossbar.

I have to say I was impressed by the crowd's reaction. Usually the stands fall silent when the visiting team scores, but this time the hall seemed electrified by Mario's goal, and some sections even began applauding. They really do know their hockey in Boston, and even though their own team's season was ending, they could still appreciate an incredible performance by one of the great masters of hockey.

After that, the game was over. The final score was again 5-1, and we were back in the finals. Later that evening, Jiri Hrdina said that he "knew even before the series began that we would win like that. While we were coming together as a team in the battles against Washington and the Rangers, the Bruins had it easy against Montreal and were able to relax and play golf. They weren't ready for what hit them."

We really did play extraordinarily well during our Boston Garden party. What's more, both teams played relatively clean the whole series, and all our worries about Ulf being attacked proved to be unfounded except for one incident when Juneau hit him with his stick. And one of the few scuffles that did take place was actually because of me, although only indirectly.

At one point in Game Four, I was skating along the boards when Brent Hughes suddenly came up beside me and slammed me into the Plexiglas, which was pretty uncalled-for since the puck was somewhere else and I was heading back to the bench. When Tocchet the "Avenger" came on right after that, he caught up with Hughes at the blue line and gave him a good hit. Then as he fell, the Boston defenseman hit Dicky in the face with his stick and opened up a gash just above his eye. Dicky got pretty pissed off at this, of course, and just went to town on Hughes, whacking him several times while he was still on the ground before the officials intervened, much to the Boston player's great relief.

After we got dressed and left the arena, we realized that we had accidentally left the conference championship trophy in the locker room. When one of us went back for it, he found the beautiful cup standing on the bench in the empty room. And perhaps symbolically, he also saw a yellow banner lying on a shelf above the lockers that someone must have brought in after the game. Written in clear black letters were the words "Kill Ulf."

The first game of the Stanley Cup finals between us and the Chicago Blackhawks was on May 26. We essentially had two days to get ready, and our main task was to figure out how to counter their bang-up style of play. A good blue-collar team, the Blackhawks did not emphasize slickness and could hack away with the best of them. And once they sensed that the constant battling was beginning to wear their opponent down, they went in for the kill.

We also knew that we were up against not only a team that had been able to coast its way through to the final series, but also one that had one of the best coaches in the NHL, Mike Keenan, who was renowned for his unusual training methods.

Keenan is a coach who insists on absolute discipline. If practice is scheduled to begin at 10:00, you had best not show up on the ice at 10:01. But Keenan's own commitment is just as uncompromising as his demands on his players. Dominik Hasek has told me, for example, that Keenan did not go home during the playoffs but stayed in a hotel in order to devote himself 100 percent to preparations for the games.

Nor are his motivational methods any less unusual. In the Blackhawks' locker room, even in the toilet stalls, hang banners with messages like "Today's the day" and "Our time has come." Keenan makes his players think about hockey every single minute, and before the series against us, he took them to a secret location outside the city so that they wouldn't be distracted by the hype. I don't even know if the players' wives knew where they were.

Keenan also has his players constantly trying to break their opponents' concentration. They screamed at us whenever we skated near their bench, and Mike Peluso started insulting and threatening us before the first game even began. I think he said he was going to sweep up the ice with me or something, but I didn't really understand him, other than that he was trying to scare me. Soon Dicky Tocchet came in between us, and Peluso backed off. Dicky doesn't have much of a sense of humor on the ice.

After the game, I heard that Peluso said that I had hidden behind Tocchet. "In Chicago," he was quoted as saying, "he won't find a place to hide," referring to me.

Game One started terribly for us, as Chicago scored the first goal after six minutes and two more before the end of the period. Their second goal came when I held on to the puck too long as the hulk-like Steve Smith crashed me into the boards. Because I'd waited until the last second, my errant pass went straight to the Blackhawks' Michel Goulet, who was in perfect position to shoot it past Barrasso. After Dirk Graham scored to put them up 3-0, it was starting to look pretty bad for us.

Bourque did manage to narrow the gap for us just before the period ended, but Brent Sutter caught us flatfooted again midway through the second, and most people thought it was over. Chicago was playing good defense, and we couldn't get into our game. And when we did get a shot off, Eddie Belfour was always there with the save.

Only as the period began winding down did we start to get going when Tocchet beat Belfour to make the score 4-2. Then just before the siren, Mario cut their lead to one with a really sly play. Looking for someone to pass to from the corner of the rink on the Chicago end, he noticed that Belfour had moved out in front of the goal. So instead of passing it, he fired the puck directly at the goalie's pad from behind, and the entire stadium watched it deflect back into the goal. We now had twenty minutes to try and tie it up.

That happened in the sixteenth minute of the final period, when I scored a goal that would make me a legend in Pittsburgh. Well, at least until the next season.

The first to reach a loose puck behind the Blackhawks' blue line, I managed to evade Graham before starting to make my move past Sutter, who surprised me by moving back toward the goal. I pulled up, then, and moved back toward the boards because I hadn't built up enough speed to make it past Sutter, and he would have easily been able to stop me. But then he made the mistake of coming at me, just as Beukeboom of the Rangers had done. One thing I've learned is that it's always easiest to get past players who are moving toward you, as Sutter was doing. With Sutter in front of me and no room behind me, there was only one thing to do: push the puck between his legs and skate around him to the side.

My new agent Mike Barnett, Jiri and Rudla Crha with Dad in Kladno. Three weeks later we would all meet up in Chicago during my second Stanley Cup victory.

I actually nudged it a little further forward than I had meant to, but I still managed to reach it with the tip of my stick and then slip around Frank Kucera on the back-hand side. Shawn McEachern was key in holding Kucera's stick in front of the goal and delaying his move toward me until I had the puck back under control. Shawn also blocked their other defenseman, Igor Kravchuk, thus clearing my path to the goal.

I waited until I was right in front of Belfour before taking my backhand shot, which felt a little weak to me until I saw Ronnie Francis raise his stick in the air. I realized then that the puck had indeed made it across the line. The game was tied, and the stadium erupted.

Mobbed by my teammates, I realized that was one goal people were going to be talking about for a while. Mario went so far as to say it was probably the most beautiful scoring play he had ever seen, and even Scotty offered his praise. But I didn't feel like I had done anything especially brilliant, and only later did I con-sider how that moment may have been the turning point in the entire series. In any case, whether I thought much about it or not, everybody else definitely remem-bered that one particular goal.

Some months later, when I was visiting Martin Straka and his family in the Ramada Inn where they were temporarily staying, Martin suddenly interrupted the conversation we were having to point at the TV set and exclaim, "Hey, it's your goal!" As I looked up at the screen, I saw myself once again weaving through the Chicago players, but the real surprise was what the announcer was saying. Though Mario Lemieux, Wayne Gretzky, Steve Yzerman and others had all scored some amazing goals during the season, none were apparently as pretty as mine, which was being designated the ESPN Goal of the Year.

With the score now tied, we felt like we were back in command. We had defi-nitely gained the psychological advantage and felt confident in our chances to pull out the victory in overtime.

As things turned out, though, it didn't even take that long. With eighteen sec-onds remaining in regulation, Chicago's Smith hacked Mario, who was skating by him. Ronnie Francis then won the face-off and passed it back to Murphy, whose shot was stopped by Belfour. During that sequence, Mario demonstrated what makes him the extraordinary hockey player that he is. Intuitively guessing that Belfour might well deflect the shot, he took a risk and abandoned his position on the left side and skated in front of the goal. If Murph had failed to get the shot off or had the puck taken away from him, then Tommy would have been alone against two Chicago players. But Mario correctly anticipated where the puck would go off of the deflection and was there to flip it back over a prone Belfour and into the goal, setting off the evening's final explosion in the Civic Arena.

We had achieved the impossible in coming back from a three-goal deficit to win a Stanley Cup championship game, and the series was probably over right then.

Chicago had played the better game, but with their certain victory suddenly taken away from them like that, they were devastated.

Two days later we won again, but I was very upset over that game. The Blackhawks had focused their defense on me the whole game, and I didn't manage to break free of their coverage for a second. So even though we won, thanks mainly to Mario and Dicky, I just stormed into my car after the game and went home in a huff.

My dad just laughed at me and said, "You think that after the goals you scored in the first game, they were just going to leave you alone? Come on, you've got to know they're going to key in on you, so you have to play smart. What have I told you a million times since little league? When one of their guys starts hanging on to you and not paying attention to the rest of the game, you have to go right up to one of their other players and let them double-team you. That way, your team has an automatic power play during the whole game. Whatever you do," he added, "don't let them get you annoyed. That's just what they're counting on." Dad, how come you're always right?

Despite my relative inability to contribute, we won that second game 3-1. Bob Errey scored our first goal even though our team had a man in the penalty box. After Bryan Marchment tied the game for Chicago in the second period, Mario won it for us with two identical goals. Both times Tocchet battled for the puck in the corner of the rink and sent it back to Mario the Man, who put it away with a vengeance.

One funny thing, actually, was after the game, when we were leaving, my parents and I and Jiri Hrdina ran into Hasek and Kucera in the hallway. They did not look happy at all to be meeting us and whispered nervously, "We can't talk to you. If anybody saw us like this, we'd be in a lot of trouble."

We laughed, of course, and asked them why. "Keenan ordered us not to talk with anybody on the other team," they answered, although they did shake hands with us quickly before running off to the Blackhawks' bus. We didn't stand together long enough for either side to betray our team secrets. Hrdina told me that he and Hasek had at least managed to exchange a furtive wink through the Plexiglas.

The Chicago Stadium was like a fortress and not one that was easily conquered. It's gone now, of course, and the Blackhawks today play their home games in the United Center, which is bigger but much less of a hockey haven than the old venue. A couple of the guys told me what it was like there at the time when the U.S. was fighting the war in the Persian Gulf. During the national anthem, literally every person in the stadium held his hand to his heart, and at its conclusion, the place erupted in a burst of patriotic thunder that gave the visiting players goose bumps.

This was the stadium that awaited us for Game Three, and the roar that accompanied our entry onto the ice was unlike anything I'd ever heard before. We knew, though, that the pressure was on Chicago and not us to come through in a big way.

The hockey that night was pretty unexceptional overall, as we just buckled down on defense and watched the superb Barrasso stop everything that came his way. Our one goal came in the first period when Kevin Stevens helped Jim Paek's shot from the blue line into the net, and that was all we needed. Three down, one to go.

Not thinking we were going to win that game, my parents had figured they could wait until we came back to Pittsburgh to see us finish the series. Now, their travel plans changed, and they flew out to Chicago in anticipation of the sweep.

We got off to a fast start in Game Four when less than two minutes into the game, I reached a loose puck in the Chicago end and sent it flying just over Belfour's glove with a wrist shot. I think his view of the action was blocked on that goal, but overall, the usually excellent Belfour had a pretty disappointing series. He let some easy goals get by him, and Keenan finally pulled the plug on him after Kevin Stevens put us up 2-1 with a simple shot that went between his legs. At that point it was Belfour out, Dominik Hasek in.

Hasek did quite a fine job and kept Chicago in the game. By the end of the second period, though, he had given up goals to Lemieux and Tocchet and the score was tied 4-4.

The final period of the season saw both teams playing excellent hockey. Hasek made a beautiful catch to foil a golden scoring opportunity for Mario on a breakaway. That big play proved to be his last hurrah, however, as he was beaten shortly thereafter by Larry Murphy, and then Francis provided the insurance. Jeremy Roenick did narrow the gap to 6-5 for Chicago with over eight minutes remaining, but we held on after that and the celebration began when the siren sounded to end the game.

That first game was really a tough hole for Chicago to climb out of, and what's more, I don't think Keenan chose the best tactics for the series. His strategy was to keep brutes like Peluso on the ice for most of the game while the better offensive players like Roenick only went in two or three times a period. Having been hardened to rough play in our series against the Rangers, we were never intimidated by the Blackhawks. On the other hand, even though we won in four straight, each individual game was a tight contest and could have gone the other way.

My parents came into the locker room for the postgame celebration, and I have photos galore of the event. Everything was similar to the way it had been the previous year. Another Cup party in the locker room, another nighttime flight back to Pittsburgh, another crowd waiting for us at the airport.

I think the only thing that didn't have it too easy that night was the Cup itself. We took it round to every bar in the city, and I suppose Jiri Hrdina and I gave it an especially hard time. The two of us played around with it until one of the rings of the Cup got pulled off, and we could look all the way inside it, where we found many notes and comments left behind by previous generations of championship

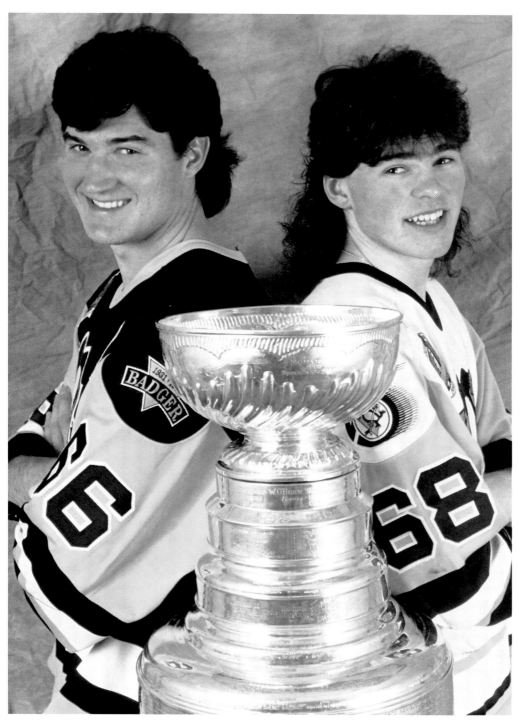

*With Mario Lemieux and the second trophy. Notice the
"Badger" badge — that's in memory of Bob Johnson.*

but that's not very important because we really did hit it off together very well. Pavlína said she was surprised that I didn't show up in some fancy car, wearing a jacket and tie acting like some kind of big shot. As for me, I found her to be exactly as I had expected. She was lovely. The next year, Pavlína took part in the Miss Universe pageant in Mexico, where I think she finished somewhere in the top seven.

I also took a two-week trip to California, where Wayne Gretzky, Brett Hull and I posed for Upper Deck and had dinner together several times with our agent, Michael Barnett. That was a lot of fun. Brett is quite a character, and he was constantly making good-natured fun of me. One time, in our dressing room, he took out a pair of scissors and tried to give me a haircut. He himself had just been to a hair stylist, and when I began to get on his case about how it looked, he came back at me with, "At least I look like a guy, unlike you."

Brett and Wayne both remembered Jaroslav Pouzar, a former Edmonton Oiler, and told me to say hello to him. For some reason they really liked the sound of his name, and several times a day, for no reason at all, they would start chanting "Poooozar, Poooozar" at me.

I really liked Los Angeles. I went to Disneyland and saw the famous Hollywood sign, swam in the ocean and got a tour of the stars' homes in Beverly Hills from Mike Barnett. I had my video camera with me and made a tape of all those palatial houses, including the one where Madonna lives. Just for fun, I started thinking about having something like that built for me one day.

After I flew back home, I took a trip to the town of Ceské Budejovice down in southern Bohemia, where Jaroslav Pouzar now operates his own sports center. I passed on the greetings from Gretzky and Hull, of course, and talked with the proud owner of three Stanley Cup championship rings about his first meeting with a then 20-year-old kid named Mario Lemieux. Mario, who played for Montreal at the junior level, had apparently approached him after an Oilers-Canadiens game once, in the same bar where the guys and I go when we're in Montreal.

Before leaving Ceské Budejovice, I did some fishing and I even caught one of the giant carp for which the region is famous around Czechoslovakia.

 Other than a few pickup soccer games, the only exercise I got all summer was playing the slot machines for hours on end, which didn't make my friends too happy. They kept asking me why a guy making millions of dollars in America has to come home and win even more money from them at gambling. But for better or worse, the one-armed bandit and I have developed an excellent relationship.

Unfortunately, playing the slot machines is not exactly the best way to stay in shape during the off-season, and by the time I started training again on August 3 with the Kladno team, I had put on more than ten pounds. When I went back out onto the ice after the layoff of a couple months, I was so slow it was embarrassing.

Before I went back to America, I received a visit in Kladno from my new teammate, Martin Straka, and his parents. The Penguins had made Martin their first-round draft pick for 1992, and he was slotted to take the place of Jiri Hrdina, who had retired after the season and joined the Calgary Flames as a scout. Naturally enough, Martin wanted to find out a few things in advance about what he could expect and how he should be preparing for his rookie season.

Not long after returning to Pittsburgh, I got a call from the Ramada Inn where the team had put Martin up for the time being. "Yeah, I'm sitting in this hotel they brought me to," he said. "Nah, I have no idea where it is." I had a pretty good feeling already that this guy was going to be fun, and I was not mistaken.

Martin and I spent almost three years together in Pittsburgh — most of it together. I was so upset when he got traded at the end of last season that I went straight in to Patrick's office and gave him a piece of my mind. Not that that changed anything.

There's almost no one else in the league who can accelerate like Straka. He actually looks like he's running out there on those skates, but his speed is something amazing. Also amazing is the speed with which he makes friends wherever he goes. The exact opposite of me. He's just a genuinely friendly guy who can find something to talk about with anybody. On more than one occasion, I've seen him meet a person for the first time and five minutes later the two of them are standing arm in arm. The two of us always lived together when the team was on the road and passed hour after hour in our room just blabbing. He was like a brother to me.

I was even willing to risk creating problems for myself with team management for his sake. Straka was unable to play right away because of lingering problems with his Czech club, and by the time Pittsburgh and Plzen finally reached an agreement, the season was already underway. Because of these complications, Martin had a hard time cracking the lineup and spent most of his time on the bench. It also didn't help any that Coach Bowman doesn't really favor young players very much.

One time when I came into the locker room, I saw Martin packing up his things. "What are you doing?" I asked. "What do you think I'm doing?" he glumly replied. "They've shipped me off to the farm." At that moment I got really angry.

Now, by that time, I had pretty much established myself on the team (I even had the second-highest salary, after Mario), and I could afford to stand up for some things, although when I look back today at how I handled the whole situation, I can't believe I got away with it.

I continued to interrogate Martin: "What did they say to you exactly?" "Nothing," he answered. "Just that I should pack my suitcase and get ready to go to Cleveland." I then calmly walked over to where his bags were and began unpacking his stuff.

After that, I summoned all the coaches who happened to be in the building —

With Grandma in the Penguin uniform — inseparable
buddies — Grandma, Robin and me.

*In the family circle. With Grandma, Mom, Jitka, Dad
and our dog Robin in Hnidouse.*

Bowman, Peterson and Smith — and launched my offense. "Now, tell me what you said to Martin," I began, "and I will tell you that he is not going anywhere."

The coaches started off by trying to convince me that it would be better for him to start out on the farm team, that there was no place for him on the team and that he'd get his chance when someone got hurt. That was my cue. "Well, gentlemen," I said, "my knee has just begun to hurt me. I don't think I can play. Martin can take my place." I then turned around and walked out of the room, leaving them staring at me with their mouths open. OK, I'd handle it all differently today, but, hey, I was young. Anyway, it worked. Martin stayed in Pittsburgh, at least for a while.

I loved having him on the team. He finally got his first opportunity to show what he could do against Calgary, freeing himself up on a number of occasions and just missing with one wrist shot. I told him after the game that he played great. Straka beamed at me and said, "And I'm not even up to speed yet."

We drove our mothers crazy because we often acted like a couple of five-year-old boys. One time when we were all home together in front of the TV set watching a tape of Game Three of our 1992-93 playoff series against the Islanders, my mother began to laugh, saying, "What were you boys doing?" With the Penguins up 3-1, the two of us were sitting next to each other on the bench, and Martin turned to me and said, "If you score a goal now, I'll throw my glove all the way up to the ceiling of this arena." "You do that," I countered, "and I'll shoot it down with my hockey stick." I then proceeded to point the handle end of my stick in the air and simulate firing a rifle with it, shouting, "Bam! Bam! Bam!" The TV cameras just happened to capture us right at that moment, and anyone watching at home must have thought we were a couple of idiots.

Another thing I had to resolve before the season began was where I was going to live. I liked it at the Casanovas' — I spoke English all the time, went to football games with the boys, and it was all really nice. But it wasn't the same thing as having my own place and being able to do whatever I wanted.

I felt like it was time for me to be able to come home, lie down in front of the television with the channel changer and take whatever I wanted from the refrigerator. I didn't have that freedom yet. True, I did have my own room, but the TV was the family's and I always had to watch what they wanted to watch. It also made me feel lonely to come home late after a game and have no one to talk to. My parents must have picked up on this because they eventually suggested that my mother come over to spend the next season with me in Pittsburgh. There's no denying that I need somebody to look after me so that I can concentrate solely on hockey. And they also realized that there was no way I was ever going to start cooking for myself. So it was decided.

We initially thought that we'd just find some place to rent for the season, but the Nemecs offered to let us stay in their place because they were going to be moving to Ohio for a time. It was a good arrangement for all concerned because they didn't want the house to be empty for so long or to let it out to a complete stranger. In turn, we got to move into a fully equipped home, complete with furniture, bed-clothes, towels and dishes.

Mom taught me how to play cards...

What you learn in childhood you can do for life. From the left, Michal, Dad, Martin and me.

After the Feast

One of my goals was to make it past the 100-point mark. It didn't look like an impossible feat. The previous year I missed nine games and despite that, I had sixty-nine points, twelve more than the year before.

I naively thought that I would get more time on the ice this season, and that Scotty would also play me during power plays: That's the key to success. If you don't get in on the power plays, you don't get any points. But Scotty didn't play me. Usually when the other team had a penalty, Mario was on the ice with Kevin and Dicky. I rarely got out there. I was unhappy about it because I knew I was worth more. Moreover, I felt like I was always warming the bench. As a result, I wasn't able to reach my goal. I gathered ninety-four points — thirty-four goals and sixty assists — and felt incredibly disappointed.

It's definitely ironic that I actually started off the career of one of the best players in the NHL, Eric Lindros. I passed him the puck for his first goal. Our first game of the new season was at home against Philadelphia. That was Lindros's first game playing for the Flyers and first game in the NHL.

At one point, there was a moment of confusion in front of our net and the puck came to me. I skated to the net from our blue line, so I was actually in front of the goalie. I could have sent the puck somewhere off in the corner and that would have been the end of it. But I backhanded it off to the left because I thought no one was there. Unfortunately, I was wrong: Lindros was there. I actually sent the puck right in his path, and Eric immediately fired it into the net. I shot it right onto the blade of his stick. He still hasn't thanked me.

I'd like to erase the memory of my third season in the NHL, except for two events. The first was an interview with the former president of the United States.

It was the beginning of November. We'd just returned from a series of four games on the road, which we finished in Tampa. I'd barely come in the door when my mom told me, "While you were gone, somebody called from Ronald Reagan's office. I think it might have been Mrs. Reagan. So I told her you were on the road and that she should call when you get back. But maybe it was a prank call."

The telephone rang again a few days later. I wasn't in a very good mood at the time. I picked up the receiver and waited. "This is Ronald Reagan's office," someone said on the other end. I wasn't in the mood for a prank call like that. I wanted to tell them to stop bugging me, but instead of that I came back with, "Yeah? And this is George Bush."

Then the woman on the other end told me that I could call back if I didn't believe that it was Reagan's office. I called back, and it turned out she was telling the truth. She asked me to call back the next day because the former president wanted to talk to me.

So I called back the next day and Ronald Reagan was really on the other end of the phone. It had never occurred to me that I would talk with a president, particularly Reagan, with whom I've always felt a personal connection, even though he never knew it.

In elementary school, I had a picture of Ronald Reagan on the cover of my student book. In the Czech school system, you have to carry a little book around with you all the time where they write all your grades. I was around twelve years old at the time, and his picture meant a great deal to me. My grandmother told me a great deal about communism, so for me Reagan was a symbol of the fight against communism. I still didn't know very much at the time, and I knew next to nothing about Reagan as a president. But that was enough for me to idealize him and stick his picture on my student book. It had the same significance for me as the initials of Alexander Dubcek on my helmet and the number 68.

At school, we learned the imperialistic United States was our biggest enemy and that they wanted war with us, while the friendly Soviet Union protected us. My parents didn't want to explain the truth to me, because they were afraid that I'd start discussing it with my friends.

It's understandable that we were never allowed to have pictures of American imperialists, let alone the president. When my teacher saw the picture of Reagan, she couldn't believe her eyes. "Jaromir! Have you lost your mind?" she screamed at me. "Get rid of that thing right this instant!" I got rid of Reagan for the time being, but after class, I put him back. This scene repeated itself a few months later, but my teacher never forced me to completely get rid of the photo.

The writers for *Sports Illustrated* had liked this story so much that they actually mentioned it in a big article about me. The former president actually heard about it. And that's how Reagan found out that this hockey player from a former communist country, now playing in the NHL, had been his biggest fan from the time he was small.

I talked with Reagan for about fifteen minutes. I told him how much I had always admired his uncompromising position, and then I asked him what he was doing these days. I even invited him to our game in Los Angeles. Reagan thanked me, but added that he would be in London at the time and would come see me play another time. When we said goodbye, I asked him if he would send me a photograph of him taken when he was president. Reagan promised me he would, and several days after our conversation, a big envelope arrived with his photograph.

The news about his declining health hit me hard. But I have to admit that I noticed something was a little off when we spoke on the phone. Sometimes he would stop in the middle of a sentence without knowing what he'd said before, and sometimes he started talking about one thing and ended up talking about something completely different. I wish him well and I hope that someday we'll meet.

I was disappointed in my playing all the way up to Christmas. Sometimes I was successful, and sometimes I wasn't. We all celebrated the holidays together, and when my father showed up in Pittsburgh at the end of the year, he didn't seem very pleased with me either. Things got worse in January. I only scored three goals, one of them sort of underhandedly, when I shot the puck from behind Calgary's goalie, Mike Vernon, and it bounced off him into the net. In Philadelphia, I was able to score only once, and only because no one was there to stop me. The Flyers had pulled their goalie, so it wasn't exactly a challenge to score.

But it was interesting that my goal into the empty net still didn't put an end to the game. As I skated along the boards and raised my hands, Mark Recchi cruised by and tried to hit me with his stick. He definitely didn't want to injure me. It was just a little roughhousing. Dicky Tocchet saw it all and took off after Recchi, and a little fight broke out at the end of the game. A few days later, Dicky and Recchi sat next to each other in the All-Star game and chatted away as if they were old friends.

The All-Star game was my other wonderful experience that season. It took place in Montreal, a city which I've always liked. This city, where almost nobody speaks anything but French, reminds me of Europe. When we're there, we always go to a bar on St. Catherine's Street or near Crescent Street and have a good time. And the Forum speaks for itself. There are definitely bigger, more modern stadiums, but the Forum has a feeling of history.

In comparison with the previous year, I was no longer a novice. My goal in the one game against Chicago had made me famous, and people recognized me on the street. It was good that Peter Bondra made it to Montreal as well, so we had a chance to talk. Bondra introduced me to his teammate at that time, Al Iafrate, who immediately grabbed my attention.

He's a hockey renegade and often scares the hell out of Washington's coach. Iafrate was one of the most popular players in Washington, not only because of his totally unrestrained manner on the ice, but also because of his outward appearance. He showed up to practice on his Harley-Davidson in a sleeveless leather jacket with the arms cut off so that you could see the head of Chief Crazy Horse tattooed on his left arm. Twice a week, he was the DJ for a rock show on the radio.

Despite the protests of the fans, Washington eventually traded him for Joe

Juneau from Boston. But Al hasn't played too much so far for the Bruins due to problems with his knee. In Montreal, however, he was still in good condition and easily won the competition for the fastest shot. The puck left his stick at a speed of approximately 112 miles per hour.

The game itself must have been interesting for the spectators and it ended with the wild score of 16-6. The game was highly criticized in the newspapers. People started talking about whether it was time to change the structure so that the players would be more motivated, like having Europe versus America or something like it.

On the one hand, it's true that we don't play 100 percent in the All-Star game, that we barely put up a defense and that the boards may as well not exist. But on the other hand, we mainly want to have a good time and have a little fun. After all, we only meet like this once a year.

The most moving part of the All-Star weekend came with the announcement that Mario had cancer of the lymph nodes. When we first learned in the locker room of Mario's condition, better known as Hodgkin's disease, we were in total shock. Nobody knew what to say. There was complete silence. When Mario walked into this depressed atmosphere, we were all embarrassed and had no idea how to act. But Mario took care of that himself. He acted completely natural, and then we all started to take things as they came.

Mario couldn't play in Montreal, but despite that, the organizers invited him to put on the uniform before the game. He got a huge ovation from the spectators. After all, he comes from Montreal. I remember that whenever we played there, he got more applause than the home players. And when he scored a goal, it was as if the home team had gotten it. In Montreal, they still consider him one of their own, even though he plays for another team.

Gretzky and Bourque handled the honorary face-off, and I played center for the opening face-off for once. I'd done this in a few other games before. After Mario got sick, Tocchet asked Bowman if he could play with me, so I moved over to center.

I did an excellent job, and when Pierre Turgeon and Joe Sakic joined me, I really duked it out with them over the puck. I even managed to score, something which I'm quite proud of. To score a goal in the All-Star game, now that's something. Sakic passed me the puck right in front of the net, and I got it past the goalie with one hand.

I also had the opportunity to have dinner with my good old pals Wayne Gretzky, Brett Hull and Michael Barnett. We've been together a few other times, mostly to tape commercials, and we always have a good time. Brett and I especially like to tease each other.

Brett is always in a great mood. I've never seen anything really irritate him. Once we had a photo-shoot in the afternoon. Mike came up to get us in our rooms and was a little nervous that we wouldn't get there on time. He was already waiting for

We see Eric Lindros on the ice pretty often. I even passed him his first goal in the NHL.

us in the elevator and told us to hurry up. Brett was walking at a leisurely pace toward the elevator when he ran into two women with their children. "Could we get a picture with you in it?" they asked. "But of course," said Brett, while Mike, who's already holding the elevator, starts tearing his hair out. "For God's sake, hurry up! We have to get photographed, too," he pleaded with Brett. "What do you mean, hurry up?" said Brett calmly. "First I have to have my picture taken here."

As the elevator doors closed, Brett and I immediately started making faces at each other. When we were together, it was just a matter of time before one of us would burst out into hysterics. I leaned over to Mike and said, "Mike, you should make a good contract for him so that he can buy a decent coat. He can't really wear that one." "If I made as much as you do, I'd buy the one you've got on," he replied. "As a matter of fact," I said, "I bought this one for a few bucks in New Jersey." "But mine is really precious. Clint Eastwood used to wear it," said Brett with a laugh.

A few weeks later I wasn't laughing any more. In February, I scored a total of three goals. But the worst thing was the game with the New Jersey Devils, when Fetisov slammed me into the boards so hard that I nearly dislocated my shoulder. I didn't play in three games, but my shoulder hurt so much I could have easily sat out five.

I came back a little early for one simple reason. I wanted to be there when Mario Lemieux returned to the ice. The doctors succeeded in halting the progress of the cancer, and after a series of radiation treatments, Mario started training again. He quickly got back into shape and announced his return as of March 2. We played in Philadelphia, and I'll never forget the welcome he was given.

The atmosphere in Philadelphia is never very friendly for the opposing team. In fact, I'd say that it's usually downright hostile. And this is where Mario was to play his first game after his illness.

When Ulf Samuelsson, Tom Barrasso and others after them skated onto the ice, they were greeted with a deafening roar of whistles. People stood on their feet, shook their fists and didn't take their fingers out of their mouths until our ears were ringing. When it looked as if everyone from our team was on the ice, one more figure came through the door. Almost embarrassed, he stepped off the rubber carpet onto the ice and slowly skated. At this moment, the entire stadium fell silent and then an explosion of applause burst out. Mario Lemieux had returned.

It was very moving to see him come back on the ice, and some of us had tears in our eyes. Except for Montreal, I'd never seen anyone before or after applaud a player of an opposing team like that. The applause lasted for more than two minutes. Mario raised his stick, waved at the crowd and, after the national anthems, was ready for the game.

Philadelphia won, but Mario managed to score. You would have thought it was the Flyers' goal, the crowd cheered so much. I didn't finish the game. I had ended up in a mob of players at one point, someone knocked my stick, which hit Lindros in the face, and I was eliminated from the game for high-sticking.

And then the problems with trades began. After the middle of March, people started speculating about who would stay on the team and who would hit the road. Around this time, the playoffs are about to begin, and various teams start analyzing the complicated mechanism that is a "team." I even overheard people talking about the fact that I might leave the team, so I went up to Craig Patrick and asked what was going on. Craig assured me that they weren't considering anything of the sort, but I only half-believed him. After all, Craig is capable of insisting that a trade is out of the question two hours before a transfer arrangement is about to be signed. He's a perfect diplomat.

Martin Straka had even bigger worries than me. There was a lot of speculation about how Straka would be leaving the club as part of a three-way agreement between Pittsburgh, Edmonton and one other club. Martin was going crazy about it, and our mothers were on the verge of heart attacks.

The guys on the team knew that Martin was afraid of being traded and started making fun of him about it. Once when we were playing Edmonton in Cleveland and were about to leave, a few of our teammates came up to Martin and told him to pack because the Oilers were taking him straight from Cleveland to Edmonton.

Eventually Martin asked Petr Klima, who was playing for Edmonton at the time, if he'd heard anything about the trade. "Yeah, I heard something about it, too," Klima told him. Martin froze with fear. "So then it's true? I'm moving to the Oilers?" he asked. "You bet," said Klima, dead serious. "The deal's already been made. They traded you for twenty pucks and five broken sticks."

Fortunately, all our fears about Martin's being traded turned out to be false. But other problems developed. They had been brewing for a long time, but everything came to a head in those few weeks.

Things that I was upset about were welling up inside me, and it was only a matter of time before I exploded. The problem was I wasn't playing at all. I couldn't understand why Scotty was putting me out there two or three times per period. And I knew that nothing was going to change. The starting five were playing well. We were constantly winning, and no coach makes changes when nothing needs fixing. It was obvious to me that I wasn't going to get on the ice. Dicky and Kevin played with Mario, and they were on the ice all the time. They also played every power play, while I sat bored stiff on the bench.

It wasn't the first year anymore when they were always telling me that I had all the time in the world and that everything would work out fine. At that time, I was a rookie, and I kept my mouth shut. Now the situation was different. I was already in my third season, and the second one had been simply fantastic. It's a terrible

With Brett Hull, Wayne Gretzky and our joint agent Michael Barnett during the shooting of commercials.

feeling to know that you can do more but don't have the opportunity to prove it. I was so angry that a few times I took off my skates on the bench and told Scotty Bowman that I wasn't going to play.

Scotty is a very strange guy. As a coach, he achieved remarkable success. His record is better than anyone else's in the NHL, and I have a great deal of respect for the man. But it's very hard to get close to him. I already mentioned the fact that there was a great deal of distance between him and the players, and I'm not disclosing what's not already known — that Scotty wasn't allowed at practices. I don't understand how such a decision could have been made, but at the request of the players, the general manager decided that Scotty Bowman would only coach us during games and that practices would be run by his assistant. I'd never experienced anything like that in my life, and I hope I don't experience it again.

You can imagine what kind of relations he had with his players, considering the bad feelings that sometimes come out during games. During heated moments between Scotty and players, I felt like I was the one taking the rap because I didn't want to get on anyone's bad side. So I kept my mouth shut, whereas the other players often seemed to be coaching Scotty.

There were decisions that he made which frustrated me. One time I was standing at the boards ready to jump on the ice because the starting five had already been on for nearly two minutes. However, they didn't want to rotate. Eventually Scotty called time-out and sent us out to replace them. We jumped over the boards, and at that moment, one of the starting five reached the bench, raised his head and just looked at Scotty. "Look, let's hold off a moment. They can still play," Scotty said all of a sudden, and we went back to the bench.

Another time that made me very angry was in one game when we were supposed to be on for a power play. Scotty sent me onto the ice, but three other offensive players jumped up behind me, so there were too many of us. Scotty had to send one player back to the bench, and he told one of the other guys that he had to wait. But that player looked back at Bowman as if he couldn't believe his ears and said, "Me?" So in the end, it was me who left the ice. When I asked Scotty if he really wanted me to leave the ice after he'd told me to go there in the first place, he just turned his head and acted as if he hadn't even heard me.

Nevertheless, Scotty respected me, even though I was young. I can only remember one time when he got mad at me. And even that time was a little comical. We were playing an extremely important game, but not in the playoffs. Three minutes before the end of the game, the referee gave me a penalty for an illegally bent blade. People do that a fair amount in the NHL. And when you know that someone's hockey stick is bent beyond the regulation angle, you wait for the right moment to use it. They caught me right before the end of the game. Scotty looked like he was about to have a heart attack. He ran to the bench and moaned, "What are we going to do?" And then his rage turned to me and he announced my fate: "That f — ing hotshot! He's gonna get fined!"

But everything turned out OK in that game. We defended ourselves during the power play, the opposing team took out their goalie and several seconds before the end of the game, I scored a goal into an empty net. In the locker room, Scotty came up to me, patted me on the shoulders and said, "Great work."

Scotty was in his own world, but I have fond memories of him. When I last met with Paul Coffey, he told me that he'd really changed, and that he was much more pleasant than he used to be. I think Coffey had some hellish times with him because Scotty never liked his playing style.

Another interesting thing about Scotty is his inventiveness. I never actually saw this, but they say Scotty used to have some interesting ways of finding out whether the players were in their rooms the night before a game. He took a hockey stick and sent a little boy to knock on the doors of every room, and every player had to sign it. Whoever's name was missing caught hell.

The internal situation on the team should have been a definite warning, but nobody took it too seriously. We weren't practicing properly and were terribly dependent on Mario — that is, on his health. Selfishly, we couldn't even imagine what we'd do if Mario wasn't 100 percent. But we didn't have a reason to worry about it. We kept on winning. The question at that time was simply this: What would hold us together when things stopped going our way?

We weren't forced to face this question during the regular part of the season. On the contrary, in a dramatic game with Montreal, we won in overtime thanks to a goal by Ulf and tied Montreal's record of fifteen wins in a row. And then came an even more outstanding game at Madison Square Garden. It was one of the best games we'd ever played.

We beat the Rangers 10-4, and Mario scored five goals. And some of them were absolutely sweet — like the one when Tommy Barrasso passed the puck all the way to the red line and Mario finished off Corey Hirsch at the home net.

We won the Patrick Division by an unbelievable margin of twenty-six points and were already looking forward to the playoffs. The New Jersey Devils were awaiting us, as well as the victor from the series between the Washington Capitals and the New York Islanders. At the time we were convinced nothing could happen to us.

The first two games went exactly according to our plans. In the second minute, Dicky slipped the puck behind Chris Terreri's back and we were in the lead. The game slowly turned into a circus for us. In the final period, even I got on the board, when Kjell Samuelsson dragged the puck behind the goal, faked to Fetisov and passed it to me in such a way that all I could do was shoot it at the unprotected part of Terreri's net. At the end of the game, the Devils lowered the margin a bit, but we finished the game without any problems.

After the 6-3 win, we went into Game Two with justifiably big heads, which after sixty minutes of that game were even bigger. We won by an incredible margin of 7-0. Everything we wanted, we got.

We went to New Jersey and won the third game. It was only by one goal. Actually, we were a little lucky in the end because Alexander Semak didn't score into an empty net after a pass from Peter Stastny. Still, every victory counts and we were leading the series 3-0.

We could afford to lose the fourth game, and we managed to do just that. I didn't finish the game because I was tossed out at the end of the second period for injuring Valeri Zelepukin. It was similar to what happened in the game not long before that with Philadelphia, when I hit Lindros in the face.

I personally don't believe that there's anyone playing in the NHL who'd intentionally want to injure someone. All the movements of the stick are the result of the action in the game, and that's exactly what happened both of these times.

In Philadelphia, I skated into the Flyers' third of the rink along with two other members of the home team. Just when I tried to get away from one, the other one smashed my hockey stick as hard he could and it flew up and hit Lindros in the face. It was just like that with Zelepukin in New Jersey. I skated up to him from behind and wanted to lift up his hockey stick — except that I was too slow. Zelepukin moved forward a split-second faster, so my stick jerked back and hit him in the face. It wasn't intentional. These things just happen, especially because it's all taking place at a very high speed.

We lost the fourth game 4-1. In order to win the playoff series, all we needed was one more win. In the Civic Arena, we were losing 3-2 after two periods, but Francis tied it up. Several seconds later, Jeff Daniels wrapped up our victory when he whisked a shot by Terreri that caught him by surprise.

So we made it into the Patrick Division finals. The New York Islanders, who had just eliminated the Washington Capitals, were waiting for us, but without their best player, Pierre Turgeon, who had been injured by Dale Hunter. Turgeon's absence increased our self-confidence even more, so we were already seeing ourselves in the conference finals.

I don't want to make myself out to be a prophet, but at the beginning of the playoffs, before the Islanders-Capitals game, I told a friend of mine that if we'd play them, it'd be for all seven games. If I'd said that in public, everyone would have thought I was crazy.

I was really anxious about that series. We'd lost our last four games with them during the regular season, and we couldn't handle their playing style — careful defense and fast breaks. Most of us didn't even consider the possibility that we could play more than five games. I knew it would be difficult, but I firmly believed that we would win and move on to the Stanley Cup finals. Especially if Mario was feeling well. Except that Mario wasn't feeling well and left after the first game.

In the first game at the Civic Arena, we started out well. In the ninth minute, Loney was catching up with Uwe Krupp, who fell just behind the net. Fortunately, Loney found Mike Needham at the last minute. For the first and last time in the game, we were ahead. Several minutes later, Vladimir Malakhov, the outstanding Russian defenseman, tied the score with a bomb to the upper-left corner of the net. Then Ray Ferraro got the better of us. We had a power play, the puck jumped over Murphy's stick and the agile Ferraro skated alone to the net to score.

The second short-handed goal came a little while later. We had another power play and lost again. Darius Kasparaitis made a nice move, and Hogue got a third past Barrasso from a moderate distance. Thanks to Daniels, we were able to shrink the margin, but against all our efforts their goalie, Glenn Healy, wouldn't let another single puck past him. He was voted best player of the game.

We lost, and for the first time it occurred to us that it wouldn't be easy. It happened exactly as I'd feared. Mario had given it a try, but because of pain, he couldn't continue. Already, our vision of the series was collapsing like a house of cards.

That was only the first game in the series, but I was already physically and mentally exhausted. That game was Sunday afternoon, and afterward, we were supposed to go to a campfire at the Nemec's. My parents were there, all the Strakas, including Martin's brother Michal, who had come over to see the finals. I wasn't up to going and went home to sleep. For the first time, I felt like we might be in trouble.

Game Two was like Game One in that Mario didn't play. Fortunately, we knew this before the game, so we were prepared. It also helped that we took an early lead. But even so, for a long time the game hung in the balance, and we only managed to tip things in our favor in the last period. I made it past the Islanders blue line with the puck, and Tocchet knocked my shot into the net. Several minutes later, Francis got the puck past Healy, and we heaved a sigh of relief.

We had two more games in Long Island, and we absolutely had to win one of them. We managed to win the first one. Tommy tended goal wonderfully. I finally got my aim back, and right before the end of the period I scored our second goal. Ferraro later closed the gap, but Mullen secured our victory in the last moments of the game, and we were set. For the first time in the series, we were ahead, and Mario, despite the severe pain he was in, was ready to play in Game Four.

Game Four started out well for us. For a long time, we kept it tied, until the middle of the game when we took the lead. I stripped the puck from Brad Dalgarno, slid past Krupp and Kasparaitis and pulled a fake on Healy. But then the race for goals began. The home team took the lead, but Loney and Tocchet managed to tie things up again. We made some fatal errors that time which cost us not only the game but the entire series. We made up for the two-goal loss, but instead of clinging to the puck and quieting the game down, we kept pushing it forward. It was stupid. We didn't need to go anywhere fast, but we acted like we'd just been unchained. That came back to haunt us. At the same time, the game was going well because we were always able to tie it up. Stevens made up for Derek King's goal on a power play, and Francis scored a goal after Malakhov's solo performance. But we just didn't learn. We were just a little scattered, and when King got his second goal of the game, it was over. At that moment, I already felt like everything had been decided.

I sensed that we were through, regardless of the fact that in Game Five we came on like a hurricane and Mario and Dicky scored two goals in the first fifty-four seconds, putting us ahead 2-0. We won without any difficulties, but we had to go back to New York.

Unfortunately, that's when my fears came true. We were losing from the beginning and just tagging along behind them. Martin Straka scored twice in the game for us, and eighteen minutes into the third period, Kevin managed to close the gap by one goal. But then we took out Tommy, and Uwe Krupp shot the puck into an empty net to seal our fate. That was it for us.

We left the ice like beaten dogs. Mario hadn't suffered so many injuries the whole season as he did from Kasparaitis in that game. I couldn't move either. Right before the end, when I tried to skate away on the right side, Kasparaitis tripped me. I limped my way to the locker room. I kept ice on my knee the whole time until the next game. Luckily it got better, so I was able to play.

But I was worried. I sensed that our performance in the playoffs was coming to an end. I could imagine the massive disappointment of our fans. We didn't have the strength to beat the Islanders. We were playing spastically, and New York clearly had the upper hand. I mean, before no one even conceived of there being a Game Five, and here we were all tied up and moving on to Game Seven.

We didn't know how to deal with the Islanders. Their toughness and unscrupulousness completely caught us off guard, and we didn't know how to react. If we'd tried to pay them back, we'd have constantly had someone sitting in the penalty box, and that just doesn't work in the playoffs. Despite the pessimistic thoughts we were having, we got ready for the final game.

Unfortunately, a shock hit us right at the beginning. In the first few minutes Kevin Stevens collided with Rich Pillon and fell on the ice unconscious. During their collision, the Plexiglas on Pillon's helmet nailed Kevin right above the nose, which knocked him out immediately. Since he couldn't control his fall, his face hit the ice and broke his nose. It was upsetting to see Kevin carried off the ice with blood all over the place. We lost a bit of our battle fervor, but we still had many chances. Only their goalie Healy was simply like a brick wall. He was impenetrable.

At the beginning of the second period, everything finally collapsed. Ulf potted a goal from the blue line, and it looked as if the lead might relax us. But that's not what happened. It was actually Ulf who made the fatal error which caused Steve Thomas to get to the puck in front of our net and even out the score.

From that moment on, things went badly for us. We were desperate to win, but we played spasmodically. In the third period, first David Volek shot one past Tommy, and then a little while later, Benoit Hogue scored the Islanders' third goal from a good distance away. It was as if we were paralyzed. We couldn't put together a single play. We tried shooting the puck deep into their zone, but they kept playing it back out. Mario played in severe pain. Kevin was out of the game, and it looked as if there was no one on the team to carry the flag and lead the attack. We were losing strength. And then, we started scoring.

It was almost a miracle that we managed to rise from the dead, and Ronnie Francis deserves most of the credit. It was at that moment when we were down, that Ronnie proved what a solid player he is. He pushed us forward and played as if it was the last game of his life.

At one point, right before the end of the game with only three minutes left to go, Murph broke down the right side, made a beautiful pass to Ronnie right in front of the net, who shrunk the margin to one goal. The stands woke up. During the next few minutes, all hell broke loose. The fans kept us going, and we focused all our energy on the attack. When there was a little more than a minute left in the game, we took a moment to catch our breath and to gather our strength for one last desperate attack. Some of us were hanging on the boards from exhaustion, but we gathered the remainder of our strength and went after them even harder.

At the moment when Murph took his shot from the blue line, the timer showed 19:00 exactly. The shot was not too high, not too fast and was headed straight for the throng of bodies in front of the net. It looked as if it would end up in Healy's gloves, but then Ronnie Francis put out his stick and redirected it so that it plopped right behind the goal line! We went crazy with joy, and the stadium could have collapsed. Three minutes before the end of the game we were losing by two goals, and now we were tied!

We literally crawled into the locker room after the third period. At that moment we weren't talking strategy. All you heard was "we have to" and "we can do it." Otherwise, everybody looked after himself to make sure he could carry himself back onto the ice. We'd had enough of the Islanders. I remember how somebody said that at that point we just couldn't lose. That thought filled my mind as I sat on the bench and panted. The break seemed so short. It was as if I'd barely sat down before we were rushing back on the ice.

Now it was overtime. We pounded the Islanders as if it was the first period, and we looked as if we were stronger. Mario and Ronnie did have chances to end the game, but Healy stopped them. I also had a good chance, but then it happened. We rotated badly and only had four players on the ice, three of them in the Islanders' defensive zone. And then the puck went to David Volek at the red line.

David hadn't had a successful season. The year before, he'd played in seventy-four games and racked up sixty points, but this year Arbour didn't play him much. In comparison with the previous year, he had forty points less, and it often happened that the coach didn't play him at all. When he went to Arbour and asked why he was only playing two or three times per game, Arbour told him, "OK, you won't play at all." So David didn't appear in several games. It also seemed as if he didn't have many friends on the team. His teammates said that he was terribly reclusive, and that although he may not have had any enemies, he didn't have many friends.

Arbour and David had been at each other's throats for quite a while, and then David did something nobody dared to do. One time when he didn't play in Washington, he sat down with his good friend Michal Pivonka, and they watched the game together. In Czechoslovakia, it was always perfectly normal for players who know each other to hang out. But in the NHL, you are limited to brief encounters after the game. It's totally exceptional for two opposing players to sit together in front of everyone in the stands.

David now had his chance in the playoffs, and to our misfortune, he paid Arbour back for the trust. The moment he got the puck, I knew things were going to be bad. Suddenly Ferraro and Malakhov shot to the front, so it was actually a three-on-one because only Kjell Samuelsson had stayed back. Unfortunately, we were missing a player at the most important spot.

Volek immediately passed the puck to Ferraro, who pulled it off to the side and waited until David was in shooting position.

If I'd been sitting in a train, I probably would have pulled the emergency brake. At that moment, I remembered the morning warm-up. David had been one of the last people on the ice, and he skated back and forth a little while longer than the rest. David took the puck and sent it into an empty net. At that moment I was behind the Plexiglas and shouted at him, "So that's the winner?" David just grinned.

It became a classic two-on-one situation as Malakhov blocked Straka on his way back, so Ferraro and Volek had enough time to finish what they'd started. Ferraro was getting into shooting position, and Kjell did what he had to do. He went after him. At that moment, Ferraro passed to the right to Volek. Volek was hovering in front of an uncovered part of the net because Barrasso had already gone to cover Ferraro to decrease his shot angle.

At that moment, David had two possibilities: hold the puck, set it up and shoot it precisely where he wanted, or just shoot it. David took the second option. He turned his hip toward the pass and, without any setup, drove the puck into the net.

As soon as the net spread out, it looked as is someone had shut everything down in the stadium. Suddenly it was as silent as a graveyard. In a split second came the whoop of the Islanders, and we knew that the battle had been won. At least we should have known. But somehow it didn't quite sink in.

I sat in the locker room and cried like a little boy. I had a torn eyelid from a hockey stick, but I didn't feel any physical pain at all. I slowly took off my gear, and went into the showers. Nobody said a word. Almost all of us had tears in our eyes. It was like a funeral. Occasionally you'd hear a muffled voice, otherwise, it was quiet. There was sadness everywhere. That's the taste of defeat. I was suddenly aware of how exceptionally lucky I'd been to get two Stanley Cups. At the time of winning them, I hadn't really been aware of how special it is. Now it began to dawn on me that victory doesn't come automatically, that it can take several years before you make it to the Stanley Cup finals.

I wanted to go away somewhere. Immediately. I knew what massive disappointment we'd dished out to the fans. I no longer thought I was untouchable, and I began to fear being traded. There was even talk about me going to Quebec in a trade for Peter Forsberg. My mother wrung her hands in despair. "I just barely managed to learn a few words in English, and now we have to move somewhere else? I won't be able to communicate. What will I do?" she moaned. Luckily, the news about me leaving turned out to be nothing but a rumor, so I remained a Penguin one more year.

During the summer, I had tons of time to think about why we'd lost. One of the causes had clearly been the excellent season. It's simply not possible to play exceptionally the whole season. We probably got too exhausted before it was over. We were like tortoises who were chasing too many hares. We had wanted to break the record for the number of wins in a row, and we succeeded. We finished the season with a record margin over the second-place team and with thirty-two points more than the Islanders.

On the other hand, we didn't have enough strength left for the playoffs, and that showed itself in the last two games with the Devils. We confirmed once again just how important Mario's health is for us. There's no doubt that he only played the series with the Islanders out of the strength of his will. If they'd been normal season games, he'd have never come out on the ice.

We had run up against a well-prepared opponent. We could have overcome them. They were no miracle team, which was obvious in the next round, when the Montreal Canadiens literally clobbered them senseless. But they played cleverly with us. They had the outstanding Healy tending goal. Their defense played well. Malakhov was fantastic, but we had the most of our problems with Kasparaitis — sort of a Lithuanian version of our Ulf Samuelsson. We let his antics provoke us — something we didn't have to do — and we didn't fully concentrate on the game.

It had happened exactly as I feared it would. They walled up the goal, waited for us and didn't budge an inch. At that time, I had no idea that two years later another team would get the better of us thanks to an even more perfect system, but the Islanders played exactly the way they needed. They were able to punish our spastic playing and lack of strategy with quick counterattacks, after which they retreated back to their zone. It was obvious that we were lacking another back alongside Murph, someone capable of passing the puck precisely or sending it into the defensive zone of the opposing team. Someone like Coffey would be ideal. But we didn't have anyone like that, which is why we on the front line felt pretty cutoff.

In both series, overall, I scored five goals and racked up a total of eleven points, which, when you compare it with the previous year, was nothing special. On the other hand, I played eleven fewer games. I had enough time to think about why I wasn't getting anywhere. But one thing was clear to me, I could already count on the fact that in the upcoming seasons I would be the target of the opposing defensemen, the same way ours focus on the opponent's offensive players who decide games.

Years have passed since the unforgettable series with the Islanders, and in that time not much has changed — at least not as far as our chances of getting another Stanley Cup are concerned. The first time we were knocked out right in the first round. The next year we made it a bit further. But what's been different in the last few years has been my role on the team. I started getting a lot of time on the ice, and my teammates expected me to win the games for them. I started thinking more about the way we played the game and tried to figure out why we weren't making it into the finals.

The Art Ross Trophy

Before the new season began, we got a new coach. They traded Scotty Bowman for Eddie Johnson, who was known as E. J. Scotty, and Bowman's assistant, Barry Smith, went to Detroit. Bryan Trottier also returned to the team, and Markus Naslund came to us from Sweden. Team management also decided to make a trade with the Los Angeles Kings — for Shawn McEachern we got one of the best fighters in the entire NHL, Marty McSorley.

Marty is an excellent guy. We often made fun of him, saying that he is like a model because he goes to the shower with five kinds of shampoo and stays there for about an hour. But he was fun. I really liked the way he was with the young fans. They could come up to him anytime. Marty's even spent some time at my house. Once my mother made dinner for us, and when she put a beer in front of him, "the giant" declared in an equally gigantic voice that he only drinks milk. And he drank all the milk we had in the house.

Once Marty and I had a contest in practice to see who could outfight the other. And I won! We held on to each other to see who could knock the other down, and because I have strong legs, I was able to knock him down first. In a real fight, Marty could give me one punch, and I'd be out like a light.

I can't handle NHL fighters. Those guys are like professional boxers. Marty tells me that the secret to successful fighting is in the first punch. Marty told me that the most dangerous one, when it comes to the first punch, is Joe Kocur of the Rangers. If he gets the first punch on you, you won't be able to get up afterward.

Every team has a few "fighters." You find out who they are when someone knocks one of their protected stars into the boards. That's when they start to fight. The probability that one of those guys will come after you is pretty small. Once one of the tough guys slammed me into the boards, and I got really angry and took off my gloves. Of course, I wasn't thinking clearly at that moment. He would certainly have beat the hell out of me, but I was so mad that I was ready to take him on. He just looked at me, made an irritated face and said, "Come on, get lost."

At the beginning of the year, I had problems with my knee and had to decide whether to have it operated on. My knee had been hurting in the previous season, but after the clash with Kasparaitis it had gotten much worse. After the playoffs, I took some time off, but as soon as I started working out again, the pain returned. I had to stop everything and have it X-rayed. After that, the doctors gave me a choice. Either I have it operated on immediately, or start on a series of exercises to strengthen my knee. I took the second option and devoted most of the summer to my knee. I would sit in an armchair with some small weights on my leg and alternate bending and extending it. The exercises helped greatly and strengthened my ligaments. On the other hand, I couldn't work out very much, so I was afraid of how I'd look at training camp. In the past, I'd always come there all pumped up.

The season started off unexpectedly well for me, although not for Mario. After the first four games, it became clear that the pain in Mario's back would keep him from playing, so we had to play more than half the season without him. While we missed him, we knew we could survive the regular season without Mario if we had to. What was important was that he be well for the playoffs.

As a consequence of Mario's absence, other players got to play more during this season. His absence certainly gave me more room to play. I had a lot more time on the ice, and I liked that. From the start of league play, I led the team in scoring. I held the lead for half the season, until Ronnie and Joe Mullen surpassed me. I was playing with them, though, so the eggs were at least all going in the same basket.

My glory day came on November 16. We were at home against Philadelphia, and there was no hint that anything extraordinary might happen. In the second period, however, we got four goals in the course of seven minutes. I scored one of them myself and assisted on two others. After two periods the score was 7-3. In the end the Flyers went home with a scathing 11-5 loss. Scoring six points in this one game is my personal record, one which I probably won't beat for a long time.

You do get the most pleasure out of the game when you succeed. Now that's no great piece of wisdom, and it's certainly nothing new. But now that I've led in the scoring for part of the season, I've come to see how this influences things. When you're doing well, your teammates start respecting you. And they let you know. Not that they go around the locker room patting you on the back, but they pass the puck to you.

It's interesting to me that if you're not doing well, your teammates turn their backs on you. It's nothing personal. They simply know you're no help. They know that if they pass to you, you'll blow it. Your fellow players want to assist whoever is capable of doing something with the puck or scoring a goal so that the team will win and they'll get a point for an assist.

Now I had the feeling that my teammates were relying on me. I got numerous passes, even from teammates who were competing with me. Of course, they could count on the fact that if I scored goals, they'd get points for assists. And points in the NHL are terribly important. They have a big effect on your later hockey and non-hockey life. It's probably what our contracts are based on.

Although we had disappointed the fans in the previous playoffs, they still came back in droves during this season. The games weren't always sold-out, but there were usually at least 15,000 fans at each game. Over New Year's, I started wondering if I was going to get as many votes to be on the All-Star team as I had last year. I secretly followed the course of the voting for the All-Star team and hoped that I'd make it again.

I knew that I'd get less votes than the previous two years. It was obvious why — we didn't win the Stanley Cup. But I had hopes to make it to New York, where the All-Star game was going to be. The voting started a little later this season, which also had influence on the number of votes received. Still, I wound up getting 209,147 votes, more than any other wing in the NHL! The third time in a row in the top five. It seemed unbelievable. It was beyond my wildest dreams — three times in a row at the opening face-off with the best players in the world.

When I flew to New York, I was thinking about where I was ten years ago. I was playing for the juniors and dreaming about playing in the first league for Kladno. But it definitely didn't occur to me that one day I'd be considered one of the top five players in the best hockey league in the world and playing in the All-Star game three years in a row. If someone had told me that, I'd have said he was crazy. And if someone had told me on the plane to New York that I actually wouldn't wind up playing in my third All-Star game, I wouldn't have believed him either. All the same, he'd have been right.

I got to New York a day before All-Star weekend started. There was a message in the hotel from Barnett that he was waiting for me in a bar near 80th street. I got there around ten. I'd barely gone inside when I knew it was going to be the kind of evening I like. There was a whole bunch of stars there, who I'd only run into when they were on the ice with helmets on their heads. This time Mark Messier didn't have a helmet on, but he was wearing a hat. Sort of a beret. Looking like a Frenchman, Mark said hello to me and shook my hand.

I was on the lookout for my agent. He was sitting at a table with Jirka Crha and Sergei Fedorov. Sergei was already a little "happy," and everyone was in a good mood. We stayed at the bar until midnight and then everyone else went to a dance club. I needed to get some sleep. After all, I was in a big race the following day.

As usual, All-Star weekend began with a photo-shoot and press conferences. Then everyone got ready for the speed-skating competition. I think Sergei Fedorov is the best in that field. He had won it twice before at the All-Star game. And it was against him that I was supposed to skate. I was really looking forward to the race, and I was feeling confident. I knew that I had it in me to beat him, and I wanted to win the competition. But it turned out differently than I planned.

The opening celebration began. Madison Square Garden was plunged into darkness, and after the opening ceremony, we skated onto the ice one after another. Then the lights came up, and we went straight to it.

And that was the problem. We didn't have any time at all to warm up. Before every game, I spend at least half an hour warming up. I have my own routine which I do regularly, and I only put on my skates after I've properly stretched and warmed up. In this case, it was totally different. In comparison with a normal season game, there was much less tension. We felt that it was an honor to be there certainly, something you don't take lightly, but the atmosphere was friendly, we were all having fun together, and the whole thing seemed like a match at the county fair. Mentally, we were perfectly prepared, but physically not at all.

I realized before the start of the race how unprepared I was. I thought, "Right now I'm about to race the fastest skater in the NHL for one lap, and I haven't warmed up at all." I started to panic and tried to use the remaining time to stretch a bit. But the ice was already empty and they were calling us for the start.

The stands went wild. Fans love this kind of stuff. That's why they put together the All-Star weekend. On one side of the red line, Jaromir Jagr, on the other side, Sergei Fedorov. The clock was ready, and so were we.

I concentrated on the start. At the moment the referee blew the whistle, I put all my might into the blades of my skates and shot forward. I knew right away that something was wrong. I felt a sharp pain in my right groin, but I kept going. Halfway around the rink we were neck and neck. I made the last turn around the net in pain and finished behind Fedorov, who won by a few tenths of a second. I feel that if I hadn't injured myself, I'd have beaten him. But at the moment, that wasn't what I was concerned about.

I felt a great deal of pain. I left the ice and went to the locker room. I took off my gear and went to the shower. I was absolutely furious. It occurred to me in the shower that I wouldn't be able to play the next day. I didn't even watch the rest of the competition. I sat on the floor with an ice pack on my leg. Then Cindy Himes from public relations arrived. "Cindy, I need a plane ticket to Pittsburgh tomorrow," I told her. "I'll take care of everything Jaromir," she said looking at me. Then she added, "But maybe I should call Craig."

I hadn't even thought about him. Craig Patrick was going to lose his mind if I left. It looked as if I wouldn't be able to play several games. At that moment, I couldn't even walk comfortably. Coffey and Sergei Fedorov came by and said, "Jags, get a move on. We're going to dinner." "I'll take a rain check," I groaned. They took one look at me, and it was obvious I wouldn't be joining them.

I wanted to get out of there as soon as possible. I limped outside and took the escalator down. I came to huge glass doors, behind which hundreds of fans were crammed. To get outside, I had to walk through them. That would of course mean being crushed by fans and signing dozens of programs, hats and photos.

The hockey fans had already spotted me and started chanting, "Jagr! Jagr!" I was in a Catch-22: I had to either bite the bullet, suffer the pain and walk through the crowd or turn my back and leave with half of New York's hockey fans mad at me.

I took the second option. I asked the organizer next to me if there wasn't another more discrete exit from the stadium. When the man nodded and went ahead to show me the way out, I could hear a deafening whistle behind me. Sorry guys, next time.

Once I was at the hotel, I got in bed immediately. I stuck a bag of ice on my leg and moped about what had happened. "Tomorrow there'll be no All-Star game for me," I thought. Instead, I was going to get on a plane to Pittsburgh.

The injury was due to my own stupidity. As if I didn't know that I shouldn't go out there without warming up. Of course, it could have been worse, but I'll certainly know better next time.

I couldn't play for four games because of the injury. It was very likely those missed games kept me from making it past the 100-point mark in scoring, and that made me mad. But I still had enough chances to hit it. We won our last game against Ottawa 4-0, but I just didn't get that last point. However, I was still number one in points on our team with thirty-two goals and sixty-seven assists.

We won the Northeastern Division and finished second overall behind the New York Rangers. Even though another team from the Atlantic Division, the New Jersey Devils, had more points, we were placed second because we had won our division. The Washington Capitals were awaiting us.

The last regular season games should have been a definite warning for us. First we got destroyed in New Jersey, where we lost 7-2. Then the Montreal Canadiens squashed us with an unbelievable score of 9-1. This wasn't a good sign right before the playoffs.

The Capitals are known as an unpleasant team, and they confirmed this right away in the first game. We lost at home 5-3. And it was a dangerously close game two days later. Fortunately, we beat them 2-1 in the second game, so we still had a chance.

But at the next game in Washington, we didn't have a chance. The Capitals had an airtight defense, and we lacked the necessary energy to bust through it. We only scored once in two games, so they beat us without any difficulty. In the first game we lost 2-0, and in the second 4-1. I could feel that we wouldn't beat them. We were completely exhausted and Mario was playing with terrible pain. In the fifth game, we were tied in the final period, and I broke away to score the winning goal. But the score was settled in Game Six in Washington. We lost 6-3 and left for vacation.

The year before we'd suffered a humiliating defeat to the Islanders. Our defeat with the Capitals was much simpler. We just didn't have that spark and had no idea what strategy to use on them. At the time, we had no idea that we would be meeting them again the following year and things would develop the same way — except there would be a different ending.

Before the game during warm-up — a few jokes and horsing around with Martin Straka.

Vacation dragged on a bit. At the end of the season, I sensed that the collective bargaining agreement between the NHL and the players would be more explosive than it had been three years ago. It looked like there'd be a strike, and when we went to training camp, that's exactly what happened. The beginning of the season was continually pushed back. It was obvious that the season wouldn't get going before Christmas. The team got together and skated several times a week, but otherwise, we just sat around bored. I wanted to go home to Czechoslovakia.

My telephone started ringing more and more often. The journalists kept asking when I'd be playing in the Czech league. Some of the Czech players had already gone back, including Martin Straka, who went back to Pilsen. "Start practicing a bit, so at least you have a routine going," my father said. I started to get really excited at the thought of returning home, but I was also really afraid.

I'd always thought that the best way to end my hockey career would be by playing at home. I've always liked the thought of reaching the end of my career around the age of thirty-five and returning to Kladno to be the old man in the league for another few years. But I never thought that I'd return so early.

I was mostly afraid of being a disappointment. During my four years overseas, I had gotten two Stanley Cups, had made it into the NHL top five three times in a row and once had had the most points on my team. My reputation followed me everywhere I went, mainly thanks to the media. Most people had heard about me, even if they hadn't had a chance to see me play in person. When I appeared in a clip on television, it was usually because I had scored a goal. Most people in the Czech Republic hadn't actually seen me play, yet they probably thought, "Yeah, yeah, here comes Jagr, the goals should start piling up." I was afraid of everyone expecting too much from me.

And I wanted to play better than I had in Italy. I was a disappointment at last year's World Championship in Italy. I was terribly tired when I got there. And as if that wasn't bad enough, our car had broken down on the way from Milan. I spent almost an entire day on the highway.

My first surprise came during skating warm-ups. I had no idea that everyone took them so seriously. I went onto the ice without my helmet and shoulder pads, totally laid-back, while everyone else was in full gear.

We started practicing power plays. "How do you play 'em in Pittsburgh?" asked Coach Hlinka. "Well, I stand here," I replied, taking a dramatic pause, "and Mario stands there. That's how we play 'em." I burst out laughing, but I don't think anybody else thought I was too funny.

The next day we were up against the Norwegians. We only managed to tie them 2-2. But the tie ensured us a place in the playoffs. We could have afforded the loss to Sweden, but then we had to face Canada and Brendan Shanahan sent us packing right before the end. I don't like thinking about it. We could have gone further.

But Italy taught me a lesson — a much-needed lesson. I thought that Europe didn't hold any surprises for me anymore. And there I was with my mouth hanging open. I needed to land in second place somewhere so I'd come back down to earth. That somewhere was Italy.

The experience in Italy helped me prepare for my return home to Czechoslovakia. I realized that I wasn't in good shape. I had been skating occasionally, but otherwise I didn't do anything during the strike. I sat around like a couch potato and gained weight. This was the state in which I was going to jump into professional Czech hockey in the middle of the season — and try to be number one.

I put myself under serious pressure to succeed. I felt like every game in Czechoslovakia would be a struggle for survival. If I didn't play perfectly in one or two games in the NHL, it didn't matter. People knew what I was capable of and they remembered my accomplishments. I was afforded the luxury to be second best once in a while. Back home in Czechoslovakia, that wouldn't be an option. Every game would be terribly important there. I had left after two years in our league and a lot had changed in that time. I'd grown as a player and wanted to show the Czech spectators what I was made of. I didn't want to disappoint them.

I thought about this on the plane on my way home. I wondered if I was up to the challenge. I knew it would take some time to get into shape and that I'd also have some problems with the wider rink. I also had the fear that as soon as I'd gotten warmed up to play, they'd be calling us back and the NHL would be starting.

There was a big welcome for me when I arrived in Prague. There was a huge crowd of people, and more journalists than there'd been after the Stanley Cup victory. Venca Cibula from the newspaper *Svobodne slovo* and his colleagues immediately handed me a fax in English which said that the strike was over, that the NHL would be starting in the next few days and that I had to return immediately. I looked at it for a moment and thought to myself, "This can't be true." "This is some kind of joke," I told them, and only then did everyone burst into laughter. They'd really gotten me good.

I wanted my big entrance to be for the Kladno fans, and it couldn't have turned out better. The visiting team was Olomouc. The stadium was already packed during practice before the game. I got my first goal in the seventh minute. Honza Blaha passed me the puck, and I sent it right into the net.

I felt like I could make a real contribution to the team. There were good hockey players in Kladno, but the team just couldn't seem to get it together. I wanted to help them. I put my all into it, and I was happy when we won. I think we actually got better.

I'll never forget the game in Vítkovice. I left for Germany for one game, where I played for Schalke 04. I flew back on the very day we were leaving for Vítkovice. Sometime in the early afternoon, I went to lay down. After the trip I was pretty worn out and had made up my mind that I wasn't going anywhere. I woke up around four o'clock and listened to all the activity around the house. My father asked me if I hadn't changed my mind, and so we just talked for a while. All of a sudden, I really wanted to play. It was around three-thirty, and I told my father to unpack my things. My father dried some of my gear on the heater, and I went into my room. I knew that I couldn't wait. They were leaving from the stadium at five o'clock. I started to get dressed and just shouted to my father, "Can you throw me my winter jacket?" We got to Vítkovice in the evening, and after a few hours in the bus, I though it might be a good idea to stretch out a bit. So I suggested we check out the local discotheque. The next day they wrote in the newspaper that we'd spent the whole night at the disco, and since we must be tired, we'd be easy prey for the home team. Except that we put on one of our best performances. At Rondo Stadium, which had been sold out several weeks in advance, we slaughtered Vítkovice 7-2. In the course of the game, the fans started cheering us on, and it reached a peak when I got sent to the penalty box. I was sitting in the penalty box, and suddenly the fans started coming down to me and handing me photos and programs to autograph. So I turned my stay in the penalty box into a little autograph signing session.

I like remembering Vítkovice, but there were games which I would rather wipe completely out of my memory. It was almost embarrassing in Pilsen, the home of Pilsner Urquel beer, and Ceske Budejovice, the birthplace of Budweiser. I was really looking forward to Pilsen, but they stuck Pavel Kreuzmann on me, and he didn't notice anything but me. He covered me the whole game. Wherever I turned, he was right behind my back. If I'd gone to the toilet between periods, there's no question he'd have been waiting outside the stall. The problem was the referee didn't even blow his whistle when he was holding my hockey stick or interfering, even when the puck was nowhere in sight. I was really irritated by that and went home after the game. I had originally planned on staying in Pilsen with Martin Straka and going somewhere afterward. When we shook hands after the game, Martin asked if I'd be coming out with him, but I was completely out of the mood. All I said was that I was going home.

In Ceske Budejovice it was similar, except that my groin muscle was hurting me. It was right before my return to Pittsburgh, so I wanted to play one last time at home, but it was a horrible experience. I fought more with myself than the opposing team and felt bad that I didn't give the sold-out crowd their money's worth.

I have the worst memories of the game with Slavie Praha in Eden. Slavie is the second Prague team, for which Vladimir Ruzicka and others have played. It was absolutely crazy. I had just come back from my triumphant Italian adventure, during which I helped Bolzan get the championship. I was supposed to catch a plane at 11:15 A.M., but they took me by car to Milan. So I flew out of there and got home around noon.

After years, again in our league during the NHL strike.

Right: There's not enough room in our league, either.

I hadn't slept the whole night. We partied until morning, and then they took me straight to the airport, so I was pretty beat. But everyone was talking about the game at Eden, and I didn't know whether or not I should play. I laid down for two hours, woke up at four and heard on the radio that the game was sold out and that everyone was looking forward to it. My father said something about it, too, so I made my mind up in an instant.

The game started at 5:30, so we had to just go. We climbed in the Mitsubishi and took off for Prague. In front of the stadium there was a massive crowd, and when the people recognized me, it got even worse. We couldn't get inside. We got there right before the start, and so I pulled the same stupid idiocy as at the All-Star game in New York. Instead of telling the coach that I needed to warm up a little, I went right out. It was as if I'd forgotten what could happen. I was bewitched by the atmosphere, in good shape and looking forward to giving the spectators something to watch.

I was scheduled to start, and being tired and not warmed up, my legs took off on their own, and I immediately pulled my groin muscle. I thought I was going to lose my mind because of the pain. I lived through the worst moments of my entire stay in the Czech Republic during that car ride back to Kladno.

The pulled muscle kept me out of commission for several weeks. The first time I was back on the ice was actually in Vítkovice.

All in all, I have good memories of that period back home. The league had grown younger. I almost didn't know anyone anymore, but it was still good to play there. I was surprised at the way some games were played perfectly. Our front line of Martin Prochazka, Pavel Patera and Otakar Vejvoda could someday play in the NHL. The three of them only need to get a little stronger. If you put Frantisek Kaberle and Antomin Stavjana with them, they would give any NHL team a run for its money. If I were to put together a Czech All-Star team from what I've seen, I'd probably stick my old junior league acquaintance Roman Cechmanek in goal.

As for comparisons between the Czech league and the NHL, there are obvious differences, particularly in terms of the style of play. There's less technique-playing in the States. There's more fighting, and there are many people in the NHL who can decide games. Czech hockey, on the other hand, is very fast, which the bigger rinks encourage. There are also a lot of young players who are good skaters. I definitely think there are a number of players in the Czech league who could succeed in the NHL.

The thing that is absolutely incomparable is what happens off the ice. A hockey player in the NHL doesn't have to worry about anything but playing the game. If you have any problems, the club helps you. If my visa expires, I go see Tracy Botsford, Craig Patrick's secretary, and tell her. Then, I can completely forget about it. She's already taken care of it. It's that way with everything. We're there to play hockey, and we focus only on that.

There's also a big difference in the health care that we receive in the States. When I returned to Pittsburgh, my groin muscle was in terrible shape. I had pulled it again during a game in Czechoslovakia, but I really couldn't do anything about it while I was there. I was able to play again after a few weeks of rest, but I was in a great deal of pain, and the muscle hadn't really healed.

There was no way to treat it back home because the health care system is a total catastrophe. I remember that once I couldn't even get an Ace bandage. If you get injured while playing in the Czech league, you have to suffer through the poor health care system like everyone else. If something happens to a player, he can take a year off. During that time, all he does is go to doctors. He spends an hour in the waiting room, then waits until a rehabilitation machine is free. Five minutes later they take him away because there are twenty other people waiting to get on it.

Another problem in the Czech Republic is the lack of ice. Every injury is treated with ice in the NHL. It looks like a refrigerator in the stadium. There are ice cubes everywhere, and immediately after the game, you put ice packs on your injuries. It's impossible to find ice back home. It's as if they'd never heard of it. Here in America, whenever my mom shops, she brings home two big bags of ice, so that I can ice my injuries at home, too.

If you get an injury here, they take care of you as best they can. Every club is extremely well equipped in this way. In the stadium we have a swimming pool, three whirlpool baths and machines which heal you using electric currents. These machines could put Humpty Dumpty back together again. Here there are specialists everywhere. We have our own doctor and several masseurs. I don't even have to leave the gates of the stadium to get better medical care than you would get in any Czech hospital. I am always amazed at how well equipped it is here. Bandages, wraps, elastic bands — there are several kinds of everything, with different thicknesses and widths. As soon as I get an injury, everybody on the team staff knocks themselves out in order to get me back on the ice. I really think that Czech athletes could use that kind of care, so that they could focus on the game and nothing else.

Thanks to the great care I received, in a matter of weeks, I was able to get past my injured groin muscle to become number one in NHL scoring. After thirteen games, I had a five-point lead over the second-place Ron Francis. It was already clear that this would be my best season as far as points were concerned. By then, I already had twenty-six.

The ones I had to beat were Joe Sakic from Quebec and Eric Lindros from Philadelphia. I had first encountered Lindros in the Under 20 World Championship in Finland. Robert Holik pointed him out to me and said, "That one there's supposed to be the absolute best. They are making him out to be a star." And then I met Lindros again, as I already mentioned, when I passed him his first NHL goal.

In the NHL, they say that he's a player who's going to dominate the league for the next six or seven years, like Gretzky or Lemieux. He definitely has the potential. While Eric is not the most fantastic skater with the best technique, there are two outstanding things Eric does have.

His most powerful weapon is his excellent shooting. He can shoot from anywhere, anytime, anyhow. He has tremendous strength in his arms. He is capable of finishing an attack with a fake, but he mainly likes to shoot.

In addition to his shooting, what makes Lindros remarkable is his physical strength. Today Eric is one of the biggest, and possibly heaviest, players in the NHL, and to take him on in a fight is like taking on a brick wall. I've never seen him lose a fight in the NHL. Thanks to his size, he can also grab the space in front of the net and score. He's also good at passing and cooperates well with his teammates. He's gotten a lot of help from the arrival of John Le Claire from Montreal. The two of them, along with Mikael Renberg, compose what was possibly the best offense in the entire NHL in that year.

I've played against Lindros many times. We often run into each other at the boards. What really impresses me about Lindros is his self-confidence. He skates on the ice as if it was clear that he's going to score three goals in the game and that it's only a question of when. He charges into every fight with the same self-assurance as when he's skating on defense. He takes off, demolishes an opposing player, slams into another and then slaps the puck to, say, Renberg. Completely naturally, as if there wasn't any other way to do it.

Lindros got ahead of me in points somewhere around the thirtieth game, and he stayed in front. After the fortieth game, I was six points behind him. I thought that the Art Ross Trophy would go to him. However, fate had something else in store.

Philadelphia was playing the New York Rangers at home when Lindros shot at the net from the blue line. It deflected off defenseman Jeff Beukeboom back toward Lindros, who was right in the line of fire. It got him right in the eye. Not only did Eric sit out the remaining two games of the season, but he was missing from the opening of the playoffs. His absence gave me the chance to go for the trophy.

In Boston, we lost 5-2, but I scored both goals. Then I scored twice in Washington, where we gave up seven. In the second period, I scored my two and caught up with Peter Bondra for the highest number of goals — except that Bondra scored twice in the final period and with his thirty-four goals became number one in the NHL.

I continued in the competition for the most productive player in the regular season, and the fight with Eric went on until the very end. Eric really wanted the Art Ross Trophy. When we played the Islanders, Eric called his brother, who actually plays for the Islanders, and didn't even bother saying hi. He just asked: "How many points does Jagr have?"

I was only one point behind Eric. I only had to match him in points because I already had more goals than he did.

We played our last game at home against Florida. It was both an advantage and a disadvantage. The home environment definitely helped me, but then the Panthers have a strong defense, and it's difficult to score against them.

We tried the whole period. I wasn't actually playing against Florida but against the clock. You can't fake out the clock. Eddie and I agreed that I could go on the ice anytime I wanted so that I could go for the trophy. After the game, Ron Francis told me that he had the flu and was feeling terrible, but that he didn't want to tell me before because he didn't want to make me nervous. "I wanted to help you," he said. "If you weren't zeroing in on the trophy, I definitely wouldn't have played in this game."

Everyone tried to help me in some way, but it just wasn't working. In the first period, I was on the ice for about fourteen minutes and did nothing. And then it happened. In the nineteenth minute, I broke free in the right corner and shot at Vanbiesbrouck. The puck rebounded right to Kevin Stevens, who scored our first goal — the goal that secured me the Art Ross Trophy because I got a point for the assist and was in first place.

I skated over to Kevin. Ulf Samuelsson and Ron Francis and the rest of the team came out and hugged me. The stadium went crazy for several minutes. I was sitting on the bench, and the scoreboard kept flashing "JAGR!!!" and the people kept applauding. I stood up and waved to the fans to thank them.

I had managed to accomplish my big goal, but the most important task was still ahead of me. In our division, we finished second behind Quebec. And even though we had more points than the best team from the other division, Philadelphia, we finished third in the Eastern Conference because the first two places were held by the winners of the Northeastern and Atlantic Divisions. The team that was awaiting us was in fifth place overall and was the one we probably wanted to play the least — the Washington Capitals.

The Capitals had eliminated us from the playoffs the previous year, and in the last game of the regular season they destroyed us without any difficulty 7-2. We had every reason to be afraid. Washington is an excellent defensive team. They have a solid defense, but even the offense connects with the defense, who can turn anything into a fast break. They're a team with the two things you need: a good goalie and people who can make goals happen.

When the Washington team was having problems halfway through the season, the Capitals coach Jim Schoenfeld made a desperate move: He called up a twenty-year-old goalie, Jim Carey, from the farm team. This turned out to be his best decision of the year. Carey turned in such fantastic performances that for a long time he was competing with Dominik Hasek for the lowest number of goals allowed. Carey is terribly quick in the net. He stops almost every first shot, but thanks to his speed, he's able to stop every rebound shot. This is terribly important. He's also big and moves well, so he covers every corner of the goal. He went from being a novice to a remarkable power, one which Washington relied on heavily in the playoffs.

The other important factor in the game was Peter Bondra. I know Peter from the Czechoslovakian league, and I spent two evenings with him in Montreal during the All-Star weekend. He's really a very nice guy, and I like bumping into him off the ice.

It was very interesting how Peter got into the NHL, and a little unusual. His father went to the Ukraine after the Second World War to work and ended up marrying there. His wife was Polish. In 1968, Peter was born. When he was three, his parents got an idea which Peter will thank them for the rest of his life. They moved back to Slovakia. Because of his background, he avoided representing Czechoslovakia. Once he was recruited to play for the Under 17 team, but then they found out that he was still a citizen of the Soviet Union and couldn't play. He had a tougher time because he couldn't draw attention to himself in the international arena. But he did it in Czechoslovakia's professional hockey league.

He got around thirty goals three seasons in a row until the scouts finally noticed him. One time Kosice was playing Vítkovice, and Peter read in the evening paper that the famous scout from the Washington Capitals, Jack Button, was coming to the game. In the game, Bondra was on fire. Kosice won 4-3, and Peter scored two goals and assisted the other two.

Button immediately showed up at another game in Kosice and waited for Peter after the game. Through an interpreter he asked Peter if he had the guts to try the NHL. Of course, Bondra nodded yes. So the Capitals drafted him.

Immediately after his arrival in the NHL, it was his speed that drew attention to him. Michal Pivonka provided him with the chance to score by passing to him, and Peter started cranking out goals. His best season was the year before last when he got thirty-seven goals and finished with a total of eighty-five points. However, people still said that he should use his talent more and that he should spend more time working on his game off the ice.

Peter took it to heart and at camp before this season almost nobody recognized him. He'd spent the entire summer in the gym, mostly working on his upper body. He'd increased his strength incredibly and came to camp totally pumped up. This immediately showed up in his game. He started winning battles for the puck, easily setting up chances for goals, and added great shooting to his already excellent speed. He scored more goals than anyone else in the NHL and looked forward to playing us. Our defense only caught the wind he left behind. It's no surprise that he often glided past them and that they were no match for him. Not that he completely got away from them. They just couldn't keep up with him. So it was the Capitals with Bondra and the outstanding Jim Carey in goal that were awaiting us in the first round of the playoffs.

There was no chance of us underestimating them. Eddie Johnston let out the unlucky prediction that we wouldn't have any problems, and the headlines carried it for the course of the series. But we players definitely did not take the Capitals lightly.

Game One confirmed our worst fears. It was tied for two periods. The game was decided at the beginning of the final period. Dale Hunter scored the tie-breaking goal for Washington, and right after that Sergei Gonchar raised it to 5-3. I managed to shrink the margin by one goal five minutes before the end of the game, but we couldn't tie it up again.

It was history repeating itself. We'd lost the first game of the previous playoffs as well. It looked like we'd lose Game Two as well. After the second period we were down 3-1 and had no idea what kind of strategy to use on them. But then our hurricane arrived at the beginning of the third period. Right in the second minute we laid siege on the Capitals' goal, and Luc Robitaille landed the puck in the net. Thirty seconds later, Ron Francis and I skated down toward one of the defensemen. Ron had the puck along the right wing while I skated down the left. Ronnie carried it out perfectly. He waited until the last moment when the defenseman turned on him and sent the puck right to the end of my stick. I slipped it into the uncovered part of the net, and the score was tied. Three minutes after that Pivonka went to the penalty box for holding, and Kevin Stevens ripped in the tie-breaking goal! A mere three minutes and fourteen seconds and we'd scored three times! We held the lead to the end of the game. In the final minute, Robitaille confirmed our win with a goal into an empty net. We won 5-3, and the series was tied 1-1.

We needed to win at least one game in Washington. But we didn't have a chance. We actually lost twice 6-2. The Capitals defense was perfect. They didn't allow us a single goal opportunity. And all they did was crank out goals. Tommy Barrasso played for the first time after his injury, but it didn't help. In contrast to the first game, it was at least tied for a while. In the seventeenth minute, I tied the score at 2-2, and it looked like we might be able to break out somehow. But in the third period, the Capitals clobbered us.

They played very tough, and constantly blew us away. In no way did they make a secret of the fact that they wanted to destroy us. The loudmouth Rob Pearson came up to me and said, "We're gonna pound your head on the boards the entire game." I replied, "Good. That's the way I like it." Ripping into each other like that is completely normal. Joe Reekie tripped me at the blue line, and I flew two yards in the air. I was glad when I landed. I skated up to him extremely angry and in a threatening voice said, "Just wait until someone does that to you." Reekie is over six feet four and, in order to scare me, said, "Oh, I can't wait." I even got into a

*All these shots come right after reaching my greatest individual
achievement — victory in Canadian point-scoring.*

fight with Michal Pivonka. He jabbed me in the leg with his stick, and I was livid. After the game, Michal told me he didn't do it on purpose. At the time I was so furious with him I chased him down the ice. When I caught up to him, I poked him a few times with my stick. Michal turned around and said, "Relax, youngster."

The worst was that we lost so easily and at the same time felt that we were the better team. The mood of the team was totally different than it had been the previous year. This time we really wanted to win, and I also think we had a good crew. Before the second game, I took everyone out to dinner to celebrate the Art Ross Trophy. It was a good opportunity for us all to go somewhere and talk about everything. It was a lot of fun, even though Len Barrie ended up in a fine mess.

When we're on the road, we often act like little kids, but we have one favorite childish ritual. When we're all around one table for dinner, a victim — usually a rookie chosen beforehand — gets a task. He has to pour ketchup on a veteran player's shoes. Naturally this happens under the table. When the ketchup has been poured, we start clinking our spoons on our glasses. This is a signal for everyone to look at his shoes. Whoever has the ketchup on his shoes becomes furious, but he has no idea who the culprit is, so he can only swear and threaten. This time we decided to roast Len Barrie. Lenny poured ketchup on Kevin Stevens's shoes. Kevin doesn't like this kind of joke. He's a great guy, but he's got a temper. We knew that if he caught the culprit, he'd probably break his face. And the moment Lenny finished pouring we started clinking. Kevin looked under the table and saw ketchup all over his shoes. And then the dance began. Kevin chased Lenny around the table. When he caught him, first he poured water over his head and then Coke. Of course, Kevin knew that we were just kidding around, but he wanted to make Lenny pay. We were falling out of our seats with laughter while poor Lenny got drenched.

We were all getting along well together, and we were sad that the series was ending. I was probably the saddest. Everyone expected me to carry the flag and turn the series around. But I couldn't. Even before Game Two, I felt the flu coming on, and I did not have my usual strength. The night before Game One in Washington, I woke up completely soaked with sweat and listened with alarm to the way my heart was beating. It was as if it wanted to jump out of my body. I was so weak I could barely make it to the bathroom. I was supposed to play hockey in this condition. Not only that, I was supposed to win the games for us. I felt horrible. I felt like the pilot of a plane heading into a nosedive with all the passengers expecting me to do something, to press a button or turn a switch so that we'd all be saved — but I didn't have the strength to do it.

Fortunately the flu went away, and I slowly began to feel better. I only hoped it wasn't too late. We absolutely had to win Game Five at the Civic Arena. After that, we had a game in Washington and one more at home. I wouldn't say it seemed unlikely. It seemed impossible.

We were losing the series 3-1 and Game Five 2-0. Halfway through the third period, Hunter was the first to drive the puck in front of the goal. He scored their first goal without difficulty. A little later, Calle Johansson shot it past Kenny Wregget from a long distance. Things looked bad. The stadium was silent, and it looked like the end — particularly when the referee sent Rusty Fitzgerald to the penalty box for high-sticking. But they didn't get a third goal. We rose from the dead.

I think that was the decisive moment of the entire series — not because I played the main role, but because it literally turned the entire game around. The Capitals never recovered from the shock. The shadow of the huge opportunities blown haunted them throughout the next two games.

The Washington players attempted to recover the period by propelling the puck around the rink. Kjell stole the puck and sent it halfway down the boards. At this moment, I broke away, and at the same time, Ronnie Francis sent me the puck by ricocheting it off the boards. I tore toward one of the Capitals' defensemen. Actually, he wasn't a back, but Joe Juneau playing defense. Juneau is an outstanding skater, and if he were to skate with me, it'd be a close race. Juneau was already waiting for me at the blue line. Then he made the right decision — he reversed and took off.

At the moment I was skating at him, I was 100 percent certain I would do a fake. I sensed that Juneau wouldn't block me, but that he would try to keep up with me to the end. I had to be faster than him. I turned from the right toward center, and the instant I got to him, I acted as if I was going to turn to the left and Juneau took off in that direction. In a split second I changed direction and with a loop in the opposite direction, I flipped the puck past his skates to the right. Because I was going fast, I was out of his reach in a flash. The only barrier left was Carey. I also indicated to him that I would loop to the left. Carey ate it up. He positioned himself in the direction of my first loop, so all I had to do was hit the empty part of the net with a backhand. I did it, and the stadium went crazy.

When I think back on it, it's possible that my method of getting the goal was more important than the goal itself. I think there's a difference between shooting from the blue line and skating from goal to goal, sending the puck to the other side and shooting it into the net. I had managed to do exactly what I wanted, and we found ourselves riding a bolt of lightning. We started believing in ourselves. This goal provided a big psychological boost, and in the locker room, we all shouted at each other that now we had to charge at them.

And we really did charge at them. In the sixth minute, Kevin Stevens tied the score and the game turned around. Hunter put the Capitals back in the lead, but at the end of the period, Kevin succeeded in tying up the score again.

It was an emotionally-charged game. Peter Bondra snared a goal to put them in the lead again, and then my second moment arrived. This time luck helped me.

Johansson tried to clear the puck from his own third of the rink with the help of the Plexiglas. He simply whacked it, thinking that the puck would wind up somewhere in the center. But that's not what happened. For some inexplicable reason, the puck bounced back. Maybe Johansson caught the wall where the Plexiglas is stiff. I can't explain it any other way. In any case, I didn't think about it too much at the moment. The puck came right to my stick, and I found myself completely alone in front of Carey.

I faked another backhand, but immediately changed direction and slapped the puck with a forehand into the open part of the net. I tied it up 4-4. I knew the deciding factor would be strength: who had the most. It looked as if it was the visiting team. Bondra sunk another goal for the Capitals, but Kevin Stevens tied it again in the twelfth minute, and the game went into overtime.

The spectators went wild. They saw us fighting tooth and nail for our lives and wanted to help out. We needed them as much as we needed luck.

But luck usually sides with the brave, and the brave one was Francois Leroux. Frankie is a real giant. He's over six feet six and is there for the dirty work. His job is to stop the opposing team's offense and move the puck to safety. He never gets involved in offense. I only saw him once on the offensive, and that was in this overtime.

Somehow the puck was bouncing between the Capitals' blue and red lines when Leroux got to it. No one knew how he got there. Frank grabbed the puck and being so energized, he took off along the boards toward Washington's net. He avoided a body check and kept going. At this moment, all of us on the bench stood up and started screaming for our lives, "Frankie, where are you going? Go back! Shoot it and run back!" Fortunately, Frankie didn't shoot it. He took the puck to the back wall, lifted his head and sent it right in front of the net. Luc Robitaille skated up to it. Luc is an absolutely fantastic shooter. He's got golden hands. At that moment, I'd have sworn to it. Luc stuck his stick out at Frankie's pass and shot it right in a corner of Carey's net. It was a goal!

We jumped off the bench and clamored over to Luc and Frankie. "Excellent, Frankie. That's fantastic! You saved us!" we all shouted. Frankie was beaming with joy. Andy Warhol once said that everyone has fifteen minutes of fame, and those were Frankie Leroux's fifteen minutes. We won 6-5 and felt that we'd win in Washington, too.

We were on a roll. The Capitals had lost their big chance, and you could see they were suffering. They kept playing hard, but suddenly we were moving up.

In Washington the game was over after ten minutes. At the forty-two-second mark, Robitaille scored. In the fifth minute, I snatched the puck from Sylvain Cote, skated the entire rink and got it past Carey with a fake. We got our third goal on a power play. We were playing five on three when Murph caught me right by the net. The goalie was lying at my feet, so all I had to do was lift it over him into

*Direct proof that not even
Michal Pivonka from
Kladno helps me out.*

*Joy from the goal that
turned around the series
against Washington.*

the empty net. Shortly after that, Robitaille collected our fourth goal. We did what we wanted to with them, and the Capitals tried their best to kill us. I preferred to stay away from the boards, and Eddie Johnston decided it'd be better to pull me out the game for the third period. We were leading 7-0. We were already calling each other names. The real master in this area is Ulf .

Ulf doesn't leave anybody alone and makes fun of everyone. When we played the Capitals in one of the last games of the season and lost 2-1 at home, their biggest tough guy, Craig Berube, who the Capitals call "Chief," came to the bench and told his teammates: "Now we've gotta play smart!" Ulf heard this and said to Berube: "They can, but you can't. I don't know how you're ever gonna be able to play smart, Chief!" Even though we lost, we fell off the bench with laughter.

The Capitals got a goal in the second to last minute of the game. It was Keith Jones who scored it, one of their fighters. Jones is always laughing and is kind of a nice guy. This time he was beaming from ear to ear because of his symbolic goal. Ulf said to him, "What are you so happy about? It's about time!"

Sometimes I exchange words with Jones on the ice. Once we had someone in the penalty box and were getting ready to play against their power play. The Capitals sent a complete line of five on the ice, and Jones was right in front of me before the face-off. I looked at him and said teasingly, "What are you doing here? Your team is on the power play!" Jones started laughing and said to me, "But I'm a power-play specialist!"

In order to miraculously make it to the second round, we still had to win at home in the Civic Arena. We took control of the game early. In the second minute, I avenged myself on the Washington players for all their injustices against me. The puck shot off toward the center line at the same time Mark Tinordi skated into me. I caught him and stuck my stick in the path of the other defenseman, Johansson. At this moment another Capitals' wing appeared, and I grabbed him by the uniform. I single-handedly got rid of three Capitals! This cleared space for the defenseman, Norm Maciver. Suddenly he was completely free. He made it all the way to Carey and gave him a fake. We were in the lead right at the beginning of the game, which calmed us down. Ronnie Francis scored our second goal at the end of the period. Even though the visitors kept pushing us and took thirty-three shots on Kenny in goal, we wouldn't let them take our victory away. A shot into an empty goal by Murray in the last minute of the period secured our lead. The game was in the bag.

I rank this series with Washington among our biggest successes. It's almost up there with the Stanley Cup. During the series, people had lost faith in us. They picked us apart on TV and made fun of us. Some people were even saying that we shouldn't even go to Washington, that we'd be better off saving the money on hotels and plane tickets. Still, we didn't give up and brought about a minor miracle. I was convinced that we were on the path to the Stanley Cup.

We still had the New Jersey Devils to contend with. The Devils may very well be the toughest team in the entire NHL. They have an outstanding defense. Scott Stevens is one of the best defensemen in the NHL. Scott Niedermayer is also outstanding, and there are others, too. The strength of the Devils is not in individuals, but in the collective team. Coach Lemaire created a system which in hockey we call a trap. The idea is that practically the entire team is on defense. That way the center zone is completely closed off, and the opposing team has great difficulty in getting past their blue line. If you can't break through, it's very hard to shoot at the net. And if you don't shoot, you can't score. If you can't score, you can't win.

It's very simple, but it works — at least for the Devils. The defensemen placed themselves along the Devils' blue line and the offensive players attacked. All of a sudden, all the players were lined up and there wasn't any way to get through with the puck. That way the Devils halted the game at the red line. It was also interesting how they shifted to the attack. It was like lightning. Suddenly it was two on one, and the Devils usually transformed their chances into goals. Such a system requires concentration and reliability. The Devils game often looked like it was mostly geared toward destruction, but it worked.

The most unpleasant Devil was Claude Lemieux. He usually strikes when you least expect it. The game is being played somewhere else on the rink, and suddenly someone hits you. You turn around and there's Lemieux looking elsewhere.

They say that when he started in the NHL, he was unbearable. He constantly fought, provoked people and poked and stabbed with his stick behind the back of the referee. He wasn't even very well liked by his teammates. He was always complaining. The food was bad; his gear wet; the bus was too cold or too hot. He was always whining about something. Recently he's supposedly been starting to change a bit.

I often got into it with Lemieux. He used to hit me without even thinking. Now he's not so free and easy about doing this, but once in a while, he'll jab me with stick and take off. Sometimes we insult each other. Once he said to me, "I was watching a news report about the hockey game with my son, and he asked me, 'Daddy, why do you play against girls? That's a girl.' He was pointing at you." I said, "Lemieux, you're full of it. You're so stupid you couldn't even have kids."

Despite his nastiness, Lemieux is an excellent hockey player. He's fast, smart and has a great shot. In the playoffs he was the best offensive weapon the Devils had. We had no illusions about Lemieux's talent.

Another great Devil is their goalie Martin Brodeaur. It's impossible to get a goal past him. I don't know how he does it, but he's always right where he should be. He spends a lot of time at the goal, so you can't fake him. He's also extremely quick. I am convinced that if the Devils didn't have Brodeaur, they'd have never made it so far.

Thanking our fans after the victorious series against Washington in 1995.

Another important player on the Devils is their captain, Scott Stevens. He's as sharp as a knife, always in the right position and a great shot. He's really the leading personality on the team. He's no giant, but he can easily go at it with Lindros, who's a head taller than he is.

And we can't forget Robert Holik. Along with Mike Peluso and Randy McKay, he's part of the so-called checking line. This trio's main goal is the destruction of the opposing team's offense. But they didn't just stop the most dangerous opposing players, they also scored the key goals. Bobby and I aren't in especially close contact, but we know about each other. I was really tickled by what he said at the end of the season. In an interview with a group of American journalists, Robert said that I'm an excellent player and that he really hoped that I'd won the overall points race. He even added, "I'm glad that one day I'll be able to tell my grandchildren that I played with Jaromir Jagr."

The Devils were moving invincibly toward the Stanley Cup, and we were the first ones to get caught in their trap.

We were already holding on by a thread in Game One at the Civic Arena, but we survived. Halfway through the first period, Stephane Richer put the Devils on the scoreboard. In the second period, Ronnie Francis tied it up. At the beginning of the third period, I put us ahead with a goal during a power play. But then Lemieux cut through our defense like a knife, tying up the score again. Fortunately, luck was on our side. The last minute of the game was approaching when Murph passed the puck from the red line to Robitaille, who faked his way past Brodeaur and netted us our third goal. We really needed that victory. We were tired out after our series with the Capitals and didn't play well. It turned out this was the last time we were to rejoice in the series.

We still had a chance in Game Two. We were losing 2-1 two minutes before the end of the game when one of the Devils' defensemen knocked my shot into the net. But we still lost. Half a minute before the finish, Stevens skated up to our goal and shot. Kenny deflected the puck, but Stevens shot it right back into the net.

We were already being upset. In New Jersey, we lost both games, the first one 5-1 and the second one 2-1 in overtime. We just couldn't create any scoring opportunities. The Devils' defense was impenetrable.

Once again we were losing the series 3-1, only this time we didn't manage to turn the tables. We just didn't have the strength. In the fifth game we took the lead when Norm Maciver shot through the wall of bodies in front of Brodeaur from the blue line to score, but Robert Holik managed to tie the game before the end of the period during a power play. Holik got the puck from the right side and fired it from the circle. The puck slipped under Wregget into the net and the score was 1-1.

Then they got two more goals, and Lemieux tipped the puck into an empty net for the fourth goal. We lost and were out of the playoffs.

The Devils were the better team, and our only satisfaction is that they ultimately won the Stanley Cup. Even if the outcome of the series looked inevitable, everything could have turned out differently if we hadn't let in the goal right before the end of the second game — or at the least we'd have lost in overtime. It was the physical exhaustion that got us — that and Brodeaur. But we weren't the only ones he stopped. Once again, it became clear just how important it is for a team to have a great goalie. Not that Kenny tended goal badly. On the contrary. Brodeaur, however, was not just good — he was phenomenal.

Being eliminated from the playoffs was tough, but we just didn't have what it takes. At the time, we had fifteen players over thirty on the team, and you could really feel it in the series. The short season definitely helped us. Who knows what it would have been like in the playoffs if we'd have had to play that many more games.

Before I flew home, I had dinner with the owner of the team, Howard Baldwin. We talked for almost two hours. The problem was that over five years, we hadn't built up the team. Most of all, we lacked a defenseman who could get hold of the puck and pass it up. The team means a lot to Howard. He's at just about every game and often comes to visit us in the locker room. He built a new practice facility for us. He really wants us to add to the other two Stanley Cups. There's a number of good people in Pittsburgh running the organization: Thomas Ruta, his brother Nick and Cindy Himes in public relations. I believed that the following season the efforts of the management and players would once again bear fruit. The fans deserve at least to see us in the Stanley Cup finals.

After the last game with New Jersey, a black cloud hung over the locker room. I showered, signed some autographs for the fans and went home with my parents. Later, Lenny Barrie called to say they were going out — to say farewell to the season. So we all went out. It was the last time this group was together. The era of these particular Penguins was over. I wouldn't be seeing some of these teammates the next season. If I did, they'd be in different uniforms.

The Year of the Rat

The 1995-96 season began long before training camp. We were looking forward to it the moment we found out that Mario Lemieux would put on the Penguins' jersey once again.

I had known that Mario would play with us since June. At that time, somebody from the team called me up at home to say that Mario would definitely be playing. I was very happy to hear the news. Mario's the best hockey player in the world, and with him in the lineup our chances of winning the Stanley Cup improve enormously. I was also looking forward to seeing how we would play together.

Mario came to camp in great physical shape. It was obvious that he had been training very hard. I think that his trainer, Tommy Plasko, helped him a great deal (Tommy is called "Guru" because he's totally bald). He understands the human body perfectly, he knows what parts of it Mario needs to work on in order to excel, and after exercise, Guru knows to loosen Mario up with a thorough massage. Guru whipped Mario into shape, and I could only widen my eyes in astonishment when I saw Mario in camp. I've never seen him train so hard. Mario was almost always in the weight room. He lifted, rode the bike, and after two months of training, it was impossible to tell that he had missed an entire season. It was incredible.

It's hard for me to say whether Mario was the same player upon his return as when he left. Only he can answer that question. But Mario's hockey artistry remains intact — the quick hands, the instincts.

Both during the course of the season and in the playoffs, Mario would say that he felt a hair slower. But I don't think he's lost a step. Perhaps, the other players were a hair faster. This season the level of play was a notch higher. Players are getting better and better because they're putting more of an emphasis on training. But Mario would be able to make up for that lost year with something else. He's brilliant at knowing how to make use of his teammates, in that he's peerless.

This year I had the feeling that I probably wouldn't regain the scoring title if Mario was going to play. But somehow it didn't disappoint me; in fact to the contrary — it made me happy. I wanted his game up to snuff.

We're too far apart age-wise to be buddies. Off the ice Mario hangs out more with Ronnie, Barrasso and other players closer to his age. But despite that, we get along extremely well. I think Mario knows how much I appreciate him being on the team.

Before the season, sometimes Mario and I would even tease each other. Mario told me it would only take him sixty games to score more points than me. He was almost right.

At the end of the lockout season, Ulf Samuelsson joked that as an opponent he'd give me a licking. Maybe he already knew he was leaving Pittsburgh. Before the season, Ulf and Luc Robitaille were traded to New York for Sergei Zubov and Petr Nedved. Zubov and Nedved were big contributors to our team.

Zubie is a huge talent. He's definitely one of the best defensemen in the entire NHL. He has great peripheral vision, he makes a pinpoint pass and he's especially dangerous on the power play. But precisely because of those things, Zubie and Mario got in each other's way sometimes.

In New York, Zubie was used to dictating the play. He was the key guy on the power play. He'd hold the puck, wait until everyone spread out and then pass it. But in Pittsburgh, it's Mario who controls the play. On the ice, he's the main guy who makes all the decisions. Consequently, Zubov and Mario's on-ice personalities clashed. It wasn't that friction arose between them, but several times Mario told Zubie not to hog the puck. Although Zubie isn't the confrontational type and usually listened to Mario, sometimes he held onto the puck a little too long taking us out of our rhythm. In the worst case scenario, Zubie turned the puck over. On the other hand, I think Mario was very happy to have Zubie on the team because a lot of the goals Mario scored came off Zubie's slick passes.

Zubie's style suits me perfectly. Even if he, sometimes, holds onto the puck too long and might even lose it, he'll come right back and make incredible passes. If we hadn't had him on our team this past season, we never would have gone as far as we did in the playoffs.

I played a role in the arrival of Petr Nedved. At least I think I did. When the Penguins traded Martin Straka to Ottawa, it ticked me off not only because we were good friends, but also because I lost a fellow countryman when he left. And that really bothered me greatly. From that moment I kept pestering Craig Patrick to bring in another Czech. It made Craig uneasy, but I wouldn't let up. Finally, I made Craig angry in Toronto at the NHL awards ceremony. He seemed angry with me, but I kept at him. And then the trade came. Craig probably told himself he'd deal for a Czech just to shut me up and get some peace. But who knows. I did have a feeling something would happen though. And it did. Two weeks before the trade was made Craig called me up and asked me about Petr: How well did I know him, what kind of player was he, what kind of character did he have? In short, Craig wanted to know everything there was to know about Petr. At that time, Craig apparently had made his mind up to bring him aboard.

Me and my idol Mario lemieux, currently the greatest hockey player in the world.

Petr has great ability, but his game can be undermined on a team that does not utilize his skill to the fullest extent. In New York, they wanted him to play a style he either couldn't or wouldn't play. They tried to change his game and it was a mistake. They wanted Petr to crash the net and slam players on the boards, and when he wasn't very good at it, they gave him less and less ice time. In my opinion, it was sheer stupidity on New York's part. After all, if you want a player on your team, it's for what he can already do. You don't want to force him to play a style that diminishes his strengths and is unworthy of his talent. In Vancouver, they let Petr play his game and he scored almost forty goals in the 1992-93 season. But in New York, they wanted something completely different from him. And they were disappointed with him when they couldn't make him into somebody else.

In Pittsburgh the approach was totally different, and it paid off. Petr was allowed to play his game, and he showed us what he is capable of.

The most impressive thing about Petr is his great footwork. Our offensive power improved dramatically with his arrival. For most of the season I played on a line with Petr and Ronnie, and we worked great together. Ronnie plays more from the end boards. He's especially good at blocking the defender behind the net, allowing me to get to the puck. At that point, I need someone quick to play it to. If he isn't quick enough, it's a disadvantage because either I have to wait for him or else I have no other option but to go it alone. But Petr is real quick, and he gets to me fast; that's why we've scored so many goals together. Another of Petr's strengths is his wrist shot. Most of the time he aims high, and it's very difficult for the goalie to pick up.

Petr and I have actually known each other since the year we were drafted, but we weren't good friends then. Still we talked almost every time that I played in New York. When Petr got traded to us, he lived at my place for a while; that's when we became better friends. Finally, I have a Czech on the team again, and he's on the same wavelength as me both on and off the ice.

When I look back on it, I think it was a good trade. True, we lost an excellent defenseman in Ulf, but we gained two players in Petr and Zubie who had a whole lot to do with our winning season.

Last year turned into boys' night out in Pittsburgh. All these young guys came aboard, and all of a sudden I had friends to hang out with in the evenings. Before their arrival, I was always the youngest player on the Penguins, but now there are guys my own age to goof around with. Besides Petr, I hang out mostly with Chris Wells, Richard Park, Magnet (Joe Dziedzic), Bryan Smolinksi and Glen Murray.

This season was my most successful of all, and in it I broke a number of records.

It began on February 23 against Hartford. Before the game Mario and I had the same number of goals — forty-eight. In the eighth minute of the game Mario scored his forty-ninth goal, even though we were losing 2-1 after the first period.

In the second period, Naslund evened the score, and right afterward, I scored our third goal. We were up 3-2. With my goal I caught up to Mario, and we needed only one goal each to reach the coveted fifty-goal mark.

Right after I scored, Mario leaned toward me on the bench and said: "Hey man, let's make a bet. For champagne. Whoever gets his fiftieth first."

Mario beat me by three minutes and forty-six seconds. At the start of the third period, the other team went ahead, but Mario evened it up in the sixth minute. In the tenth minute I scored the winning goal, but I had already lost the bet. However, I became the first Czech player to score fifty goals in a season, and in any case there's no way that Mario's winning the bet could disappoint me. I still haven't bought him his champagne, though.

On February 28 we played in Florida. Several games before that I knew that I would have the chance to set the record for most points scored by a European in a single NHL season.

The standing record of 139 points was held by Peter Stastny who recorded the feat in the 1981-82 season while playing for the Quebec Nordiques. During his era, Stastny, who emigrated across the Atlantic with his brothers Marian and Anton, was one of the NHL's best players.

I tied his record in a game against St. Louis on a night when Mario once again distanced himself from me in our battle to win the scoring race. Before the St. Louis game, I had scored three points against the Rangers in New York, and I was only one point behind Mario. But Mario would rack up five goals and two assists against St. Louis, leaving me in the dust. That was the beginning of the end for our friendly competition concerning the scoring title.

But in Florida I scored my sixtieth goal of the season and broke Peter Stastny's record upon reaching 140 points. Now, only Mike Bossy stood in my way.

I broke his assist record for a right wing — eighty-five — in Ottawa. A few days later, in Boston I became the right wing with the greatest number of points ever in a single season. In the second period of the final game of the regular season, I passed the puck to Mario for his sixty-ninth goal and thus recorded 149 points. Mike Bossy's record was history. When I returned to the bench, my teammates congratulated me — Mario, Petr, Ronnie, the trainers, and after the game, even the journalists.

The season ended well for me. I had scored sixty-two goals and eighty-seven assists. My 149 points put me in second place behind Mario, who ended up with twelve more points than me. It was also great to receive the 1995 Dapper Dan Award as best sportsman in the state of Pennsylvania. I still don't think I realize just how significant that award really is. I am very honored to have been chosen.

Until the last moment it was uncertain who we would face in the playoffs. For a long time it looked like it would be the defending Stanley Cup champion New

Jersey Devils. But when they didn't even end up making it, the first round was decided in favor of our old friends — the Washington Capitals.

They worried me, but I didn't think they'd be as difficult an opponent as in the previous year. Brendan Witt, Steve Konowalchuk and Joe Reekie were out with injuries, and Keith Jones didn't play until Game Five. In addition, this year we had Mario on our side, so we didn't expect the Capitals to give us a run for our money.

But a cold shock of reality awaited us in the very first game, even though it started off so promisingly. Petr Nedved scored two goals in three minutes and that settled us down. Unfortunately, Peter Bondra, a constant thorn in our side, narrowed the lead right before the end of the first period. At the start of the second period, Kaminski did something stupid and was sent to the penalty box. Ronnie Francis capitalized on the power play, burying a puck behind Jim Carey. Then Tomas Sandstrom made the score 4-1, and it seemed like we had them in the bag. Only we made the mistake of keeping on the offensive. I think that we were worked up by the media. If you don't score a single point for several games in a row, they start writing in the papers that you're playing badly, that you're struggling and in a slump. Therefore, despite the score, we kept on attacking, instead of being content with the lead and defending it. The warning lights were flashing. First Sylvain Cote and, toward the end of the period, Todd Krygier each scored for the Capitals. All of a sudden, we didn't know what style to play. Because we kept attacking, Washington kept getting odd-man breaks. Sergei Gonchar tied the score at the halfway mark of the final period, then Krygier scored another goal against us and, finally, Michal Pivonka's shot into an empty net put us out of our misery. We had gotten what was coming to us.

In the second game, the same thing happened all over again. Again we took an early lead and again we were unable to bring the game to a successful conclusion. The Capitals were able to close the gap on our two-goal lead. History was repeating itself. We definitely played better than in the first game. We had chances to score but Olaf Kolzig, who replaced Carey in the first game and had gotten the nod in the second game, was spectacular. It's hard to get the puck past Kolzig, especially because of his size advantage.

The decisive moment came at the halfway mark of the third period. In a classic two-on-one rush, Pivonka came up from the left side and faked a pass to the right, smartly waiting for Zubov to come at him. But Sergei held his position, and it looked as if Pivonka would have to shoot. But Pivonka demonstrated great peripheral vision, and sensing Bondra was coming up behind him, Pivonka sent him a timely pass. Although Bondra's first shot was blocked, he still had enough time to pick the puck up along the backboards, come around front and shoot it past Barrasso. Washington took the lead.

We still had hope with 15:03 left on the game clock. Pivonka got four minutes for a high stick and we had a power play. However, the Capitals sacrificed their bodies like martyrs. They hammered us, they dove to block shots and, tenaciously, defended the goal. In the final minute, Pivonka sealed our defeat, again putting the puck into an empty goal.

It was beginning to look pretty bleak for us. We went to Washington knowing that if we lost once there, which at the time seemed quite possible, we would be in a critical situation.

Despite everything I never stopped having faith. Up until then, Washington had outplayed us, exhibiting a fighting spirit and a greater thirst to win than we had. On the other hand, we definitely could have won both games had we played smarter. Before the games in Washington, one thing was clear — if we didn't change our system and play defense, we would have little chance of winning the series.

In the opening two games, I went through a crisis. It wasn't clicking for me, and I had problems with my skates. Whoever hasn't played hockey can't understand how important such details like skates and sticks can be. I'd had the same pair of skates for the whole season, and by the playoffs they were completely worn out. And now I had to make a decision: either keep playing in the old pair I was used to, but which I hadn't been able to sharpen for a long time (it felt like I was skating on plastic), or get new skates and wait several games until they were properly broken in. You can't imagine how big a difference there is between types of skates. For example, Bauers are completely different than CCM's; they're set at a different angle. CCM's are better for forwards because their angle leans forward, and it drives you straight ahead. They're more stable. I was still waiting for the new skates and started playing in them only during our series with the Rangers. I have Bauers with a specially-raised heel, so they're angled like CCM's, and they suit me perfectly.

Before the first game in Washington, we told ourselves that we needed to get the lead early and then close them down. Our strategy worked perfectly.

In the ninth minute of the first period, I took the puck from Mike Eagles in the neutral zone, crossed the blue line and dropped it behind me for Mario. He stepped over the blue line, passed it to the other side and an approaching Ronnie Francis scored our first goal. By the end of the first period, Glen Murray had opened the lead to 2-0, and we were playing better.

Mario orchestrated everything. He advised us when to come up and how to attack the goal. He constantly rallied us, and above all he set an example for us in the game. At the halfway mark of the second period, Dave Roche increased our lead, and Kevin Miller scored our fourth goal soon afterward. Mario assisted on all four goals. At that point in the game, the outcome was clear, and Cote's goal was incidental. In the end we won 4-1, despite our nineteen shots on a shaky Carey compared to the thirty-one shots Barrasso had faced.

Wayne Gretzky in his older age is still excellent.

We had taken our first step, but we needed another win. When we rode from the hotel to US Air Arena for Game Four, it never occurred to me that we would be playing the equivalent of more than two games in a single night. It was a first for me.

At the beginning of the game, things didn't look good for us. In the first period, Pivonka scored a goal for the home team to give Washington the lead. At the halfway mark of the second period, Bondra increased the Capitals' lead to 2-0, and the clouds started gathering over our heads. However, before the end of the first period we saw a ray of hope. We were playing short-handed, and Dale Hunter and Frankie Leroux were cozying up in front of our goal. Francis got the puck at center ice and we came at them two-on-two. I raced toward the Washington goal along the right wing and was going faster than Sergei Gonchar, who was skating backward. I was waiting for Ronnie to deliver the puck, and he sent me a prompt pass which gave me just enough time to aim. I shot it past Kolzig's stick side into the bottom-right corner. I wasn't very confident since I hadn't scored a goal in about six games in a row. After I put the puck in, I skated around the net and looked at the referee to make sure he hadn't blown the play dead because of the pushing and shoving in front of the net. Luckily, he hadn't, and so we had cut the Capitals' lead in half at 2-1.

A moment later, something gave us even more incentive. Krygier cross-checked and then speared Mario. Frustrated by the Capitals' tactics, Mario could no longer turn the other cheek. He whacked Krygier with his stick and then went after him. And the referee ejected Mario for instigating a fight! We considered it a great injustice, and Dan Marouelli's ruling brought the team even closer together. In the locker room we rallied each other and felt we could still turn the game around even with Mario lost to us for the game.

Midway through the third period, Petr Nedved evened the score with his renowned wrist shot, bringing us back into the game. Nobody scored for the rest of the period and overtime loomed. Surprisingly, I felt fine physically; I had gotten a lot of ice time during regulation, but I was raring to go.

At the outset of the first overtime, I got a scare. I was penalized two minutes for hooking, and I was shaking at the thought of the Capitals winning it on the power play. But mom, who was watching the game on TV in Pittsburgh, was taking it even worse than me and immediately called home to dad in the Czech Republic to tell him I'd been penalized. Mom was really afraid the Capitals would score on us. Luckily, our defense won out.

At the beginning of the second overtime, Petr Nedved had a huge chance, breaking in alone on Kolzig, but the Washington goalie stoned him. In the sixteenth minute, the game and possibly the series hinged on Kenny Wregget, who had replaced Tom Barrasso in net when Barrasso had to leave because of back spasms. Marouelli actually called a penalty shot on a controversial play when he ruled that we had intentionally removed our net from its moorings. Kenny squared off against Joe Juneau.

The tension mounted in the building. Juneau pushed off from the red line and approached the goal with great speed. The ice was already bad by then, and it was obvious he would have to shoot. Kenny came out a little, stretched and caught the puck! We breathed a huge sigh of relief.

During the breaks between the overtimes, we were brought pizza in the locker room; some of us were starving. It's not surprising since on game days we eat lunch at about one o'clock and then for the most part we don't eat anything. Mario served the pizza in the locker room, but I didn't have any. Amazingly, I didn't feel hungry, and anyway I wasn't even in the locker room.

Since the lockers are small at the US Air Arena, I always go into a spare room to lie down and put up my legs so that they're higher up than my body. That's how I relax best. When I sit down, I feel like a sardine packed next to the other players on the bench, and then I get even more tired. So I always lie down next door to the locker room for the first ten minutes and then I join the others. At that time, the coaches usually come in and give us tactical advice; before that nothing is said. Everyone just relaxes. That's been my routine since the start of the playoffs.

In the locker room between overtimes, there was a strong fighting spirit although we were all really tired, but we believed in ourselves. Even though Mario had been ejected from the game, he walked around and rallied us. He spent most of his time with me. Maybe he thought that I would win the game. He coached me on how to play against Mark Tinordi, who continued to stay glued to me throughout the overtime. "You have to change speed on him," Mario said, "he's not able to react quick enough. Slow down and then take off fast." As the game went on, I began to gain more confidence. I started getting around Tinordi and because of it, I noticed that he was beginning to drop back.

Tinordi and I were an inseparable pair throughout the series, and once in a while we even exchanged words. One time I got a pass and immediately sent it over to Francis before Tinordi could come up on me. Somebody hooked Francis from behind, and the referee sent him off the ice. I went up to Tinordi and said, "See, you blew it again, you're always too slow!" Tinordi looked at me, and instead of responding aggressively replied with a totally serious expression on his face, "But it wasn't my fault, I had nothing to do with it!" I burst out laughing.

When it seemed as if the game would never end and they'd be serving us breakfast in the locker room, the decisive moment came. Tinordi blocked Petr's first shot, but his subsequent wrist shot went through a maze of players, up over Kolzig's shoulder and into the net! I didn't even have the strength to raise my arms. We jumped on Petr although we still couldn't believe we'd won it. It was less than a minute before the end of the fourth overtime. The arena clock showed the time of day: 2:15 A.M.

We didn't get home to Pittsburgh until shortly before daybreak. I had a message from mom on the table asking me when I wanted to wake up. That's our routine. If I come back late and she's already sleeping, I leave a note telling her when I want to get up for practice. I definitely wouldn't wake up on time on my own. But this time I didn't have a single thought about waking up, and beneath mom's question I wrote, "Never, I'm dead."

The next day I couldn't even move. But I knew that the lactic acid remaining in my muscles was causing the tired feeling, and the best way to remove it was by exercising. So I went out to shoot some baskets behind the house and also to do a little cycling.

In Washington they wrote in the newspapers that we had celebrated as if we had won the Stanley Cup, but I knew the series was over. I was firmly convinced we would win the next two games.

In the fifth game we were focused from the very beginning, and we soon took the lead on a goal by Mario. Then we scored a pair of slightly lucky goals and it was all over. At the end of the game, I also scored a fluke goal. I was coming up along the right wing and sent the puck in front of the net. Only I sent it too close to the goal, and it looked like Kolzig would get to the puck. But someone in front of the net changed the puck's direction, and it slipped by Kolzig into the net. Not a very pretty goal, but it counted. We won 4-1 and were on our way back to Washington. This time we arrived under completely different circumstances; we were on top and confident. We also had a better start in Game Six.

In only the second minute of the first period, Zubov found Mario beautifully on the power play for our first goal. A while later during another power play, Mario held onto the puck, I skated out from behind the net, and Mario sent me a perfectly timed pass. I came out in front of Kolzig and put the puck between his legs and into the net. A moment later, Ronnie scored our third goal and it was more or less over.

The home team, however, continued to battle, and at the start of the final period Gonchar narrowed our lead to 3-2, but we held on until the end and put a tough hurdle behind us as we finished off the Capitals.

After the first two games of the series, it hadn't looked good for us, but we began to play better defensively, to fight harder and to play smarter. The Rangers were next.

We were confident, but on the other hand, we knew the Rangers were an experienced team that had managed to close out the Canadiens after trailing them two games to none. We had a good chance against the Rangers if we played well defensively and used our quickness. The Rangers' style suited us much better than the strong defensive style of Washington. We knew that Messier and Company opened it up more, and we were relying on odd-man breaks, especially since their defensemen weren't very fast.

An intriguing subplot during the Rangers' series was that two of our key players, Sergei Zubov and Petr Nedved, had been traded to us by New York before the start of the season. We'd be facing our old friends Ulf Samuelsson and Luc Robitaille, and for a change, Ulf would try to shut us down.

I won't reveal any dark secrets when I say that I respect Ulf and that his style works well against me. I've already said many times that I consider him to be the best defensive player in the world. It's very tough to play against him. He's got excellent footwork, and he's quick on his skates. When we skated backward in practice, nobody was as good at it as Ulf was. Also, he never falls for moves between the legs or short fakes. He always plays the body. He doesn't play the puck; he comes straight at you. It's really tough to get around him, and if you succeed, you can at least expect to be hit hard. Ulf isn't soft on anybody.

If he's mean on the ice, he's great off it. I still like him just as much as when we played together. After the first game of the series, Ulf and I ran into each other at a bar and talked a little. But we teased each other the entire series. Before the games in New York, Ulf told me, "You've got a lot to look forward to. We've got a plan in store for you." And I said to him, "Then you'll have to chase me around the whole rink. I'm in great shape!"

The first game at home began well. I scored the first goal off a power play on a pass by Mario. It wasn't a set play. I was across the ice from Mario and went to the front of the net before Mario got the puck to me. Mario also got credit for helping with the second goal.

I carried the puck to the left wing and picked up speed. Surprisingly enough, nobody paid attention to me, they were all pursuing Mario. Mario blocked off Beukeboom and all of a sudden I had an opening. I shot the puck across the goal and banked it in right off the post. Now we were up 2-0.

It seemed like everything was working in our favor. The Rangers narrowed the lead, but we scored another goal right afterward and again led by two goals. But Peter Sundstrom caught us napping, and a moment later, Sergeo Momesso evened the score. Shortly thereafter, my big moment came.

I had been on the ice for a long time, Kevin Miller gave me the puck behind the net, and I only wanted to get rid of it, especially since three Rangers were gearing up for me. One stood across from me, Bruce Driver came up to me and wanted to slam me against the boards and the third was coming up from the side. I stopped and all three missed me. I took back off, and all of a sudden, I had open ice in front of me. Driver was waiting for me at the blue line, but since I had picked up speed I got rid of him with a quick fake and waited for Brian Leetch to reach me.

Even before I deked Driver, I knew that Mario was coming up behind me on the left. It was impossible to miss him. He was shouting like a madman. I skated in

The back Joe Reekie mixed me up with his wife.

Battling for the puck with the captain of Boston, Ray Bourque, who still ranks among the best backs in the whole NHL.

with the puck toward the goal and kept Mike Richter and Leetch's attention centered on me. Leetch couldn't wait anymore and came at me. I made a little fake to the right and stopped. At the same time I sent the puck to Mario, who only had to get his stick on it. He had nothing but open net in front of him, and he buried it.

The second game was one of the worst we played all season. We thought that maybe the Rangers would just self-destruct. We began halfheartedly, our defense was playing poorly and we created few opportunities. After the first period we were losing on goals by Robitaille and Bill Berg, and when at the start of the third period Alexei Kovalev made it 3-0, we finally began to realize we were on the verge of losing the home ice advantage. After two periods it was a blowout. The Rangers were ahead 5-1, but at least we narrowed the lead. First Smolinski scored on a spin-around move, and then it was my turn on the power play, and we began to hope. But we couldn't manage to score another goal. Jarri Kurri scored the Rangers' sixth goal into an empty net and the series was tied at one.

Madison Square Garden awaited us. We went there with one strategy. Get ahead quickly and then play cautious defensively.

We wanted to win badly, and perhaps Mario wanted it most of all. Even on the bus from the hotel to the arena, he came back to sit with us and went over the power play. He told us how we had to play it to produce more goals. Mario was convinced that in these games the power play would be the difference. We agreed that we needed to connect more with each other. If Mario was on one side and I was on the other, we shouldn't pass across the box because it would be too risky. We also shouldn't play the puck in a circle because in that formation we'd be standing still and it wouldn't be dynamic enough; even though sometimes we score goals that way, like in Game One against the Rangers. But Mario proposed that I should stay behind the net and come toward him, similar to the play we used when we scored an important goal in the first game in Washington.

Right before the game, E. J. must have had one-on-ones with all of us. The day before he had called Ronnie, Petr and me together, and for an hour, he explained what he wanted from our line for the third game. At the time we had no idea that we wouldn't be getting any ice time together. I don't know whether everyone was surprised or if Mario, alone, had guessed it, but E. J. switched us around right before the game. I played the entire first period with Mario. I was also double-shifted, so I was almost always out on the ice.

Mario and I have never played much together — once in a while at the beginning of my NHL career, and in later seasons occasionally on the power play, but otherwise never. We play well together, know each other instinctively, and can complement each other on the ice.

But I think it's better for the team if I'm on a different line. Mario can play with anybody and make him into a star. However, I contribute more to the team when

I play with Ronnie and Pete. Francis adjusts his game to accommodate me. He covers for me defensively, sets picks and creates room for me. Ronnie seems inconspicuous because he doesn't appear to excel. Instead, he tries to make me excel. But Francis does so many things well. He is an unselfish player who sacrifices himself for the good of the team.

Ronnie and I play exceptionally well together but sometimes it definitely helps to change it up for a while. Such a change is useful, and moreover, it surprises your opponent. And that was confirmed in the game against the Rangers. All of a sudden, Mario and I were on the ice together.

The home team didn't expect it. They were ready to stick Ulf on me and Messier was supposed to play against Mario. Furthermore, the Rangers had last line change, and they expected to have the advantage of matching lines. Only our coach switched everything and Colin Campbell, the Rangers' coach, was unable to react.

We flew past the Rangers right from the start and won the game in the first period. First Tomas Sandstrom hit a shot off the face of Ulf Samuelsson into the net. The goal was credited to Mario who was the closest Penguin to Sandstrom even though it didn't appear to touch Mario. Right after that, Chris Tamer found Mario beautifully and it was 2-0. And before the end of the period, we had banged in a third goal. The Rangers weren't moving the puck well. I picked it off in their zone with lots of time and room and passed it to Sandstrom who drilled it into the open part of the net.

But the Rangers still were able to prolong the suspense. At the start of the second period, the home team scored two quick goals, and we had to defend our lead until the end of the game. We pinned the puck behind the net and dumped it out. The tactic could have come back to haunt us, but we didn't give New York any dangerous chances, and Kenny was excellent in goal.

The start of the fourth game was also promising. Dziedzic carried the puck into the Rangers' zone and fired, it deflected off Smolinski in front of the net and ended up on my stick. I was at a wide angle from the net, nevertheless, I fired it immediately and hit the open goal. It was only the fifth minute of the game, and it was exactly the kind of start we needed.

Then Messier was waiting for me. He probably had determined he had to do something. He realized we were outplaying the Rangers and a lot was expected of him. He waited for me and hit me in the neck with a cross-check from behind. The puck was nowhere near us. He gave me a real wallop. I was lying on the ice for two minutes without being able to move my head. My teammates helped me to the bench, and I tried to pull myself together.

When I returned to the ice, a smiling Sergio Momesso came toward me and with feigned concern asked, "Did Mark hurt you? Should I call your mom?" That made

I'm the Montreal team's favorite. As they say, proof that hockey is no stroll in a rose garden.

me forget the pain a little, and I told him, "Not at all — I'm OK. But why don't you stay on the ice a little longer and help out our team?" Momesso didn't say anything back. Maybe he didn't know what to say.

At the start of the second period, Petr Nedved scored our second goal with a pretty wrist shot. But the Rangers still made a drama out of it when Graves cut the lead, and we went into a defensive shell for twenty minutes. But then Beukeboom made a huge mistake. He sent a cross-ice pass from his defensive zone; Murray perfectly intercepted it and was completely alone in front of Richter. He drilled the puck over Richter's glove into the net, and at that moment it was all over. At the end of the game, Mario scored our fourth goal into an empty net, and after the 4-1 victory, we returned to Pittsburgh for what turned out to be the last encounter of the series.

It was a historic game for me. I got my first playoff hat trick.

We were confident before the game. We knew that we couldn't lose and that it would be decided on our home turf who'd go on to the next round. Right away Mario scored our first goal from the wing, and at the start of the second period, I increased the lead to 2-0. Zubov brought the puck deftly up the right side and centered it to Mario. I had wanted to get off the ice for almost two minutes and had been practically dragging my legs behind me. When Mario got the puck, I was just crossing the blue line. If I'd had more strength, I probably would have already arrived at the goal. I had enough room ahead of me, so I sped up. I could sense that Mario knew I was approaching, and he sent the puck to me without hesitation. I came in alone on Richter and because I was a little to the right, I had to fake to the other side. I shifted the puck to my backhand and lifted it under the crossbar. It was there for the taking!

We were leading by two goals, but it wasn't over yet. Messier dented our lead, but Mario scored our third goal right after that. There was a sliver of space just big enough to fit a puck between the post and Richter. Mario found it perfectly. But the shootout continued. Momesso narrowed the score again, and a moment later, Peter Sundstrom tied it up. But then I had two of my biggest moments of the playoffs.

Petr Nedved won the face-off and sent it back to Neil Wilkinson, who fired right away. Richter knocked the puck down in front of the goal. Again Petr tried to shoot it, but his shot hit Richter and was deflected out — right in front of me. It was luck, but I also get some credit for following the puck. I was in the right place at the right time, and I didn't have any problem banging the puck into the exposed net. Before the end of the third period, I scored my third goal. I took off from center ice, reached the Rangers' zone and tried a slap shot because I knew Richter was screened. The arena erupted, and I realized I had my hat trick. Caps started raining onto the ice, until the entire surface turned into a garbage heap. The referee ended the second period even though thirteen seconds remained. They were tacked on to the final period.

Now we were fired up. Smolinksi scored our sixth goal and Mario added his third goal of the game to round out the scoring. We won 7-3 and the Eastern Conference finals awaited us.

However, our victory over the Rangers didn't come without a cost. In the final game we lost Ronnie. A shot from Adam Graves broke a small bone in Ronnie's instep, and he knew right away it was bad. I've already mentioned several times Ronnie's importance to me on the ice. He's indispensable to the team, and his absence wasn't only felt by the defense but also on the power play. Francis plays the left point and works the puck from there together with Zubie. Ronnie doesn't have a super shot, but he doesn't need it. His strength is his ability to make accurate, timely passes. And his experience. He's unflappable and doesn't lose his cool when his point is pressured. He has good instincts. He's not the type of player who goes to the net to bury the puck. We have other players who fulfill that role. Ronnie's value is his ability to work the puck down low, to set up the shot.

After the game when journalists asked me about the injury to Francis, I was really sad. I said that it was a big loss for us, and I meant it. We would sorely miss Ronnie.

The Eastern Conference finals. Florida. A very tough team. The Rangers' game suited us because they play a man-to-man defense, and we know how to exploit it. If you can get around your defender, all of a sudden you're free. Nobody else will come at you. But Florida plays a kind of zone defense, where they all help each other out. You fake out one Panther and there's another one on you. It takes a lot of commitment to play it, and it must be physically demanding because all five players must have a superb defensive game. But New Jersey won the Stanley Cup playing it, and Florida didn't do much worse with it this year. Florida's defense doesn't suit us well. We were already convinced of that from the series against Washington, which plays a similar defense.

Personally, I play better against teams that defend man-to-man, not zone. I always score a lot of points against teams like Buffalo or Boston who use man-to-man coverage. The same thing goes for the Rangers. That's why it never occurred to me that we could lose to them.

But against the Panthers' defense, it's tough. There's only one formula that exists. Good communication. When I have two players on me, somebody has to be open. And he has to reveal himself right away. Or shout. Everything's decided in the neutral zone. If each of us knows where the other is, the zone can be beaten.

Before the series against the Panthers, a great deal of bad blood resulted from a statement I made indicating I would rather play against Florida than Philadelphia. The Florida players even brought the newspaper clippings into the locker room and hung them up for motivation. However, I never had any intention of criticizing the quality of my opponents with that statement. But I'm still convinced that

Senator Martin came to say goodbye to the local girls — the trade was too fast.
Next to Martin stand Neckar and Bonk. All the way on the right is Michal Straka,
who played the 94-95 season in Cleveland.

Philadelphia would have given us an even tougher time of it. The Flyers' style doesn't suit us at all. We don't have physical hockey players. Philadelphia would have worn us down and then finished us off. We had played poorly against them in the regular season, and we've always had a lot of trouble beating them. And we'd never beat them without Francis.

Our line always plays against the Flyers' best, and we've always managed to handle Lindros and Company — mainly because of Ronnie. In five-on-five matchups, we always beat them, but without Ronnie we lack a defensive specialist. The Flyers also have good defensemen. Petr Svoboda and Eric Desjardins are good skaters who play up front as well as back. Kjell Samuelsson is a classic defensive defenseman, and they also have other good blue liners like Kevin Haller. It would have been tough to play against them.

I was surprised that Philadelphia didn't get past Florida. I think the Flyers beat themselves. We watched them before our series with the Panthers. With the kind of talent the Flyers have, they should have just gotten the puck into the offensive zone and gotten to work. Instead they tried to carry it all the way to the goal, and the Panthers waited for them at the blue line and scored their goals off counterattacks.

I couldn't believe my eyes when I saw the mistakes Philadelphia made. They would pass the puck in the neutral zone, then somebody would leave it behind him and three Florida players would take off with it against one defender. Furthermore, Lindros wasted all his energy in physical duels. He battled with the Panthers and wore himself out. They smartly switched up on him and totally exhausted him.

I spoke with Eric in Boston during All-Star weekend. We had already sort of become friends and talked to each other every once in a while. Mostly about hockey, of course. I said to him, "Why play so rough all the time? You only wear yourself out, and then you don't have enough strength in front of the net. If you weren't always looking for somebody to kill, you would definitely score more goals." "You're right," he admitted. But then he immediately added, "If I don't play rough, then nobody will. On the ice, they expect me to do the dirty work."

Florida played Lindros smart, and they got to him. It was up to us to learn from Philadelphia's mistakes.

We can't say we didn't know how to play them. Still, they ran us out of the rink in the first game. We played horribly, and the long break before the series contributed to that. After our victory over the Rangers, we had to wait an entire week before the next game. We lost our rhythm. It was most apparent in our weak passing. We didn't control the puck at all in the neutral zone and couldn't create anything over their blue line. The Panthers patiently waited for us and then countered against our porous defense.

Still, I was looking forward to the series. I believed that somehow we'd be able to penetrate their defense. I was also happy to see my friend Martin Straka whom I hadn't seen for a long time. He had ended up in Florida after detours to Ottawa and the Islanders. During the season I spoke to him on the phone from time to time, and our moms spent time together on the road.

During the series I had hoped to have lunch with Martin, but he was afraid to. He said that the coaches checked to see whether he was in his room, and he feared they would find out he was visiting with the rival Penguins. He was also conscious of how his teammates might feel. The Panthers' team was getting ready for me, and so Martin felt that we shouldn't be hanging out. We barely had any contact throughout the series. In the first game, I tried to speak to him, but he didn't react much. One time we jabbed each other a little before a face-off. Otherwise, there were none of our typical antics.

We didn't start the first game of the series off well. In the second minute, Dave Lowry took a shot that ricocheted off Zubov into our net. Toward the end of the period, we gave up another one when Tom Fitzgerald beat Wregget in close.

In the second period, Fitzgerald scored his second goal and it was more or less over. We couldn't manage to complete passes, and when we finally got in front of their goal, John Vanbiesbrouck worked his magic. At the time, I didn't, yet, realize we would not be able to solve them for an entire series.

In the final period, there was still a ray of hope for us. Dave Roche passed to Kevin Miller who scored to narrow the lead, but that was all we could muster. Lowry and then Scott Mellanby sealed the Panthers' victory. We lost 5-1 at home. Not an inspiring start.

In the second game Barrasso got the start. Our strategy was to play a patient defensive game and wait for them — not to open it up like in the first game. First secure our defense and then try to score goals.

Our strategy worked, even if we were a little lucky in the first period since the Panthers could have easily scored two goals. But fortunately, we were the first to score. In the eighth minute of the second period, the puck ricocheted to Zubov and he found space between Vanbiesbrouck's stick and the right post.

And then Mario came back on the ice. At the start of the period he was holding back, and I started thinking there was something wrong with him. Exhausted and dehydrated, Mario stayed in the locker room after the first period. The pace of the game was fast, and Mario had definitely had enough. He was battling an intestinal flu and remained below hoping the doctors could fix him up.

Sometime around the ninth minute of the second period, Mario reappeared on the ice to a loud cheer, and a moment later I scored my only goal of the entire series. Actually, the scenario was similar to the first period when I passed from the wing to Mario, and he had one whole side of the net open. Only he shot a small fraction of a second late, and Vanbiesbrouck had enough time to cover the shot.

This time we were on the power play, and the puck bounded to the corner of the rink toward Mario. I took off toward the goal and realized I was all alone. Luckily, Mario spotted me on the other side of the ice. He sent me a cross pass which I shot on the fly. Vanbiesbrouck tried to move right to left, but it was too late. We now led 2-0.

But the game still wasn't won. Right at the start of the final period, we left Ray Sheppard totally open in front of our net. After only twenty-nine seconds, he had cut our lead in half at 2-1.

But we didn't let them take the victory away from us. Petr Nedved cut into their zone with the puck, left if for Chris Tamer, Vanbiesbrouck deflected his shot and Mario sent the puck into the net for our third goal. That moment decided it. Bill Lindsay brought Florida within one goal at 3-2, but we stuck it out and with the victory evened the series at one.

Miami was next. I felt confident on two counts. We were unbeaten on the road in the playoffs. We also figured Florida would open it up on their home ice which would give us more offensive chances.

The Panthers actually opened up even more than we'd expected and were almost offensive-minded. But their defensive play continued to be solid.

Again they scored on us right away. In the second minute, Ray Sheppard crossed the blue line, let it rip and surprised Barrasso. But by the end of the period, Smolinksi managed to tie it up. At the start of the second period, we took the lead. I was fighting my way to the front of the net, when the puck slid off my stick. But Petr was right behind me and flipped the puck perfectly under the crossbar. We led 2-1.

The home team began feeling besieged. We shut Florida down in their zone and were getting chances. I felt if we scored again, the game would be over. But the worse possible thing happened. We weren't able to hold the lead. There was a flurry around our net, and the puck went to Radek Dvorak. He nailed the upper corner from a sharp angle.

Dvorak scored, but really he shouldn't have been playing at all.

In the first period Zubov received four minutes for sticking Dvorak in the face. Radek was shaken up and lost three teeth. Few players would have been able to play after that, but Radek returned to the game. Overcoming the pain, Radek scored a pivotal goal to knot the contest at two.

Again the match was up for grabs, and the game of nerves began. Unfortunately, we were the ones who lost it. In only the first minute of the final period, we couldn't get the puck out, and Stu Barnes got his stick on it behind Barrasso. A little while later, Barnes scored again, and we were in big trouble. We barely had any scoring chances the entire period and managed our first shot on goal only at the sixteen-minute mark. Meanwhile, the home team fired twenty-three shots at Barrasso.

Martin Straka finished us off. He tipped in Gord Murphy's shot from the blue line and the game was over. It didn't look good for us. We totally disintegrated in the third period and another loss would seal our fate once and for all.

At the start of the fourth game, I was seeing stars. First, Barnes high-sticked me in the face along the boards. I crumpled to the ice. I had a busted upper lip and blood was running from my nose, but after a while I was able to get up. My team-mates helped me to the bench, and soon I was back on the ice. But a few minutes later I really got clocked. Petr had the puck on the right-wing boards. I went to the front of the net and called out to him. Petr spotted me too late, and the pass was behind me. I had to wait and spin around to get the puck. When it finally arrived, Mike Hough, racing in from the wing, slammed into me with his shoulder. It was a clean check, but it was from my blindside, and I wasn't expecting it at all. For a while I didn't even know where I was. I was knocked out for several seconds and lay unconscious on the ice. When I finally woke up, I felt an excruciating pain. When Hough hit me, I had bitten my tongue. I don't even know how I made it back to the bench. I was in terrible pain, and my head was spinning. I pulled off my helmet and crawled to a corner of the bench. I was in bad shape, but I wanted to keep on playing. I tried to return to the game in the last minute of the period but was shaky on my feet. Still, I knew I'd be able to finish the game.

During the game I heard a lot of snickers coming from the Florida players. Bill Lindsay came up to me and said, "Hey, we're not interested in you wallowing around. Do it at home but not here." Even though I usually get into those kind of debates on the ice and often even start them myself, this time I wasn't in the mood to jaw and just told Lindsay to shut up. But he continued, "Shut up, my ass. You guys knocked three teeth out of another Czech, but unlike you he doesn't make theatrics of it and just keeps on playing. If you're such a wimp and can't take it, then go back to your bench and quit playing." Luckily at that moment, the refer-ee dropped the puck to resume play, so I didn't have to listen to Lindsay anymore.

In the second period I had a great scoring chance. Martin Straka lost the puck in our defensive zone, and somebody sent it to me at the red line. I picked up speed and came in alone on Vanbiesbrouck — as if on a penalty shot. I knew I shouldn't deke on such bad ice, so I shot on his stick side. But it was too low, and Vanbiesbrouck knocked it aside.

I soon had the chance to regret it. In the eleventh minute, Terry Carkner took a shot, and Lowry, positioned in front, tipped it nicely past Barrasso. What we had tried to prevent at all costs had happened anyway: Florida took the lead. We had a couple of chances before the end of the period, but Vanbiesbrouck didn't let any-thing get by him.

In the final period of the game, Florida kept us tied up in our defensive zone, and we got to their goal only sporadically. The game appeared to be over.

However, at the halfway mark of the period, lightning flashed straight out of the blue. Zubov started the operation from behind the net. Tamer carried it into the Florida zone, leaving it for Nedved, and then Brad Lauer tipped his shot into the net! It was all tied! It had all happened in only a few seconds, and I was the only Penguin on the ice who hadn't touched the puck.

When we evened the score, Florida was shook up. All of a sudden they didn't know how to play because they weren't ahead anymore. And so we tried to finish them off. At one point, Mario shot the puck on net and it went almost completely over the goal line. But Vanbiesbrouck managed to cover it up, and the referee ruled it "No goal."

The moment finally came in the seventeenth minute. Mario orchestrated a brilliant rush down the left wing and cut across to the net. Vanbiesbrouck was able to deflect the shot, but Smolinksi pounced on the rebound, jamming the puck home! We were literally raised from the dead. At the end of the game, Straka had a good scoring chance, but we held on and won the game.

After the game I wasn't feeling very chatty. I was still spitting blood on the plane ride back to Pittsburgh, and I couldn't speak. But, still, we had won the game.

We were back in the series and we went into the fifth game with a good deal of confidence. And we played it to a tee. We started off by applying pressure on the Florida goal and capitalized quickly. We soundly outplayed them and fired seventeen shots at Vanbiesbrouck in the first period. We scored our second goal at the end of the second period. It was the exact same scenario as in Game Four in Washington, when Ronnie sent the puck to me on the fly, and I fired the puck past Kolzig from the right wing. This time I had the assist. I sent the puck to Petr on the fly, and he drilled it off the wrong foot past a startled Vanbiesbrouck. Now we led 2-0, and our destiny seemed clear. Right before the game ended, Sandstrom scored an empty-netter, and for the first time we led the series.

We believed we'd win the series in Florida. For the first time we didn't have to play catch-up and could approach the game calmly, whereas our opponent was only one defeat away from elimination.

But we didn't take advantage of our opportunity. It was the first playoff game in which I felt truly tired. All of a sudden, it caught up to me. That I hadn't been scoring didn't bother me all that much. I was convinced I would break out of my dry spell. Besides, I felt I wasn't playing badly. I was getting chances and had two assists in the fifth game. But I must admit I was getting fed up with my lack of scoring. The spark in me was missing, and I felt I wasn't playing totally up to par.

We started the game off poorly, and again, we fell behind. Mellanby, hooked by Tamer, bumped Barrasso, and the puck ricocheted off him into the net. Miller tied it up at the beginning of the second period, and then we actually took the lead. Zubov held onto the puck in the Florida zone in his incomparable way until J. J.

Daigneault appeared. Daigneault's cannon shot was tipped by Dziedzic and we led 2-1. Unfortunately, the Panthers managed to tie it up at the end of the period, and it started all over again.

Play went back and forth. Both teams had chances, but we were the first to give up a goal. Straka crept through our defense, fired the puck with Lindsay alongside him and the shot sailed by Barrasso under the crossbar. Less than three minutes later, however, Sandstrom tied it back up on an outstanding play by Mario. Mario picked up the puck at the blue line, put it between Robert Svehla's legs, picked it up again, passed it to Murray who sent it back to Sandstrom and it was all tied up.

But a moment afterward, the game was decided. Smolinski lost a defensive zone face-off, and Rob Niedermayer sent it back to Terry Carkner who blasted it from the point. Meanwhile, Smolinksi had forgotten about Niedermayer, who followed up the shot for the score. Six minutes before the game ended, Florida scored again, and we couldn't catch up.

It would come down to a seventh game. We didn't prepare for it in any special way. The night before, Eddie Johnston told us to think about what else we might be able to do better. Otherwise there was nothing special in our preparation. I don't think it would have done much good if we had prepared differently. Your nerves are all worked up, and lots of advice won't sink in at that point. We knew one thing for certain: Whoever got the lead first was going to win — it was Florida.

I didn't see it clearly because I was making for the net. Zubov held onto the puck for so long in the Panthers' defensive zone that somebody poked it away from him. Brian Skrudland sent it to Hough. Leroux dove in front of Hough attempting to break up the pass but missed, taking himself out of position. Suddenly, the Panthers had a two-on-one against our only defender, Zubov, who had somehow managed to get back as fast as lightning. Hough passed to Robert Svehla, who waited for Zubie to come at him and for Barrasso to close off his shooting angle. Svehla smartly passed the puck to Hough who put it into the open side of the goal. Symbolically, the game clock read 13:13.

Florida had jumped ahead of us. We wanted to even the score as soon as possible but couldn't make it happen. The Panthers played good defense and also had a guarantee in Vanbiesbrouck. Once the puck hung on the goal line, another time we couldn't finish off a scoring chance from two yards away. It was all in vain.

But finally we got what we were hoping for. At the start of the third period, we had a power play. I took a shot from the right side, the puck bounced off Mario to Nedved, and Pete lifted it under the crossbar. It was all tied up!

All hell broke loose in the arena. The crowd urged us on, and we came back to life. All of a sudden, we started shutting Florida down, and the Panthers couldn't get out of their own zone. At that moment I strongly felt that we had them beat, and we would earn the right to play for the Stanley Cup.

But in the seventh minute the shock came. Fitzgerald crossed the blue line and fired the puck at the net. It seemed like a harmless shot, but Neil Wilkinson tipped it, changing its direction, and the puck ended up in the net. There was dead silence in the arena. We felt the end coming. I stopped believing we could stage a comeback when Johan Garpenlov put Florida up 3-1, but it was Fitzgerald's shot that shook us up. We couldn't believe it.

Later in the newspapers, a lot was said about how Tommy had lost the game by giving up such an easy goal. That's complete nonsense. First of all Fitzgerald's shot was tipped, and in my opinion, Tommy was even better than Vanbiesbrouck in three of the games. Tommy was definitely playing behind a weaker defense than his counterpart, and despite that he kept us in the series. His weakest moment came at the worst possible time, but in no way do I blame Tommy for our defeat.

After Fitzgerald's goal we kept on trying and had several chances. Mario probably had the best opportunity to score. I fought to the front of the goal from the right side and sent the puck through a jungle of bodies to Mario who was laying low near the left post. But because he only saw the puck at the very last instant, he wasn't able to steer it into the open goal. It grazed his skates and ricocheted off the back boards in front of the net from the other side. I nearly got my stick on it, and if I'd been a bit quicker with my hands, I could have put it in the net.

Some of the crowd had already left for home, but many of them stuck it out until the very end. In the final minutes, we repeatedly attacked the Florida net, but it wasn't meant to be.

I know the moments after you get eliminated all too well. Some guys head straight for the showers so you can't see them cry, others sit silently on the bench and stare straight ahead. We were so disappointed. If somebody had told us before the playoffs that a single game would separate us from the finals, we probably wouldn't have believed it. But now we could only feel incredibly frustrated at how close we had come.

But in retrospect, our elimination wasn't such a big surprise. I think we had been a little overrated. Just because we had three of the top four scorers in the league during the regular season didn't mean that we'd automatically win. The playoffs are a totally different game.

Florida played us smart. They covered Mario and me flawlessly. On the other hand, I don't think we played so badly. But we weren't scoring. Florida's defense executed superbly. Definitely better than ours. But it wasn't just Florida's defense; their forwards also came back and played conscientious defense. Vanbiesbrouck was excellent, but if the Rangers had been playing in front of him he definitely would have given up more goals.

In the end, I think that Francis's absence tipped the scales. I've already mentioned how important he is to my game. His injury made it necessary for us to shuffle our lines, so Petr and I always had somebody different playing with us. Ronnie has always sacrificed his own on-ice creativity for me. On the other hand, he knows that if I play well then he too will be a beneficiary. In addition, Ronnie always helps me a lot when I'm not playing good hockey. I had something of a on-ice crisis against Florida, but if Ronnie had been on the ice and given me the puck a couple of times, nobody would have noticed. I would have scored a couple more goals and everything would have been different. But instead, my game suffered in Ronnie's absence.

In fact, this year had a feeling of déjà vu to it. Last year when we lost Ulf in the last game against the Capitals, we sorely missed him against the Devils. This time it was Ronnie.

I was the last one to leave the locker room. I was down in the dumps, but I knew I had nothing to be ashamed of. I had broken a number of records in the regular season, finished second in the scoring race behind Mario and helped the team make it to the Stanley Cup semifinals.

In my very first two seasons, it was amazing to have won the most coveted trophy in the NHL. I realize it more and more as time goes by. The desire to hold the Stanley Cup above my head once again gets stronger and stronger all the time.

I also realize I'm playing on a totally different team now. Of course, I'm still wearing the Penguins' jersey, but I'm surrounded by a revolving door of new faces. It's incredible that at only twenty-four years of age, I already have so many hockey memories. When I think of it, only Mario, Ronnie and both goalies, Tommy and Ken, are left from our Stanley Cup team. And that's it. All the others are gone. Some of them are my opponents, others have completed their hockey careers.

My famous teammates. During my five years in Pittsburgh, I must have gone through dozens of them. I have good memories of all of them. But of the ones I like most, I have to put Mario in first place. Actually, he's not my teammate. I'm his.

And I am extremely grateful that I've had the chance to play with him.

Mario and Company

Mario Lemieux was my hero from the time I saw him play in the World Championship in Prague. Now I can admit it, but a year and half after I arrived on the team I had a little secret. I carried his picture in my wallet. If one of my teammates had found out, I'd have been the laughing stock of the team. He was a god to me. I still get nervous when I'm around him, as if I was asking for his autograph or something. He's a player from a different planet. He was already having problems with his back when I arrived in Pittsburgh. He couldn't practice because of the pain. And then he would show up and score three or four goals per game. I always watched him closely and tried to copy him. I was constantly thinking about why he's such a good hockey player.

First of all, he's extremely smart. I don't think he's ever scored a goal by standing in front of the net and just shooting it in. He stands away from the net and waits for a ricochet. He doesn't just skate up to the net without thinking. He waits until the puck ricochets and then he whacks it into the net or passes. He's extremely fast, even though he doesn't look like it at all. As soon as he takes off, you won't catch him in a million years. I'll never forget what he did to Bourque from the Boston Bruins during the conference finals when we won our second Stanley Cup.

He always wants to be the best. That's another thing I admire about him. We were playing in Anaheim once and Mario made it to the net twice and didn't score. That never happens to him. Right after that, he got the puck at the blue line and took off toward the goalie. But a defenseman caught him from behind and stole the puck! That was the last straw. Mario immediately stomped off to the locker room, and after the game announced that he was taking a two-month vacation. He knew that his health wouldn't allow him to play 100 percent, and he didn't want to do anything on the ice less than that.

Mario can hold onto the puck and pass it exactly where he wants it to go. I've never seen anyone who can set up a play like he can. He's so good at skating and finding ways to get open that you can almost always pass to him. It looks like he's hanging out at the blue line for no reason at all, even though his stick is behind the line. All of those passes are right on the edge, but never offside. It must be really unpleasant for an opposing team to take him on during their power play. He's got such long arms and an incredible reach, so it's not very easy to get past him. His hands are terribly fast and he steals a lot of pucks.

It's also amazing how well he works his hockey stick. In a split second he's got the puck and is moving it down the ice. He's twice as fast as the rest when it comes to moving the puck. Sometimes Mario gives me advice during games. When I got a couple chances and blew them once, he came up to me on the bench and said, "Try aiming a little higher." Or else: "Just wait a little, and you'll definitely get him."

Mario didn't play for a whole season, and I was just dying to see him on the ice again.

Unfortunately, I never played against Wayne Gretzky at his peak, so I can't compare him with Mario, but he's still a fantastic player. I was crazy about him from the moment I got a poster of him. Maybe I was just impressed with his image because I never actually saw him play.

He's a little older these days, but he still plays superbly. It's unbelievable the way he pulls the same fake and everyone around him acts like they're seeing it for the first time. I'm glad that I got to know him, thanks to Mike Barnett, and had dinner with him a few times.

When we play in Los Angeles, we often chat before practice. I'm the last off the ice, and he's the first. He invited me to his place in Los Angeles, and it's fantastic. Some day I'd like to live like that.

Another model for me is Ron Francis. He's definitely the most underrated player in the NHL. He's extremely intelligent. A while back, he was offered a scholarship at the prestigious Cornell University. He may be the most important player on the team. He totally lets go on the ice and is extremely hardworking. Even though he's not in the spotlight like the big stars, I think he's one of the best players in the NHL. He's terribly modest and is acknowledged by everyone. He's a leader on the ice, and when the team doesn't succeed, it's usually he who pushes the car out of the mud. I think he's got a lot of character. He's also willing to sacrifice. He can arrange anything. When I wanted to have a dinner party before the game in Washington to celebrate my winning the Art Ross Trophy, I said something to Ronnie, and he took care of everything. He arranged it all. Or my new car. I wanted a Mercedes and said something to Ronnie. In a short time, I had my new car.

Ronnie and Mario are probably the only players I talk with during the game. We discuss game strategy. We really get along and Ronnie's pretty funny. Before Game Five against New Jersey, we decided that if I made it to the net with the puck, Ronnie would be right behind me, and I'd pass it to him at the right moment.

The situation we discussed came about. I made it to New Jersey's red line with the puck and aimed right between the two defensemen. Unfortunately, they started moving toward each other and it became clear that I wouldn't make it past them. So I stopped right where I was. When Ronnie reached me, he obviously wasn't counting on my stopping. To our detriment, the Devils got hold of the puck. I think it was Claude Lemieux who ultimately scored. In the locker room, Ronnie came up to me and said, "So what do you think? Should I still skate behind you?"

Of my other teammates, I have to name Ulf Samuelsson first. He's a great guy off the ice. Really nice. I always had a good time with him. On the ice, however, he's totally crazy. I didn't even like playing against him during practice. He's so out of control that everyone's afraid to go near him. He treats every practice as if it was the Stanley Cup finals. When we go two-on-one, almost no pair finishes a play with him. Ulf either checks one of them or intercepts a pass. He never lets a player get past him.

Sometimes he'll scare us. He skates right at you, shouting things the whole time. You're so scared, you get rid of the puck as fast as possible. Then Ulf laughs and gets a big kick out of it.

He's the kind of player everyone wants on his team. He'll easily keep attempting to score goals one minute before the end of a game that was lost in the first period. And off the ice, he's a hell of a lot of fun. There's not a day that he doesn't pull some practical joke.

You always have to be careful around him. Ulf might be getting his hockey stick ready in the locker room and heating it over a flame. When the blade is hot enough to be flexible, he comes up to you and sticks it on your leg. You're not expecting anything, and suddenly you feel a terrible pain. You turn around and there's Ulf cracking up.

Or doorknobs. You go to the locker room, turn the doorknob, and it's covered with black shoe polish. In the corner, you see Ulf observing his shoes with great interest. Eventually, he can't take it anymore and bursts out laughing, and you know who the culprit is.

Even the referees are the butt of his jokes sometimes. I don't remember who we were playing, but the referee skated right in front of our bench and leaned against the boards. Ulf reached over and poured water down his pants. Fortunately, he didn't find out about it for a while. For the rest of the game he rubbed his butt and couldn't figure out for the life of him why it was all wet back there.

Ulf poked fun at all of us. Most of us knew that at some point he'd come around. That's what Kevin Stevens thought, and he was right. Kevin was sent to the penalty box for five minutes, which of course irritated him. When his penalty was up, he skated toward the bench assuming that he would return to the ice because he'd been sitting out for five minutes. But at that moment, the whole team got penalized for too many men on the ice, so someone had to go to the penalty box. When Kevin reached the bench, Ulf told us, " Watch this." He then shouted to Eddie Johnston loud enough for Kevin to hear, "Hey coach, send Kevin. He needs a rest!" Kevin did exactly what we expected, he turned red and exploded: "But I was just there!" Then the entire bench burst out laughing, including Coach Johnston.

Ulf's best friend on the team was his fellow countryman Kjell Samuelsson. Kjell is thirty-eight, but he's still a very good player. Just like Ulf, he won't shy away from anything. If he gets a hockey stick in the face and ends up with fifty stitches in the course of the game, he returns to the ice. Kjell is around six and a half feet tall, and, next to Uwe Krupp, may very well be the tallest player in the NHL. Because of his height, he comes across as being extremely clumsy, but it's tough to get past him. When he extends his arm with his stick, it covers a great deal of the rink. When I stand next to him I feel like a dwarf. Once when we played Tampa, Petr Klima came up to me and said, "Hey, tell 28 that the basketball game's tomorrow."

One of the toughest customers on the ice is Kevin Stevens. On the ice, he's totally crazy. He swears at everyone who gets in his way: opponents, referees, teammates. It's like he's in a trance. But I really respect him. He's one of those players who challenges everything. He never got anything for free. He wasn't born with the kind of talent the other NHL stars have. He worked his way to the top by hard work and persistence.

His best weapons are his readiness and energy. He can shoot from any position and rarely fakes. He often doesn't even look at the net. He just wants to shoot that puck at all costs, and he usually scores. It's very difficult to get him away from the puck because he weighs well over 220 pounds. Off the ice, he's a great guy. I was really happy when he came over to my house once.

Dick Tocchet has a similar playing style. The club traded him to Los Angeles. He was a hard worker and battled his way to many a puck at the boards. He was a good fighter, too. I never saw him lose a fight. Dick was always extremely friendly to me, and if someone gave me problems, Dick skated up ready to get involved.

Joe Mullen is a hockey legend. It's incredible what he can still do at age thirty-eight. One of his best weapons is his shooting. He has extremely strong arms and can shoot exactly where he wants, even right off a pass. If the puck bounces in the goalie crease, it's usually Joe who sends it into the net. He can flick his stick twice in the space of half a second. He's also a real family man with an exceptional sense of fun. After they traded Martin Straka to Ottawa, we became roommates on the road and were always playing video games on the hotel TV.

Tommy Barrasso tended goal for two Stanley Cups. Tommy is a good goalie who is absolutely fantastic with his stick. He's probably the best in the NHL in that respect. It's very difficult to work with him during practice. The moment he hits the ice, nobody's allowed to take a shot at him. He spends a lot of time practicing alone. He often works out in the gym or spends time riding an exercise bike.

Grant Jennings was an interesting character on the team. He's extremely muscular, which is why we called him "Meat." Meat was an extraordinarily talented and friendly guy. He even has his pilot's license and often flies these days. I think he may be the laziest player in the NHL. Not even a tow truck can get him off his rear end. Four of us had to pick him up and push him just to get him moving. He constantly complained that he was underpaid. When we told him to practice more, he said that he was paid for games, not practice.

The way he answered questions was famous. It was always, "Huh?" or "What?" We started repeating our questions, so he'd have a chance to figure out what they meant. Whenever we asked him a question, we always asked it twice. "Meat, are you coming into the city tonight? Are you coming into the city tonight?"

Once Meat really distinguished himself. When I think back on it, I can't help laughing. We were playing a good team and were on the attack. We lost the puck in the opponent's zone, and they went on a three-on-two against us. Meat and Marty McSorley were retreating from the three offensive players. And then all of a sudden, it was a three-on-one. Meat had completely vanished. Fortunately, they didn't score. During a break in the game, Marty came up to the bench where Meat was sitting and asked him, "Meat, where in God's name did you go?" Meat then said the magical words which sent the entire bench into hysterics: "I thought I was injured."

I also really liked playing with Troy Loney. He's not on the team anymore, but he's the kind of player you need to have at your side. He fought at the boards and freed up many a puck for me. I always had the feeling that as soon as he was on the ice, I had twice as much room.

I have good memories of Jay Caulfield, too, the one who actually "welcomed" me to Pittsburgh. I remember when I arrived at the stadium and saw this giant in the doorway, I turned around and ran. I told myself: "I don't need to play here." We quickly became good friends. Jay started playing hockey when he was sixteen. Before that he played football. He couldn't do a whole lot with the puck. He was just your classic fighter, and he taught me how to box. He was completely crazy when it came to practice. We started a little group that always played two-goal scrimmages after practice.

That hadn't been the norm in Pittsburgh, and I couldn't understand why. Basically, we started playing scrimmage games after my arrival in Pittsburgh. In my opinion, practice games are terribly important. You can only develop your confidence and self-awareness by practicing. How are players who have been out of commission for a long time supposed to believe in themselves during one-on-ones when they haven't even tried it in practice? You've got to rehearse everything in practice over and over again. But that's not the way things were under Scotty Bowman. These days I usually stay on the ice after every practice, even on mornings when we're warming up for a game, and I play two-on-two with the team's alternates.

We used to have an absolutely fantastic group of alternates. Martin Straka, who didn't play that much, was among them. We always looked forward to our scrimmage matches. Even if I had to play in a game in the afternoon, I still played the scrimmage with them. Jay Caulfield really got into it. One time, we were looking forward to the scrimmage game so much that Martin and I literally jumped out of bed so that we'd get to the stadium. When we lost, Jim Paek and Ken Wregget marched around with their hands above their heads making fun of us. So the next match we made sure to get our revenge.

Jay just loved those games. We were in the playoffs — I think it was against New Jersey — and we were in the locker room getting ready. When we went out onto the ice, Jay came up to me and Martin and said, "Boys, let's bust our butts and win tonight. But don't get too tired. We've got a game tomorrow." I got such a kick out of that that I was still laughing during the game.

Luc Robitaille, who arrived in the course of the season, is an interesting character. Luc is definitely not God's gift to skating, which is probably the result of a difficult operation he had on his ankle several years ago. He's the kind of player with amazing intuition and incredible hands. He's always in the right place at the right time. You can't learn that. You're simply born with it. When he was playing for the Kings, he scored lots of goals, and he keeps shooting them in Pittsburgh. He's an extremely nice guy. The journalists like him because he talks to them. Sometimes we make fun of him about it and send the journalists right to him, saying, "Go see Luc. He'll tell you."

The way he prepares his hockey stick is very interesting. The first third is covered in white tape, the second in black and the last third white again. He doesn't worry himself about quality when it comes to the wrapping. He wraps it worse than a gorilla would. In every game he has his leg wrapped from the ankle to the groin. If he played in the Czech league, no one could afford him because of the bandages he uses. They'd probably rather cut off his leg.

These are the players who were so important to our team.

In the NHL there are a lot of outstanding hockey players, and sometimes I have no problem just plain watching from the bench. Besides Lindros, there's the absolutely top-notch Sergei Fedorov, who's incredibly fast and has a good sense of strategy. I also like Pat LaFontaine from Buffalo. It was interesting to watch him go at it with Alex Mogilny. On the other hand, Dave Andreychuk's style leaves me cold. He gets most of his goals by slipping the puck in behind the goalie's back. His playing doesn't grab me, but it's very effective. I prefer more artful plays, but I have to admit that Dave's goals count, too.

Observing offensive players is definitely interesting, but I mainly have to focus on defensemen. After all, they're the ones I have to overcome in order to score (for the most part). I actually don't play against defensemen. I play against myself. When I'm physically fit, in tiptop shape and have confidence in myself, I'll take on the best back in the world one-on-one. But if I'm in a slump, even the clumsiest oaf can stop me.

I have an advantage because of my long reach. If I'm going fast enough and manage to shake off the defenseman, I can go far and can always control the puck. I was able to do that in Game Six of the playoffs against Washington. I came from the right at Calle Johansson, who's not very tall. I took the puck to the right and, with one hand, slipped it between Johansson's legs. I reached out and caught it on the other side. Washington's defenseman just couldn't reach that far. Unfortunately, I got too close to Washington's goalie and wasn't able to shoot. But if I'd gotten that one, it would definitely have been a great goal.

I play my best against the best and most famous defensemen. It may sound paradoxical, but the reason is quite simple: They're never on defense. Gretzky's slogan explains it all: "There's no money in defense." Players like Coffey from Detroit or Brian Leetch from the New York Rangers are always somewhere else. As soon as their front line has the puck, they're after them bringing up the rear. That's why they have so many points, but it's also why they let in so many goals. Even when they're excellent skaters, they can't get back fast enough.

It has to be very difficult dealing with backs like Ulf Samuelsson. They don't leave you an inch of space and constantly cut you off. Ulf's contract expired last season, so he was always teasing me. "Just wait. They won't sign me on, and next year we'll be playing against each other. Get ready for a good fight."

It's also not too hard against huge, slow players. They're not very agile and are easy to escape. For instance, I like playing against Mark Tinordi from Washington. He often checks me, but I have a good chance to outskate him. It's a lot worse when they're excellent skaters and rough at the boards. That's an unpleasant combo. That's what Chris Chelios is like. But the most unpleasant back has to be Washington's Silvain Coté. He's fast, agile and extremely tough. He almost never fouls. He doesn't need to. He's always there on time, and it's extremely difficult to get past him.

Ray Bourque from Boston, Scott Stevens from New Jersey, Darius Kasparaitis from the Islanders and Uwe Krupp from the Avalanche are also excellent on defense. Normally we encounter the same players during a season. So if we play Boston, I know that Bob Sweeney is waiting for me. With Montreal, it's Lyle Odelein. I also regularly take the ice against Joe Reekie from Washington and Kevin Haller from Philadelphia.

When someone is covering me and won't leave my side for a second, I always break toward another player to get him out of the play. I often have mini-duels with defensemen. I try to get by them one at a time, and even if it doesn't work the first two times, maybe it'll work the third. It might take a little longer with one defenseman, and it works right away with another. Usually if I get by a defenseman without much difficulty, the coach pulls him out and sticks someone else on me.

Hockey wouldn't be hockey if there wasn't a little fun on the ice now and then. Sometimes we threaten each other, and other times we terrify each other. It's part of the game. Once I ended up at the boards that way when Chris Chelios attacked me. He's one of the best players in the NHL, but until recently, he had the reputation of being one of the nastiest. There was a time when approaching Chicago's net and encountering Chelios meant crawling back to the bench on all fours. And that was if you were lucky. In the worst cases, the doctor got the stitches ready. Recently, Chelios has calmed down a bit. Chicago really depends on him, so he doesn't want to end up in the penalty box for some stupid reason. There are games in which he's on the ice for more than thirty minutes and is all over the rink. He covers the area in front of the goal, so that he can immediately take the puck to the opponent's third.

Once we were playing Chicago and a scuffle broke out in front of their net. Everyone grabbed a player and waited until the referee broke it up. It was Martin Straka who had Chelios that time, and he gently begged him not to join the fight. "Relax, Cheli," Martin said. Chelios simply couldn't believe that Martin, who is by no means a terrifying person, dared prevent him from joining a fight. He told Martin, "Shut your trap, pipsqueak," and skated away unhappily.

I've never had any problems with Chelios — except for one occasion when we were going at him two-on-two and he grabbed me at the boards, stuck his stick under my chin and said, "Move and I'll stick this through your face!"

There are players I always talk to during games because it's fun. One of those is Paul Broten. He's in Dallas now, but he used to play for the New York Rangers. He always turns to me in the game and says, "You're playing horribly today. Where'd you whoop it up last night?" Sometimes Broten is assigned to cover me. In one game he wasn't playing and Mario got a goal. In the next game, Broten came up to him and said, "You only got that one because the coach had me warming the bench!"

Bernie Nicholls from Chicago is also a load of fun. During games, he always shouts at me, "Wait up! Don't go anywhere." Or: "Where are you going? Don't run away!" He doesn't make a science of hockey either, and I usually like to joke around with him.

But number one in the NHL's fun department is Petr Klima. Every time I think of him, I crack up. He has no problem speaking to me on the bench throughout the game. He'll come up to the wall and start making fun of me. Or during skating warm-ups. He'll skate to the center of the rink, lean on his hockey stick and babble away until the game starts. When they play Calgary and he sees Frank

Musil warming up properly, skating from board to board, he can't keep from laughing. Klima shouts at him, "Frank, you've gone crazy! Stop, please stop!"

When I play against him, he always comes up to me and asks, "How many goals have you scored?" He listens to my answer and replies, "That's all? I can score that many on one foot with a beer in my hand." He likes to come up to me before face-offs and say, "You guys have so many injuries that they actually let you play?"

Once we were playing Edmonton and things got kind of wild, and the fans started throwing coins on the ice. Klima started collecting them with his stick. When he had a fistful, he came up to me, gave me the coins and said, "Take this. You'll finally be able to get yourself a real meal after the game."

Klima is the biggest fun-lover in the world, but once Martin Straka really pulled one over on him. In the season before last, Martin was outstanding and led the NHL for shots on goal. But then Martin had a bit of a slump and started scoring fewer goals. That was around the time we played Tampa. "Hey youngster. You've got dust on your stick," Klima said to him. He had no idea that it was Martin who'd be laughing after the game. Martin scored a goal and had three assists, racking up a total of four points for the game.

It was actually Tampa who became the victim of Peter Bondra's big day. He got six goals in a single game and was able to do just what he wanted on the ice. Klima came up to him before a face-off and said, "Look, you better not skate so fast. If the cops catch you, you're gonna get a hefty ticket."

Frank Musil of Ottawa is another Czech hockey player who's a pretty good jokester. He always smacks me a few times as soon as I come off the ice. Frank's a little slower, but he's extremely strong and very difficult to escape from. He likes to trap you with his stick and doesn't let go. He's sharp as a knife and during a game doesn't care who's who. As soon as someone gets in Musil's way, he makes them regret it. I can't even count the number of times Frank checked me into the boards so hard I could barely breathe. And after the game he'll say, "You know, I've got to rough you up a bit. Otherwise you'd slip away from me." He was even rougher with Martin than with me. Straka is smaller and more agile than me, so the defensemen have a tougher time catching him. Frank goes after him in his special way, and when he catches him it's worth it. Straka has trouble getting up off the ice. Frank rubs it in a bit by saying, "Wake up. Wake up. Stop fooling around down there." Or when there's a break in the game, Frank goes up to Straka and says, "Hey, slow down a bit. How many times have I told you. Do I have to beg you?" Frank is one of the few Czech players who I call on the phone during the season. We also talked a lot when we were home in the Czech Republic during the strike.

Dominik Hasek is a chapter in himself. He's been doing an outstanding job tending goal for the last three years and has become one of the best goalies in the NHL. In Chicago, he had it tough. Mike Keenan preferred Eddie Belfour, and

At the edge of Pittsburgh I bought a house and my guard dog Luci belongs to it (left). In the picture with us is agent Jirka Crha, until not long ago an excellent goalie in Germany.

It's a lot of work with fan mail. Mom helps me out the most.

when Dominik got into the goalie's crease, he had the feeling that he couldn't make a single mistake. If he screwed up, next game Belfour would be in goal. That's what goalies hate the most. It looked like his bad luck just wouldn't disappear. When they traded him to Buffalo he was injured, and right before he got better another outstanding goalie arrived in Buffalo, Grant Fuhr, who got several Stanley Cups while in Edmonton. But then Fuhr got injured, and Dominik didn't leave the net.

Whenever we Czechs in the NHL get together, Dominik actually comes up pretty often in our conversations. It's incredible, the things that happen to him. The best was probably the 1987 Canadian Cup when he pressed the alarm button in a hotel in Calgary. Even though it was a few years ago, I still have to laugh about it. I must have heard the story ten times, but the first time I heard it from Hasek himself was two years ago during Christmas. Buffalo was playing in Pittsburgh, and I invited Hasek and Risa Smehlik to my place for Christmas dinner.

"In the hall where our room was, there was a little red button — the fire alarm, and it really irritated me. So whenever I went by it, I kind of pressed it a little," explained Hasek. "One time I pushed a little harder than usual and, all of a sudden, these sirens started wailing. I started freaking out. I had no idea what to do. People were running out of their rooms, and pretty soon a hotel manager was running onto the floor with a walkie-talkie. I told him that it was a false alarm, that I'd accidentally set it off. He just looked at me and said, 'It's too late. The firemen are on their way.' When I reached the ground floor, I was petrified. The main door was open, and the firemen were unraveling the firehoses in the direction of the elevator. I ran after them frantically. I cut them off and, waving my hands around, shouted, 'No fire!' The sad thing about this comedy was that people were fleeing their rooms. They even had to carry out our masseur, who was suffering from kidney problems at the time. He cried out in despair, 'Leave me alone! I don't want to go anywhere. I'd rather die!' Eventually everything was explained, and the firemen called off the alarm. Meanwhile, I was feeling like a total idiot."

He's one of the few active hockey players with a university education. He studied at the Education Faculty, specializing in education and history, but sometimes he acts like a little boy.

He used to have an old Skoda car at home. Once he tried to get into it, he turned the key back and forth — it's a wonder he didn't break it — but he just couldn't get the door open. Then he got so mad that he started kicking the tires and swearing. This went on for about twenty minutes. Then he went back and forth between swearing and trying to open the car until one of his teammates asked if it was actually his car. Hasek thought for a moment, stepped back, looked at the car and said, "You know what? You're right. There's something odd about this car." His was a few yards away.

After a few years in the NHL, Dominik brought a beautiful Porsche home to the Czech Republic. A few days later someone stole the hood ornament off it. "The car was in front of the house, and I saw some kid taking the hood ornament off. I kept watching him, and it never occurred to me that he was stealing the ornament off my car. When it finally dawned on me that it was my car, I ran downstairs, but the kid with my hood ornament was long gone," Hasek told us, and we were completely in stitches.

I know an even better one from Vladimir Ruzicka. When he and Hasek were in Moscow for the World Championship, they took the elevator to the first floor, and Dominik had a portable stereo with him, which he put on the floor of the elevator. When they got out, Dominik was so absorbed in the conversation with Ruzicka that he forgot about the stereo. He realized it after they were out of the elevator. He pressed the elevator button, but by the time it came back the stereo was gone, and Hasek was totally bummed.

I'm always really happy to see him. He's a great guy and I always have a good time with him. When he was at our house for dinner, he'd had a beer, and I asked my mom to bring another. Dominik didn't want any more beer and started munching on a carrot, which is of course good for your eyes. Then I said to my mom, "You'd better take that carrot away. Do you want him to stop all my shots?"

Vladimir Ruzicka is also one of best known jokesters. The best was his verbal exchange with my former teammate, Paul Stanton. Now Paul's in Boston, but this incident happened when he was still in Pittsburgh in a game against the Bruins.

Stanton was trying to provoke him during the game, so that he'd break his concentration. During one face-off, Stanton said to Ruzicka, "Just look how stupid you are. You've been here for four years and you still haven't learned how to speak English properly." Ruzicka didn't bat an eye and toppled him with a great comeback: "It's true. I speak English like you play hockey."

Michal Pivonka, another player from Kladno, is known for his dry wit as well. The start of last year's season went poorly for him. He didn't score a single goal for several games. When he finally got one after about fifteen games, his teammates welcomed him back to bench with an incredible roar. Michal acted as if nothing had happened: "That's what you're supposed to do, isn't it?"

Michal makes fun of everyone. When I was talking with Czech journalists after a game against Washington, he came over and told them, "Leave him alone. He's completely stupid. He won't be able to tell you anything." When we were losing in the series against Washington, right before the face-off, Michal would skate over and remark, "Yeah, sure. Just try it." Jokes like the one he pulled on Martin Rucinsky while he was still with the Nordiques are completely normal for him. Rucinsky had the puck in the center zone, crossed the red line and was passing the blue when he was startled by a hearty shout, "Ruca!" He left the puck behind.

Before he had a chance to figure out what had just happened, he had already skated for a few more seconds without the puck. At that point, he turned around, and what did he see? Michal with the puck happily rushing toward the Nordiques' net.

Another player who I'm careful of is Roman Hamrlik. He grew into one of the best defensemen in the NHL, and in addition to his offensive abilities and great shooting, he's also known for his energy. He certainly doesn't spare me, although sometimes I have the feeling at the boards that he could be harder on me if he wanted. Unfortunately, Roman signed a contract for two million a year with Tampa. We could really use a fantastic defenseman like him. But more importantly, he's a super guy.

During the six years I've been playing in the NHL, I haven't had any problems with any Czech players — with one exception: Franta Kucera from Hartford. Once we were playing Hartford, and someone kept holding me back. I couldn't get away from whoever it was, so I jabbed him as hard as I could with my elbow. I got him right in the face. It turned out it was Franta Kucera who was on the receiving end. He flew into a rage. He took off his gloves and wanted to start a fight with me! Fortunately, Kevin Stevens came up and prevented a potential Czech versus Czech battle.

I was looking forward to playing against Ottawa, particularly when Martin was there. There's a whole Czech colony there, so when the Senators played in Pittsburgh, I brought Martin, Radek Bonek and Standa Neckar home with me to play some pool.

Neckar is an easygoing guy, but a very unpleasant defenseman. He is short and stocky, so he's got a low center of gravity and wins most of the battles he gets into. He's also incredibly fast and terribly difficult to get past. In December 1995 he turned twenty, but he's already on the ice more than twenty minutes a game. I'm convinced he's going to develop into an outstanding defenseman.

I also like seeing Martin Rucinsky. He had a good season last year after he was traded from the Avalanche to Montreal. Martin witnessed a holdup in a department store two years ago. He had already gathered a bunch of things in his shopping cart when some robbers ran into the department store and shouted, "Everyone on the ground!" The only problem was that this was in Quebec. It was in French, and Martin didn't understand. He didn't pay any attention to them because he thought someone was just having an argument. He was rummaging through the shelves when one of the robbers came up to him, stuck a pistol to his head and shouted at him that if he didn't get down immediately, they'd blow his brains out. It could have been Chinese and Martin would have known exactly what the guy meant. He immediately got down on the ground. He was so scared that he stayed there long after they'd gone. And I don't blame him.

JAGR
My Life in the NHL

For a professional hockey player in the NHL, every day of the season is like all the others. There are two main ingredients for good performance: responsible preparation for games, which includes practice, sufficient rest and a healthy lifestyle. The other is diet, which is no less important.

I'm lucky in that respect because my mother takes good care of me. She's with me the whole year in Pittsburgh and cooks and prepares food for me every day. It may sound like it's not that important, but the fact is, if you don't eat right, you won't have energy and strength.

So what does a typical day look like? I wake up at different times, depending on when the warm-ups or practices are scheduled. It usually takes three tries to get me up. First my mom wakes me up around nine, then again a half hour later. I usually make it out of bed around nine forty-five. Breakfast is always the same: coffee, bread, ham and waffles with whipped cream because they're substantial and have lots of calories. After breakfast, I go to the stadium. If we have a game, I usually get there some time before eleven o'clock. Then I eat a light lunch and then sleep two hours or so. If we don't have a game, I can really stuff my face.

Our kitchen table is never without cakes and cookies, something which I'm really crazy about. I've got a sweet tooth and can gulp down a huge block of chocolate in one sitting. I really love the Czech wafer cookies from Karlovy Vary. I'm addicted to them. Sometimes I eat a whole box. I used to drink a lot of Diet Coke, but now I prefer Gatorade or water.

Even after games, mom's got dinner on the table for me. If I hang out at the Sports Arena or Chauncee's, mom at least leaves a sandwich out. But that's only if she doesn't wake up. Usually she can't sleep if I'm out, and as soon as she hears the car or gate, both of which make a little noise, she wakes up immediately and runs downstairs to heat up something.

On the day of a game, I wake up in the afternoon around four o'clock. Mom makes me coffee. I munch on some cookies. Then I put on some energizing tunes. My favorite groups change from time to time. I used to rock the house with Guns N' Roses, but now I'm into other bands.

In the living room I've got a hockey stick with weights on it. I play with it for a while, strengthening my arms and getting ready for the game. During the game, my actual stick seems so much lighter. Someone once told me that Gretzky warms up for games by taping three pucks to each side of his stick and swinging it around.

Then I go into my bedroom and get myself together. It's time for my secret ritual. Then I get dressed in a suit. In the NHL you have to go games in a suit and tie. Around five o'clock, I head for the stadium.

The team meets at six o'clock. Before that, I prepare my hockey stick and sometimes chat with my teammates. We don't joke much. Everyone keeps to himself and gets ready for the game.

After the players' meeting, I start warming up. I start with stretching, but before that I heat up my leg and groin muscles. I have a hot water bottle which I use as a hot compress. When I was home in Kladno, I had to improvise, so I poured boiling water into a Coke bottle. When my leg muscles are warm, I put on sweatpants and run around a bit. Just around the Civic Arena. No one's there yet, of course. I run up and down the stairs, stretch thoroughly and get warmed up. I never get completely sweaty — only in Florida, where it's ninety degrees in the stadium. Sometimes I put my legs in cold water. It really helps. Coffey taught me that. On the day before games, he spends thirty minutes in a hot bath and then takes a cold shower. I started doing that, too. I did it twice and felt like I'd been reborn. Sometimes I do it at home after games when I can't sleep because of pain and exhaustion.

The last thing I do is put on my gear. We always enter the rink in the same order. Most games start at 7:35 P.M., but we go on the ice at 6:50 P.M. Then we leave the ice by 7:10, so that there's exactly twenty minutes before the official entrance onto the ice.

I go on the ice before Mario. He is the last one. I skate to the boards about three meters from the goal crease and wait until the puck comes to me. I try to score a goal from that angle. When I make it, I usually score in the game.

It always looks the same. Someone tosses the puck to the goalie, who sends it to me, and I pass it to Mario. Mario takes a shot and goes to the locker room. The rest of the team follows him after a while.

Most players take off their skates, but I only loosen mine. The coaches aren't in the locker room. They arrive two minutes before we hit the ice. We psyche each other up and enter according to the set order. It's always the same. I wait until everyone's out and then I follow. I kiss the cross around my neck and my hockey stick, and then I go to it.

One unpleasant aspect of the NHL is traveling. During the season, we spend half the time away from home. We see almost nothing of the cities we visit. We usually fly the day before games. We check into our hotel, go out to dinner together and then play cards in our rooms or watch TV. We've usually already seen the movies they show in hotels. We usually stay outside of the city and don't go out anywhere. It's not such a great idea to go out, and I never go out when I have a game the next day. Then again, we couldn't even go anywhere if we wanted to. It's at least half an hour by taxi into the city. In the morning, there's breakfast and skating warm-ups. Then we have lunch together, and afterward, we nap. Then we ride to the stadium, and immediately after the game, we either fly home or head to another city. I never see anything of New York because we always sleep in New Jersey and only go to Manhattan for games or practice.

I prefer playing in the south — in Florida or California. I like being in sunny, hot weather. Everything seems happier. I envy Klima. Even in the winter, he can wear short pants and drive in his car with the roof open to the beach. But they usually have problems with the ice in places where it's warm. Bad ice isn't only in the south, though. They have bad ice in Washington and Madison Square Garden in New York, where you can have basketball one day and hockey the next. Their ice is really low quality. It's soft, slow, tough to pass across and even more difficult to control the puck on. The best ice is in Canada, especially in Edmonton. The ice there is like a frozen pond. No place really bothers me. The only place I didn't like playing was probably Minnesota because no one came to the game.

Thankfully, I don't have any problems with flying. I sit down, put the seat back, and in five minutes I'm sound asleep. The plane may not have even taken off, and I'm already in dreamland. We fly hundreds of thousands of miles, but it's not that bad. It's definitely more pleasant to fly from Pittsburgh to Los Angeles than to sit for six hours in a bus going from Kladno to Ostrava.

After the games they sick the journalists on us. I think the American journalists have much better conditions for their work than Czech journalists. Usually there's a short press conference with the coach, and then the journalists can come into the locker room. They can come up to the players and ask questions to anyone they want. They have thirty minutes. After that, the locker room is off-limits. In some places, they adhere to the thirty-minute rule strictly. In other places, they let them stay longer.

I must say that I have an odd relationship with journalists. At the beginning, I didn't speak with them at all. That was mainly because I wasn't capable of forming a sentence in English and I felt embarrassed. Now it's a little better. Since my position on the team has changed, I feel that I have a responsibility to speak with them occasionally, but I'm never at ease. I've acquired something of a bad reputation because I sometimes say two or three sentences and then leave.

But I don't want to come across as an idiot. It's always the same. A pack of journalists swarms into the locker and they all ask the same things. "What do you have to say about the game?" "How did you feel about your play tonight?" "How was the opposing team?" And so on. Unlike my teammates, I just can't talk to them. It seems to me that I say the same things over and over again, while the other players can say the same thing in five different ways. They have much bigger vocabularies than I do and know exactly how to express things. I can't do that, which is why I don't like talking to them. But if a journalist comes up to me and asks for a longer interview, I usually say yes. In that kind of situation, I have time to explain everything. After all, I like talking about hockey. But I only do interviews when there's time, and I have a chance to think about what I want to say and how to say it. I have one irritating quality. I want to be the best in everything, and if I'm not the best, I don't do it. That's the case with English. I know I can't do it, so I don't even try. I don't want to be the butt of anyone's laughter. And you never are when you're the best.

It's different in the Czech Republic, where I can talk with anybody I want whenever I want because there's no language barrier. A lot of sportswriters there even have my home phone number in Kladno, and they call me up all the time. Not once in my five years in the NHL has anyone ever dared to call me at home. I also simply know the Czech sportswriters better, so I trust them. Plus there are real obligations on my part toward people who are interested in hockey and want to know more about the NHL, and it is through the sportswriters that I can reach them and can talk almost directly to them.

Good relations with sportswriters are, however, one of the keys to success in American sports, and I can understand that. If the media guys like you, they can provide real support even when you're slumping. Being a good communicator can make life in the NHL much easier.

The most important thing is always your play itself, but I have to admit it's not the only thing a player has to take care of.

Image is incredibly important in the NHL, and part of every player's image is his personal appearance. When I first came over, I was really surprised by the unofficial dress code that all the players adhered to. I mean, my previous wardrobe had consisted primarily of jeans, T-shirts and denim and leather jackets. Now I had to wear suits. Designer suits. When Martin entered the league, I saw how the guys on the team looked at him like some kind of backwater hick because of what he was wearing. If your clothes don't have the right label, then you are going to be made fun of, and even if a suit looks and feels just as good as one from a more prestigious outfitter, it won't pass muster if it's not the real thing.

When I left for America, I had three suits, but that wasn't enough. I really need seven or eight to get me through a season, and every summer I buy a couple of new ones right at the Hugo Boss factory. They have a great selection there, and it's cheaper than buying the suits in the stores. Actually, six new suits that I had ordered in Montreal just came in, each with "Jaromir Jagr" written in the lining.

*I play tennis just like hockey —
with great verve... but the results
aren't quite as good.*

*Without an ergometer, I
couldn't even begin to
imagine summer training.*

My personal preference is for black, sometimes dark blue, suits in softer, lighter fabrics and white shirts. Even my T-shirts are always either all white or all black. I buy all my own ties in America, and they tend to be pretty conservative, nothing too loud or flashy. Most of the ties I get as gifts I never wear.

Shoes I also buy only in America, and they last a long time. I thought about this recently and realized that I barely ever take a single step in them. Like most Czechs, I walk around barefoot or just in socks at home, I play hockey in skates, and I go from place to place by car or by plane. The only real action my shoes get is when I walk to and from my car at home and at the arena.

The old saying that the clothes make the man seems to be truer in America than anywhere else. But still, I have to admit that I still feel most comfortable in jeans and a white Gap T-shirt. Out of superstition, I still buy all my underwear in the Czech Republic each year, although by now I've gotten used to the American style as well. When my Pittsburgh teammates first saw me in my Czech underwear, they almost died laughing and asked me if I'd borrowed them from my sister. Or somebody else.

They say that popularity is a double-edged sword, but I don't really mind it at all, even if it does bring with it certain restrictions. In Pittsburgh, for example, I cannot do my own shopping because I get recognized and it's chaotic when people form a crowd around me. It's even worse at the bank, so my mother has to do all my transactions there for me. When I did go in one time, it created such a scene that the police had to call for reinforcements to make sure that in all the commotion no one actually robbed the place.

But I don't mind it at all when people stop me on the street and ask me for an autograph. It would definitely be worse if they didn't. Of course, when I'm rushing off to practice or something, I don't necessarily have time to stop and sign for everybody who happens to want one right then. On these occasions I tend to just hurry off. Similarly, when I'm in a store and a crowd of fans gathers around me, I usually try to escape as quickly as possible. I don't know, it doesn't seem quite right somehow for me to give out autographs to ten people and let forty more walk away disappointed and upset that they didn't get one, too.

What can be more annoying is when I happen to be with someone else and people still come up and ask me for an autograph. It's a little uncool when I'm chatting with a pretty girl at a club and a crowd starts to form around me. If these fans get so persistent that I give in and start signing, the girl usually gets annoyed and walks away. Likewise, if I'm out talking with a group of friends, I don't really need to have strangers come and push photos of me in front of my face for me to sign.

And the worst is when fans come up to me while I'm eating. One time I was at a pizzeria with my mom, and a group of people with photos approached me just as I was biting down on a hot slice. They didn't even want to wait for me to finish chewing and wipe my hands.

These are all exceptional situations, though, and usually I try to accommodate everybody — especially after games. Tickets are expensive, and I know that some people travel over 100 miles to see their favorite stars in person.

Having a famous name can make life a great deal easier in all sorts of ways. One Pittsburgh bar owner, for example, told me that my party's tab is permanently on the house at his establishment. During one stretch of games at home, Martin and I went to the same place for chicken sandwiches after every game, and the management would not let us pay for them. That kind of thing is definitely nice in one way, but it's also embarrassing. I don't think anyone likes to feel like a freeloader, and we usually end up leaving a tip corresponding roughly to the proper cost of the meal itself.

I get in free to every club in Pittsburgh and usually get drinks sent over to my table from other guests at these clubs. This makes me feel awkward, usually. It would be impolite not to accept, after all, but at the same time I feel silly accepting when I can afford to buy my own.

One nice perk is that whenever there's a basketball game or concert in the city that I want to see, all I have to do is walk up to the Civic Arena box office after practice the day of the event and tell the person there that I'd like two tickets. And even if it's sold out, I get them.

Bon Jovi's group invited me back to their dressing room when they played Pittsburgh. I was really bummed then that I didn't speak English well enough to be able to talk with them about very much, but they were all very nice. What surprised me most was how short John Bon Jovi is. He looks so much taller on MTV. Mainly, everybody in the band looked worn out. It struck me how demanding that kind of tour must be.

The members of Metallica sent me a T-shirt, and a female journalist who I have a good relationship with has set up a get-together between me and them. The guys in the group are apparently real hockey fans and began following me after my second All-Star game. They left me a message that they'd like to meet me when Pittsburgh plays in San Jose, which is not too far from San Francisco, where they live. I called them back and they picked me up from my hotel. I had a lot of fun with them.

After one particular practice, the race car driver John Andretti, who was friends with one of the guys on the team, came into the locker room to say hello and specifically wanted to meet me.

Paul Stanton once introduced me to the management of the Sands Hotel in Atlantic City. When I mentioned casually that I wouldn't mind visiting after the season ended, they went overboard in rolling out the red carpet. First they sent me two plane tickets, although given the size of the room they put me in, they should have sent ten. I almost got lost in there, not to mention almost drowning in the whirlpool. I was on a penthouse floor that regular hotel guests didn't even have access to and had to use a special key in the elevator to get it to take me there.

A hotel limousine drove me to and from the airport. My incredible room was free, as was all the food I wanted anywhere in the city. All the expensive restaurants in town were overbooked, and I saw how even rich businessmen had to wait for more than an hour before being seated. I made a reservation for 7:30 but ended up getting delayed and not showing up until almost 8:00. And yet there was my table, still empty and waiting for me when I finally arrived.

Mom brought me down to earth a little when I told her about the trip. "You can be sure," she stated, "that they wouldn't have given you that kind of treatment if your name wasn't Jaromir Jagr."

My house in the Pittsburgh suburbs is beautiful, and it's exactly the kind I'd always imagined living in. It has a three-car garage, a pool table in the basement, a modern kitchen and a nice living room. Upstairs are a bathroom and three bedrooms, not counting my own. In the bathroom adjoining my bedroom, a mirror covers one entire wall, and there is a shower and a small whirlpool bath. Really, I live in all the comfort I could possibly want. Some of my teammates have much more luxurious homes, but my mother, my dog Lucinka and I are very happy in our home.

If I wasn't a hockey player, I'd probably have a different lifestyle. People ask me if I think that's fair. And actually I do. I worked hard to reach the top. For many years hockey was the only thing in my life. But it is not the game of hockey that got me where I am today. I did that myself. Hockey was the way I got there. And, yes, now that I have done what I set out to do, I am reaping the rewards that go with that achievement. Just as a player ends up having as many fans as he manages to win over, so it is with everything else. Everything is earned.

Every month or so, I take home a big crate full of about a thousand letters from my fans around the world. Most of these come from North America, but there are others from the Czech Republic, Sweden, Norway, Switzerland, Holland and elsewhere. I've even gotten fan mail from Australia.

Most of the letters are written by children and teenagers. The ones that include self-addressed stamped envelopes containing a card or picture for me to sign are the easiest to take care of. My mother used to go out and buy envelopes and stamps and tried to answer all the letters sent to me.

I can't fulfill requests for jerseys, baseball caps, banners, posters, pucks and the like. I don't have these things at home.

I don't respond when people send me a number of cards to sign just so that they can then trade or sell them. It sometimes happens that in one load of mail I'll get five letters from the same person, each containing ten cards he wants signed. Often they don't even try to hide their intentions. One guy even tore a single piece of paper into three pieces and just wrote "Sign these cards for me" on each one and put them in separate envelopes.

Most of my North American fan mail comes from Pittsburgh, naturally, followed by Washington State, Toronto, Montreal, New York and the province of Saskatchewan.

I dislike the letters asking me for money. From the former Czechoslovakia come direct pleas for financial assistance. People in the U.S. and Canada, on the other hand, tend to "offer" me the chance to "invest" in all sorts of projects that they've got going. The Czech letters say things like "Send as much as you think would be appropriate" or request specific sums, usually $400 for some reason. I dislike it when people write things like: "...so we don't think it should be any problem for a person as rich as you to send us $2,000. You can afford it."

But this kind of letter can also be pretty funny. One guy actually wrote me and said: "My brother and I have a big building under construction, but we've run into difficulties and don't have enough money to finish it. If you could just lend us $10,000 now, we guarantee that we will pay you back in full within thirty years' time, maximum."

Not everyone wants something, of course. I also get a lot of very nice letters. When the local sportscaster Mike Lange happened to mention during a game with Winnipeg that I was looking for an English tutor, I received a large number of serious offers from experienced teachers of English as a second language.

The fan mail really helped me out a lot during my first season in Pittsburgh. Even then, I was already getting about five letters a day, and knowing that the fans liked and were rooting for me was what kept me going through that difficult period. I also started receiving various gifts and good luck charms, flowers, and even cakes for my birthday. The best was when it came out on TV that I happen to like Kit Kat bars. Soon I was just deluged with them. To this day, I have not yet eaten all the Kit Kats that came during that first wave. And they're still coming.

Sometimes I can tell that a letter comes from a child whose family is not very well off, and these letters move me. Maybe a kid will send me just one Kit Kat bar because he can't afford anything more, but he still wants to give me a little present. Then there was a wonderful letter from the mother of a four-year-old girl who apparently loves to watch me play on television. After I wrote the family a letter back, I got a package from them containing a photo of little Kristina and a video cassette of her providing commentary while watching me on television.

And I love letters from children with advice on how to play better. Mark from Toronto wrote me recently, for example: "I've noticed that when you're on the ice you create a lot of opportunities for yourself. What's also good is that you pass to Martin a lot, and the two of you play well together. You seem like brothers. I think that's great. I don't know what it is, though, but it seems to me like you don't know how to convert all of your scoring opportunities. Sometimes you look like the greatest player in the world out there, but you really do get a lot of chances. I don't want to offend you or anything, but if I were you I'd try doing what Mogilny did last year: shoot fast from up close. When somebody gave him the puck, he just hit it as hard as he could. I think you have a lot of talent, but you're still not making the most of it yet." Thanks for the tip, Mark.

The letters from teenage girls are something else completely. Eighteen-year-old Shannon of Pennsylvania wrote: "You're looking really sexy this year. You have nice muscles. I liked your picture in *Sports Illustrated.*

Kristina from Canada sent me a perfect letter. I guess in one sense she was making fun of my terrible English, but the idea she came up with was totally original. She wrote her letter in English words but using Czech phonetic spelling. To a native English speaker the following sentences are meaningless: "Aj get e dykenery from dze lajbrery tu traj end rajt ju e leter. Aj sot it wud b najs. Aj vil dast du maj best end aj houp it iz rajt." But for me, her words are much easier to read than "I get a dictionary from the library to try and write you a letter. I thought it would be nice. I will just do my best and I hope it is right."

Another letter, from a Vietnam vet in Pennsylvania, touched me deeply. "When I read about you," he wrote, "I understood that the people in your country were also fighting for freedom, just as we sacrificed our loved ones to help the Vietnamese people fight for freedom in theirs. I have enclosed in this envelope the Purple Heart that was conferred upon my brother Terry Taylor in memorial. I believe that the spirit of this medal will help you to achieve success in your battles on the hockey rink."

Every letter I receive means a lot to me — even if I have to admit I don't finish reading all of them. Sometimes a single letter will be about ten pages long, but I almost never get past the third page. All this reading has also taught me a very interesting lesson. That I still don't understand English at all.

When I first joined the NHL, I couldn't speak a word and had to try and just figure out whatever I could by listening. Now I find I understand virtually everything that I hear. But written English is still a foreign language to me. I look at words on the page and have no idea what they mean. Then someone reads them to me and it's like "Oh, OK."

I always try to read the newspaper articles about the Penguins and our games, and I am getting better it. But it's still not usually long before I turn to the stats and standings page, where it's all perfectly clear to me. The thing about the mail is that every letter is different, so it's often impossible to use the ones I've read before to help me with the latest batch.

All in all, mom and I have done a pretty good job at responding to the letters I receive. I wish I could write a personal answer to every one, but it would really be impossible to do so for even a fraction of them. Even the letters from the Czech Republic, which I have no problem reading, would be impossible.

Toward Another Stanley Cup

People back home often ask me what America is really like. But I can't really answer them because I don't know. As a foreigner, it's impossible for me to assess this country.

My situation is completely different from those of the millions of other people who live here. All I do is my work, which also happens to be my favorite activity in the world, and I get paid very well for doing it. I've never had to go through hard times here. Sure, there were a few difficulties at the beginning, but those were nothing like a real struggle to get by. I never even had to play on a farm team and experience the anxiety of waiting by the phone in some small town for someone to finally call and tell me to pack my bags and get ready to fly to Montreal. Thankfully.

Is America a difficult place to live? Well, yes and no. It all depends on where you are and what you're doing. Success is very important because with success comes money, and money, I've come to realize, is the standard by which everything is measured here. A person with money is worthy of respect. I know that sounds like an empty statement, but it's true. What interests people about other people here is how much money they have. I guess this is because America is supposed to be the land of opportunity. Everybody has the same opportunity as everyone else, and it's up to each individual to make something out of it.

I see these principles play themselves out every day in Pittsburgh. Before coming to the NHL, I was used to players watching the coaches out of the corner of their eye during practice so they could take it easy when they knew no one was looking. That doesn't happen here. The guys I play with now constantly go at it as hard as they can, not to impress anyone else, but for themselves. That's why they even stick around and work out when practice is over. They want to be all that they can be. Every player is eager to do whatever it takes to be successful.

Success ensures an easy life and all the benefits that go with it. America seems to me like a fair country because most of the money ends up with those who deserve it and not in the hands of speculators and con men as it does in most other countries.

Being involved in nonstop competition does, of course, have its downside. Genuine friendships are hard to come by. Americans are conditioned to behave in

*"Get up you lazy good-for-nothing, you haven't
skated enough yet," says my niece Pavlina.*

Look how nice it is lying down. "Relaxation with Pavlina."

certain ways. When someone says "Hello, how are you?" it's often not because he or she really wants to know. People here are more reserved and protective of themselves. To be caught off guard looking tired or irritable just one time can do irreparable damage to an image that may have taken years of hard work to cultivate.

I know a lot of people in America, but my real friends are back home. That's why I always look forward to returning to the Czech Republic. It's simply more fun for me there. Real friends are made when you're growing up, hanging out and getting in trouble together, before anyone has anything to be envious of.

The people I can be myself with are the guys from Kladno. Like Jarda Krulich, who didn't begin playing hockey until fifth grade, but hung in there and became a solid junior player. We did passing drills together in practice. Jarda always complained that his parents never came to watch him play. And then one day his mother showed up for a game, and I took the puck away from him and scored a goal. She walked out after that and didn't show up again. Now, whenever we get together, Jarda says things to me like "Remember that goal you scored against Most? When we won 1-0?"

People in America never tell me to shut up or anything like that when I'm going on about something. That's just not done. I'm sure that sometimes they think to themselves, "What the hell is this guy talking about?" but everyone just nods in agreement like they're completely interested in what I'm saying. I guess they're afraid I'd get mad and not want to talk to them any more if they expressed what they were really thinking. The truth is, though, that I'd appreciate it. Honesty is one of the things I value most. When I'm with my friends and start blabbing away, they just let me have it: "Hey, Jardo, take it easy. Your jaw's gonna hurt in the morning."

It's difficult for me to make real friends in the circles I move in here. You can't always tell who would really be there for you if things got bad and who is just interested in you because you're popular. There's no question that some of the people I've been close to were more interested in my name than in me as a person. This has led to a number of disappointments, and as a result, I have since tended to close myself off and turn inward.

Many of my friends in America are young women. I like their sense of independence, which you don't find as much in Czech women. American women are also quicker to say what they really think. I'm also impressed by how spontaneous they are. When they want to talk with me, they just come up and introduce themselves. That kind of direct approach is refreshing.

Currently, I am not planning on getting married. But if I ever do, I doubt it will be to an American. We wouldn't speak the same language, and I don't think I'll ever learn English well enough to hide the fact that I'm from somewhere else. I'll always feel like I can't say exactly what I want. But nobody knows what might happen. After another five years of hockey here I might to see things differently.

Bryan Trottier once said that I learned most of my English from girls, and I guess that's true. I've spent a lot of time hanging around with them. Essentially, there are two bars in Pittsburgh where I go after games, so everyone knows where to find me if they want to. Sometimes there are crowds of young women there waiting just for me. Often when I play video games, they stand behind me and hand me quarters.

And then they call me on the phone. I guess I've given out my home number a couple of times, and it seems to have gotten distributed along the network. At the beginning, I was glad whenever anyone called me, and I could easily stay on the line for two hours. But today, I find I have less time than I used to, and I often have to say I'm simply too busy to talk. When dad comes over at the beginning of each season, he always ends up forced into the role of my chief secretary. He's funny because he completely ignores such American conventions as saying "Hello" when he picks up. It's one thing if Mike Barnett or Jirka Crha or some local sportswriter is calling, but once he hears that it's a girl (as it usually is), he gets tough and answers in his inimitable English: "Sleepink" or "No home."

Also, some of these girls don't seem to think too much about what might be a good time to call me. Mom tells me that sometimes they even call in the middle of a game. Really, you'd think that if some girl was interested in me, she might be able to figure out that I'm not likely to be at home right at the moment when the Penguins happen to be playing in Buffalo.

Sometimes, people who are envious of me say to me that the only reason I attract so many girls is that I'm a famous hockey player. That hockey is the only reason they're interested in me. These comments don't offend me, really, because basically I agree with them. But the thing is, hockey is what I do. It's part of what I am, just like my body, my hair, my face or anything else. I worked hard to learn to play the way I do, and I've earned whatever benefits I get from it.

Every gift or talent compensates and is compensated by something else in life. That's the way the world seems to work. We all know people who have suffered terrible misfortunes but then gone on to outlive almost all of their contemporaries. You can't influence the hand you're dealt or what number the roulette ball lands on.

Look at Mario, for instance. He has enormous God-given talent that puts him above the rest. But life is difficult for him in other ways. His back has been giving him problems for a long time, and in recent years it has gotten so bad he couldn't even play. I've seen him writhe in pain in the locker room. During games, he clenched his teeth, and sometimes he could barely turn around. And no one knows the cause. He's been examined and operated on, but the best doctors in the world still can't figure it out. I don't think they will. Either Mother Nature will take pity on him and provide relief or she won't, but it's not up to the doctors.

And then there's his lymphoma. Mario lives an inordinately healthy lifestyle.

Eats right, doesn't smoke, doesn't drink. It's as if he's paying the cosmic price for his great hockey talent with his health.

You can't have only good luck. That's how it often works out. Or, vice versa, I'll play terribly one day. But then I still have faith that the score will balance out, and maybe next time I'll get two goals.

Of course, I never forget that luck favors the prepared. Every one of us has a chance to achieve in life. And there is a difference between the kind of luck at work in games of chance, and the good fortune that is only realized when you help make something positive happen. I look at good fortune in the short-term perspective, in the here and now. Good fortune means being able to do something I want, like skating down the ice and making the perfect pass or picking up a hat trick. But none of that would happen if I didn't work for it.

Nevertheless, I do take sudden good fortune with some reserve because you never know if what seems like good fortune may actually turn out to be a bad thing. Just like a temporary setback may prove in time to be a blessing. I was miserable when I got that ten-game suspension for knocking over the referee, Ron Hoggarth. But then I realized that for all I knew something even worse might have happened if I had played in those games. Sometimes bad things happen so that we can learn from them, even if the lesson is actually learned some time later.

For instance, my first two years in the NHL were injury-free. I didn't get hurt for the first time until a game against the New Jersey Devils in my third season, when Slava Fetisov knocked me into the boards so hard that I got a contusion in my shoulder. As a result, I missed three games. But when I thought about it later, I realized that I had received a warning the night before.

For no reason at all, I had woken up the night before at three in the morning, and I felt sick as a dog. I hadn't eaten anything bad, just the same stuff I always eat. But there I was, throwing up all night. I should have heard the voice whispering to me, "Don't play tomorrow!" But I didn't. I played, and I paid for it.

I don't see losses as tragic events. And bummed though I was when we were eliminated from the playoffs, I got over it soon enough. Everything happens for a reason, including losses. Fate has something to do with it.

It also depends on who you are and how you act. If you act badly toward someone, it will come back to haunt you. Not necessarily from the same person you wronged, but from somebody else. And if you help someone, then you will find someone to help you when you need it. I truly believe this.

I also believe in natural and supernatural forces. I like to read fantasy and science fiction literature. The books I brought with me to Pittsburgh this year deal with UFOs, and I am reading them now. I am also intrigued by unexplained phenomena and discoveries like the ancient structures in Peru that could not have been built by man. They really pique my curiosity. Someone, or something, that we don't know anything about has been here before us.

My relation to doctors is also interesting. I believe they can help us with ordinary illness, but the powers of their methods are not limitless. With all the money that has been spent on scientific research, there still remain so many things that we don't know. Nature is mysterious. Again, look how many doctors have been unable to determine the cause of Mario's back problems. And I'm not even talking about diseases like cancer and AIDS.

I believe that the key to health can be found only in nature, and that's why my family and I rely principally on natural healers, like Pavel Síma. Síma is a former athlete himself, a decathlete. Four years ago, he was suffering from intestinal cancer. After he recovered with the help of alternative medicine, he began prescribing herbal treatments to people himself.

My initial consultations with Síma two years ago made me interested in learning even more about the kind of work he does. I started seeing him because of pain in my groin muscle and swelling in my knee, and he determined that it was the congestion in my right urinary duct that was causing the pain in my knee through the connecting blood vessels. He prescribed special exercises, self-massages and combinations of herbs and allowed me to eat only natural sugars. He also identified the upper cavity of my left respiratory passage as an additional weak spot. The pus emanating from this area was damaging my kidneys, but further herbal treatments were also successful in ridding my body of the harmful matter.

My mother and I now keep a store of herbs with us in Pittsburgh and use them for various ailments. At first I didn't believe in the miracles of healing and greeted reports on this treatment with skepticism. But then I saw how helpful these treatments were, and not only with hockey injuries.

Disease and illness are what I fear most in life. The pain of a failure on the rink will pass. A loss can even turn out to be positive because no defeat is final and the road to victory has to begin somewhere. But illness is the worst. There's nothing you can do about it but ride it out. Injuries are tough, too, but to a certain extent they can be avoided.

A wise man once said that a great human tragedy is that people regard the present moment in their lives as a kind of dress rehearsal or rough draft. They are always waiting for something better to come along and saying to themselves, "I still haven't started my real life, the best is yet to come." But unfortunately, that's not the way it works, although I can't say that I don't end up entertaining such thoughts myself from time to time.

Sometimes I wonder if I couldn't be happier. At twenty-four, I've already won the Art Ross Trophy and two Stanley Cups as well as the hearts of hundreds of thousands of personal fans, not only in Pittsburgh and Kladno, but across the U.S.

and Canada, as well as in Italy, Germany and perhaps elsewhere. I have a great professional hockey contract that has already ensured me financial security for the rest of my life. And yet, recently I've been thinking more and more about the limits of what I can do.

It used to be, for example, that I never went to bed at night. Even after playoff games, I would head to the local bar, not to drink (I actually don't like alcohol), but just to be among people and have fun. I'd stay out until dawn before going home for breakfast and then turning around and heading out to practice. Then I'd sleep all afternoon. That was my lifestyle. It was OK at the time because I had energy to spare. I guess it didn't have too negative of an effect because we did win the Stanley Cup in each of my first two years.

But that lifestyle is all over with now. I need my sleep. As much as it pains me, I never go out the night before a game. When someone calls me in the evening with an invitation to go out, I do really want to go, and it's sometimes frustrating to feel like everyone else is out having a good time except boring old couch potato me. But I resist because I know I have to save my strength for the next day.

Simply put, I take care of myself. I know what I can and cannot do. And I know that as I get older, I'll be able to do less and less.

Although I've already had many great moments in my career, I do still believe the best is yet to come. All my happiest memories are related to hockey: winning the Stanley Cup, finishing first in the league in scoring, turning around the series against Washington, assuming a position of greater responsibility on the team in Mario's absence and leading the Penguins into the division finals. These are all moments and achievements I remember with great joy.

I would love to be able to relive these experiences, but occasionally I get the feeling that I'm sacrificing too much for my success in hockey. When I wake up in the afternoon and realize that I've just slept through another day, not because I was tired, but because I want to be fresh for that night's game, I sometimes ask myself if it's really worth it. To give up so much for those few, fleeting moments of glory. I would have a much more interesting life if I was willing to settle for being just an average NHL player.

But I'm not willing to settle for less. I want to be the best and to accumulate more of these moments and more of these memories. All the practicing, the working out, the hours of busting my butt on the ergometer, the days of self-imposed house arrest pay off whenever...the goalie is down. I flip a backhand shot past him into the net, and the arena explodes as my teammates surround me. The crowd is still on its feet when I get back to the bench and sit down, savoring the moment. And then the hall echoes with the words of the PA announcer: "The Pittsburgh Penguins' goal scored by number sixty-eight...Jaromir Jagr!"

Conclusion

On the podium stood Eric Lindros. Right there where I had hoped to be standing. He had just been awarded the Hart Trophy for the league's Most Valuable Player in the regular season. I had really wanted to win it, but then again so had Eric. The Hart is the most prestigious trophy awarded to an individual player.

Eric was beside himself as he thanked everyone who had helped him earn this distinction. He almost made it through his speech, but just before the end came the moment of truth. Whenever anyone asks me how important the Hart Trophy really is, I answer, "Remember Lindros." It was like the realization of his childhood dream. Of course, winning the Stanley Cup is the ultimate triumph, but the one who wins the Hart is the best player in the game.

And Eric Lindros knew that. He knew his parents were somewhere in the room watching him. He knew that all of Canada and the United States were watching him. He could feel it. The honor of being recognized as the best player in the National Hockey League slowly began to dawn on him. Now, Lindros is a big boy. He'll hang players out to dry who try to take him on and then turn right around and score a goal. But this occasion was too much even for him. As his acceptance speech concluded and it looked like he was just going to make it through without losing his composure, it hit him. And the result was inevitable.

His chin began to tremble, the tears rolled down his face and his voice broke.

Eric Lindros was crying.

I am sitting on a plane which will soon arrive in Prague. It is Thursday, June 13, 1996. I had a good year. I was second to Mario Lemieux in points. I broke a few records. More than half a million fans voted for me to play in the All-Star game in Boston. We got to the semifinals of the Stanley Cup, barely losing in the seventh game. I was very happy Mario was able to come back and show what makes him the best player in the world. I remember when I saw him for the first time ten years ago on TV. I was just a junior when Mario excelled at the World Championship in Prague. I never thought that a decade later I would be betting with him about who would score fifty goals first in an NHL season. But there are still flashbacks to Toronto, July 6, 1995. Exactly a year ago, I was, for the first and last time, nominated as one of the three best players in the NHL.

I still see the ceremony like it happened today. Entering the hall the first guys I met were the rookie of the year candidates — Jim Carey, Peter Forsberg, Paul Kariya. "Hello," I said. "I'm Jaromir Jagr." Of course they knew that already, but I was starting to get these American courtesies down pat. I still remember when I met Gretzky for the first time, he came up to me and introduced himself. As if I didn't know.

Soon the room was filled with honored guests. I was already seated when I heard a voice behind me calling, "Jaromir!" I turned around, and who was it but Paul Coffey. Coff. How that guy helped me. It had been a whole year since I had seen him. "How could you loose to the Devils?" I teased a little. We both were laughing. We had the same experience.

Eventually, Ronnie Francis and I began to make our way toward the auditorium. We stopped for a moment at the men's room, where we ran into Eric Lindros. "Hey, guys," he said to us. "Wait up for me outside." As we stood in the hall waiting for Eric, who should walk by but Craig Patrick. I decided to play a little joke on him.

"Craig," I quipped, "I've discovered a new player. He'd be great for us. You've got to draft him."

Hearing this information, the GM's eyes began to widen. "Sounds interesting," he replied. "Is he big?"

"Like a mountain."

"Where'd you see him?"

"In the men's room. Just now. Wait a sec, this might be him coming out." The doors opened and out stepped our new prospect — Eric Lindros. Craig Patrick had to laugh.

After passing through the auditorium doors, we all split up. Ronnie and I exchanged a wink before he headed to his seat. I really hoped he would win both of the trophies he was up for. He's such a nice guy and really an excellent team player. I wouldn't have been at the awards ceremony without him. Still standing at the door, I lost sight of Lindros for a moment before I heard him calling out to me, "Hey, Jag, good luck!"

"You, too!" I replied, each of us knowing what the other was referring to. The MVP.

The ceremony began, and Dominik Hasek received the Vezina Trophy, awarded to the league's best goalie, for the second year in a row. Hasek was also a nominee for the MVP award, along with Eric and myself. Without him, Buffalo probably would not have reached the playoffs. Hasek and I were actually standing

The most prestigious prize — the Hart Trophy — all three of us wanted: Eric Lindros, Dominik Hasek and me.

Ron Francis helped me most to victory in Canadian point-scoring, NHL 1995! Together we rejoice at receiving these trophies.

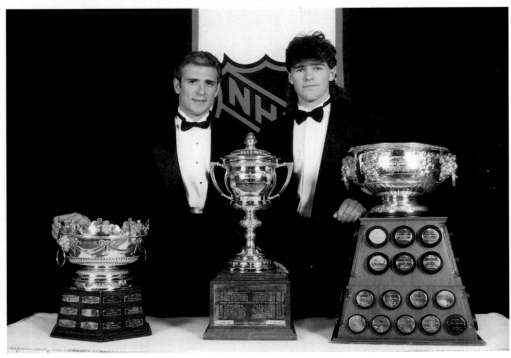

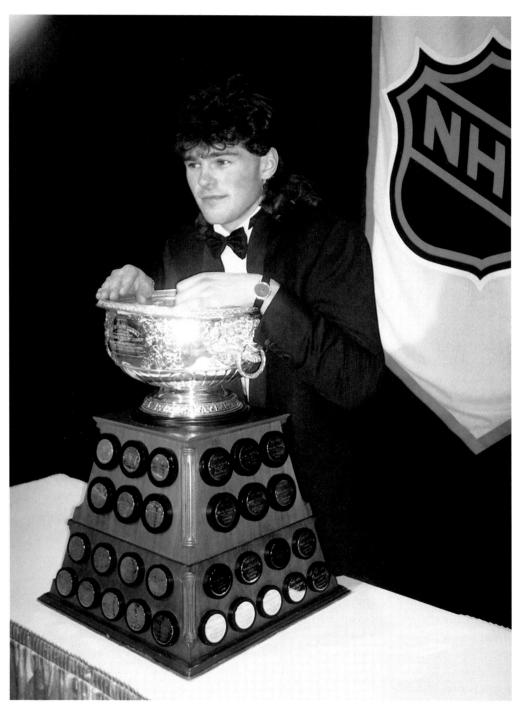

…it's mine! (Art Ross Trophy 1994-95)

right next to each other without even realizing it at the press center just a little earlier. After a few minutes, I looked over and noticed him, and his face lit up. "Hey!" he said. "I didn't even know it was you there. I thought it was Mike Peluso."

Now it was my turn in the spotlight, as I stepped up to receive the Art Ross Trophy as the league's leading scorer. I was very happy but also very nervous. Despite having rehearsed my acceptance speech over and over again, I suddenly found myself at a loss for words. But after a moment I remembered about half of what I had prepared to say.

"First of all," I began, "I'd like to say that the only reason I won the Art Ross Trophy this year is that Eric Lindros got hurt and missed the last few games of the season. Otherwise, I'm sure he'd be up here instead of me." The audience applauded loudly. "I'd like to thank everyone who has helped me get to where I am today: my parents, the Pittsburgh organization and my teammates." I was so nervous that I forget the last group of people I'd planned to thank, which were the fans.

Winning the Art Ross Trophy didn't compare to winning the Stanley Cup, but it was prestigious, nonetheless. Obviously, I was proud of having led the league in scoring during the season, which no European player has ever done before. Since 1981, the only players to earn this distinction have been named either Gretzky or Lemieux. But now, for the first time in fifteen years, the winner went by a different name altogether: Jagr.

I had a hard time falling asleep that night because I couldn't stop thinking about the award I had just won. And, really, I had won it. No one had selected me, there was no voting involved. I had earned it on the ice. From now on the record books would always show that the Art Ross Trophy went to Jaromir Jagr.

I kept thinking about the moments in the auditorium. If I had won the MVP, I realized, I don't know what I would have said. I hadn't prepared for that eventuality. It's OK, though, because I didn't win it anyway. Eric Lindros did. I couldn't stop thinking about how he stood up there on that podium.

The captain turns the fasten-your-seat-belt sign on. We will arrive soon. A few weeks rest and then it starts again. We'll be getting ready for the World Cup. Certainly, it will be the best hockey tournament in history. Maybe I will play for the first time in my life against Mario.

And then I will go directly to camp. Suddenly, I realize that four years ago, after the Canada Cup, I also went directly to Pittsburgh. That season, I played my best games of the playoffs. I have the fondest memories of that year. We won the Stanley Cup. I really want to hold the Cup over my head again. To hold it with Mario and parade it around the ice of the Civic Arena. I can't imagine a better feeling.

But there is one other thing that I want. Secretly. I've wanted it for a long time. That's why Toronto is so often on my mind. I dream of being recognized as the best hockey player in the world. Just once. To hear people say that right now it's Jaromir Jagr who is the absolute best. I'm thinking about it the whole flight back from Pittsburgh.

I've had a very happy life so far, largely because I've always known exactly what I wanted. And now, as my plane slowly begins its descent over Prague, I realize that I still do.

I want to cry like Eric Lindros.

Photo Credits

All photos are from the Archives of Jaromir Jagr except:

page 73	Jiri Kolis
page 77	Jiri Kolis
	Jiri Kolis
page 140	Beverly Schaefer
page 177	Dan Levin
page 201	Jiri Kolis
page 209	Denny Cavanaugh
page 213	Denny Cavanaugh
	Denny Cavanaugh
	Denny Cavanaugh
page 216	Denny Cavanaugh
page 226	Dan Levin
page 231	Dan Levin
	Dan Levin
	Dan Levin
page 234	Dan Levin
page 251	Denny Cavanaugh